N. - 6.1989

D0504679

DIVIDED WE STAND

DIVIDED WE STAND

Working-Class Stratification in America

WILLIAM FORM

University of Illinois Press
Urbana and Chicago

This book is printed on acid-free paper.

Library of Congress Cataloging in Publication Data

Form, William Humbert, 1917–
   Divided we stand.

   Bibliography: p.
   Includes index.
   1. Labor and laboring classes—United States—History.
2. Social classes—United States—History.   I. Title.
HD8072.5.F667   1985   305.5′62′0973   85–16537
ISBN 0-252-01168-6 (alk. paper)

For Joan Huber

Contents

List of Tables

Preface

Most of my research has centered on stratification issues in industrial and economic sociology. In my earlier studies, I was struck by the fact that only a minority of employees in automobile manufacturing worked on assembly lines. Moreover, the workers in this mass-production industry differed widely in their skills, beliefs, and behavior. Later, I studied auto workers in four countries that varied in the extent of their industrialization. I asked whether exposure to similar sociotechnological work environments would lead workers in different cultures to respond similarly to a host of situations they faced in the factory, community, and nation. Although the problem was more complicated than I had imagined, I found that skilled, semiskilled, and unskilled employees in each country responded to their social worlds somewhat differently. When I compared the behavioral profiles of the three skill groups across the four nations, I detected the largest differences in the more industrialized countries. After I published this finding (1973), several colleagues criticized it in print or wrote me heatedly that I was wrong to suggest that industrialization might increasingly divide the working class. Although I relished the exchanges, I realized that my colleagues had an investment in the idea that the working class should become more homogeneous and more united.

Clearly the internal structure of the working class merited deeper study. I found that while American scholars disagreed on who is in the working class, almost all of them agreed that the class had become more homogeneous with increasing mechanization. They also agreed that the working class had not become politically united nor had it spawned a socialist or labor party. The enormous literature on this topic suggests that many scholars, disappointed in the American working class, permitted their political views to govern their observations. I found the literature full of untested assumptions, ideological posturing, and overdrawn generalizations. This book represents both an attempt to examine the literature with

minimal bias and an attempt to launch studies that measure the
types and sources of working-class tensions.

Sociological literature is rich in theories of class formation, but
no theory sufficiently explains the failure of the American working
class to become a cohesive status group and party. Martin Lipset
has contributed most to our *historical* understanding of this failure.
My observations center on the contemporary situation as they attempt
to measure current class cleavages. I hope that the measurement of
class cohesion and cleavages will be applied to earlier periods so
that we may improve our theories of class formation and dissolution.

Quite early in my work I had to decide which class segments to
examine. My approach to the problem reveals my theoretical
orientation. I decided to look for class fragments that could be
distinguished along parallel economic, social status, and political
lines. I assumed that the most important class division is economic
and that research must first deal with earnings and unemployment.
The questions then include: Are economic cleavages more or less
distinct? Do economic cleavages parallel status, power, and organizational differences? Parallel cleavages would clearly retard political mobilization. My judgmental selection of class segments was based
on what appeared to be variations in labor market organization—
including occupational skill—the closure of labor submarkets, labor
union protection, and ascribed worker characteristics that affect
job security. The strata I examined, therefore, include the foremen,
self-employed manual workers, skilled or craft workers, nonskilled
employees in oligopolistic industries, nonskilled employees in competitive industries, and the marginally employed.

The data for these essays are derived from the 1970 census,
governmental and nongovernmental surveys taken during the 1970s,
and two original field surveys. Unfortunately, the 1980 census abandoned the 1970 skill categories, thus making the 1980 census unusable
for my purposes. Since the data in my sources were not gathered
according to my criteria, I spent much energy trying to make the
data comparable. When I began the research, I did not intend to
write a systematic monograph, but when my notes began to form a
coherent if incomplete picture of working-class division, I decided
to fill in as many gaps as I could. Hence, this book.

In Chapter I, I review the sociological literature on the American working class and discuss some issues that I had to ignore in
the empirical research. The chapter does show that no one has
systematically used a Weberian framework to locate divisions within
the working class. I also demonstrate in Chapter 2 that the economic divisions are deep and persistent. Chapters 3, 4, and 5 briefly

examine the history and present economic and social status of three aristocracies of labor: foremen, self-employed manual workers, and skilled craft employees. I show how each group differs from the rest of the working class and how these differences may impede political cohesion of the class.

The lower half of the working class is also divided into three strata. Chapter 6 shows how labor unions may have had the unintended effect of further dividing semi- and unskilled workers into relatively affluent and impoverished segments; moreover, these economic effects may have exacerbated ascriptive sex and race divisions within the class. In Chapter 7, I analyze the topic most central to all my work: the impact of technology on social stratification. I demonstrate how modern technology is adapted systematically to subordinate women, preventing them from filling jobs that management and unions have reserved for men.

Chapters 8, 9, and 10 ask whether stratal economic and status differences have political consequences. Chapter 8 examines the Perlman thesis that workers know their economic self-interests, pursuing them without regard for political class interests. I develop a comprehensive set of questions to measure economic ideology and ask whether the working class systematically differs from the middle class. Then I examine whether consistent ideological differences divide working-class strata. Finally, I determine whether the economic grievances of strata are transformed into grievances against the government, other classes, or other groups.

Chapter 9 explores the question of whether unions successfully socialize their diverse members to follow the political instructions of the leadership. It examines local union politics for evidence on whether different strata agree with the political stand taken by their officers and the liberal coalition in the Democratic party. In Chapter 10, I examine the political stand of the six strata in a number of national elections. Here I examine the standard questions in political research: the extent of stratal voting participation, the extent of strata loyalty to the Democratic party, social-class identification, and trends in political behavior. Finally, I consider these questions: How much variation in the class's political behavior is stratal in character? Does this variation affect election outcomes?

Chapter 11 compares economic, social status, and political divisions of the French and the United States working classes. Its purpose is to compare class segmentation in working classes that vary enormously in class consciousness and political ideology. The analysis exposes some myths but leaves many questions unanswered.

Chapter 12 briefly reviews the book's findings but focuses

primarily on the future of the American working class. I examine the strategy that labor unions may follow in the uncertain future and how coalition members in the Democratic party may respond to that strategy. The book ends with a prediction that a divided working class can more successfully attain class objectives when larger social movements composed of blacks, Hispanics, and women involve organized labor in the pursuit of common interests.

Acknowledgments

This book got started because some of my friends did not like a conclusion of my earlier book which reported on my research on auto workers in four countries. I tentatively suggested that the more industrialized the country, the less cohesive is its working class. The idea that the working class could become more internally stratified over time went against the grain of both Marxist and other sociological traditions. I decided to investigate how the contemporary American working class is divided. The deeper I got into the problem, the more fascinating it became. For this reason, I owe a debt of gratitude to my friendly critics.

My dual appointment in the Department of Sociology and the Institute of Labor and Industrial Relations made the University of Illinois an ideal place to work, for I had the stimulation of colleagues in both departments. I should like to thank both Melvin Rothbaum and Walter Franke, directors of the institute, for their support and encouragement. They provided me with graduate research assistants who performed their assigned chores with grace and enthusiasm. Other colleagues at the institute who deserve special acknowledgement include Larry Kahn, Francine Blau, James Scoville, and Milton Derber. As a true scholar and friend, Bernard Karsh, who also held a joint appointment at Illinois, helped me by being critical of almost any idea I presented to him. David Bordua and Joe Spaeth in the Sociology Department helped in opposite ways. As a myth buster, Bordua pushed me to explore deeply ideas that I had approached timidly, while Spaeth always asked for logical and statistical proof. Joan Huber read all of my articles and this manuscript. She helped me in the entire range of intellectual activity by suggesting new ideas, criticizing pet ideas, and offering suggestions for writing, rewriting, and rewriting.

At Illinois, I was fortunate to work with five graduate students who became colleagues and co-authors: Robert Bibb, David McMillen, George Putnam, Claudine Hansen, and Gary Miller. Other graduate students whose help is gratefully acknowledged include Stephen Lyons, William Urton, Debashish Bhattacherjee, and Kevin Conlon. In France, Jean Pierre Bonafé acted as my graduate assistant, companion, and interpreter of the local scene. I am grateful to him and to his colleagues at the University of Lyon for their hospitality and help; in particular, I should like to thank Phillip Bernoux, Jean Saglio, and Jean Bunel.

Early versions of some of these chapters profited from the informed comments, criticisms, and suggestions of Lewis Coser, Otto Larsen, Hubert Blalock, and Steve Rytina. I extend special thanks to Wendell Bell who read the entire manuscript and gave me detailed suggestions for improving it. At Ohio State University, Simon Dinitz, Saad Nagi, and Kent Schwirian listened patiently and offered sage advice, much of which I was able to follow.

This research was supported by assistance and grants from the National Science Foundation (SES 79-20053), The Research Board of the University of Illinois, and the departments of Sociology of the University of Illinois and the Ohio State University. Anice Birge and Cindy Maher were especially helpful in preparing the manuscript for publication.

I gratefully acknowledge permission to publish material that originally appeared as articles or chapters in the following sources. I cite below the original titles of the pieces and the chapters in which they appear in this book. In all cases, the selections have been rewritten, revised, and restructured to fit the design of this study.

"Sociological research and the American working class." 1983. *Sociological Quarterly* 24:163–84. (Chapter 1).

"Economic cleavages in the American working class." Co-authored with George Putnam. 1985. *British Journal of Sociology* 36:1–33. (Chapter 2).

"Self-employed manual workers: petty bourgeoisie or working class?" 1982. *Social Forces* 60:1050–69. (Chapter 4).

"Conflict within the working class: the skilled as a special interest group." In *The Uses of Controversy in Sociology*, ed. Lewis A. Coser and Otto N. Larsen, 51–73. New York: Free Press. (Chapter 5).

"Women, men, and machines." Co-authored with David B. McMillen. 1983. *Work and Occupations* 10:147–78. (Chapter 7).

"Working-class divisions and political consensus in France and the United States." In *Comparative Social Research* vol. 4, ed. Richard F. Tomasson, 263–93. Greenwich, Conn.: JAI Press. (Chapter 11).

DIVIDED WE STAND

1

Heritage of Working-Class Studies

Prior to the Great Depression, sociological interest in the working class was slight and episodic. From 1855 to 1930, the *American Journal of Sociology* listed only twelve articles on the subject. Thirty other articles on "workers" dealt mostly with poverty and working conditions. Then the Lynds' (1929) study of *Middletown* stimulated an interest in the working class that, as the economic depression deepened, spawned a variety of studies. Corey's (1934) *Decline of American Capitalism* predicted that declining wages would spur a proletarian revolution, but in *Insurgent America*, Bingham (1935) predicted that the Depression would demoralize the working class, hastening its merger with the middle class. Soon after, the Lynds' (1937) *Middletown in Transition* described how the Depression was eroding working-class confidence in the American dream. In the same year, Davidson and Anderson's (1937) path-breaking *Occupational Mobility in an American Community* concluded that class lines were hardening, while Dollard (1937) demonstrated in *Class and Caste in a Southern Town* that the lower-class culture of blacks and whites had solidified long ago. In *The Proletariat*, Briefs (1937) argued that the effectiveness of the Social Security program would determine whether the working class would revolt.

The CIO's attack on craft unionism led some scholars (e.g., Hardman and Neufeld, 1951) to conclude that a self-conscious working class had finally emerged in the United States. The 1937 automobile shutdown strikes in Flint (Kraus, 1947), rubber workers' strikes in Akron (McKenny, 1939), violence in steel (Brooks, 1937), and general labor unrest led Hartmann and Newcomb (1937) to conclude that *Industrial Conflict* could be reduced only by an attack based both on the scientific method and democratic idealism. But Jones's (1941) brilliant study of *Life, Liberty, and Property* in Akron

1

revealed that a self-conscious, radical, native-American working class was now ideologically ready to oppose middle-class dominance. In the same year, Warner and Lunt's *The Social Life of a Modern Community* concluded that the lower classes were a permanent cultural feature of American communities, a finding that was to be replicated often in the next decades.

World War II softened working-class militancy as organized labor and business cooperated to defeat the Axis powers. Union strength, however, continued to grow. Centers' (1949) national survey at the end of the war (1945) concluded that workers were still class-conscious. Challenging *Fortune*'s (1940) prewar survey showing that manual workers identified with the middle class, Centers demonstrated that they not only identified with the working class, but they also had an anti-business ideology. As Centers had predicted, unions continued to grow and became politically aggressive in the postwar decade (Calkins, 1952). Scholarly interest in labor surged: several universities founded institutes for the study of labor and industrial relations; industrial sociology emerged as a subfield; the Industrial Relations Research Association was created; and research on labor blossomed at Yale, Columbia, Chicago, and elsewhere (e.g., Walker and Guest, 1952; Chinoy, 1955; Seidman, et al., 1958). Mills's (1948b) study of labor leaders as the *New Men of Power* climaxed the faith that many intellectuals had in labor's political potential; perhaps more important, it also signaled some doubts.

In the second postwar decade, Mills's skepticism that labor would challenge the status quo seemed vindicated. Leading European and American social scientists (Aron, 1955; Bell, 1960; Lipset, 1970) predicted that class ideology had waned with rising working-class affluence. Two Republican party victories led some scholars to conclude that the working class had become conservative and would meld into a new "middle mass" (Wilensky, 1960). Despite such opinions, in 1962 Harrington rediscovered massive poverty in the allegedly affluent society, and soon Hamilton (1965) and others challenged the view that affluence had made workers politically conservative.

In the third postwar decade (1965–75), interest in the working class was rekindled by labor militancy. Grass roots revolts and wildcat strikes protested poor working conditions and the relentless pressure to increase production. An aroused rank and file also directed its anger against bureaucratized union officers who appeared to be more interested in enforcing collective bargaining agreements than in resolving workers' daily grievances and struggles for work control (Hunnius, Garson, and Case, 1973). Racial unrest, student protests over American violence in Vietnam, and white-collar union-ization had generated a new political climate. The Paris worker-student uprisings in 1968, the ensuing strikes in Italy, and the 1972 Lordstown revolt in the United States led some social scientists (Gorz, 1973; Denitch, 1973; Mallet, 1975; Weitz, 1975) to conclude that this time (Ollman, 1970) a radicalized blue- and white-collar proletariat was mobilizing to seize power in all mature capitalist countries. Studies of blue-collar workers blossomed (Shostak and Gomberg, 1964; Shostak, 1969; Levitan, 1971). Sheppard and Herrick (1972) proclaimed that American workers were robots no longer, and Aronowitz (1973) concluded that, although (unionized) workers had been given *False Promises,* they might be able to radicalize themselves. Even the government (U.S. HEW, 1973) worried that *Work in America* was in deep crisis, and that something had to be done to tranquilize the alienated working class. Levison (1974) announced that America was not a middle-class society, and that the manual *Workingclass Majority* would make government respond to its needs.

The end of the Vietnam War and the ensuing economic reces-sion dampened worker unrest and social science interest in the working class. Yesterday's working-class activism now seemed to be another *Failure of a Dream* (Laslett and Lipset, 1974). By 1980, economic depression, shrinking union membership, and the declin-ing political influence of organized labor led many scholars to conclude that the working class had lost its last opportunity to seize power.

The political yeast of the 1965–74 decade nevertheless contin-ued to leaven in the universities. A generation of young sociologists dedicated to a Marxist analysis of capitalist society heralded Braverman's (1974) *Labor and Monopoly Capitalism* as a rallying point for working-class research. Braverman's themes indeed sug-gest the framework for this chapter: the growth of the working class, the inexorable deskilling of labor, management's scientific exploitation of workers, and rising worker alienation. Braverman did not address the fifth theme of this chapter, the political mobilization of the working class. This chapter assesses the postwar literature on five questions: Who is in the working class? Is the working class becoming deskilled? Is work discontent increasing? Who is winning the class battle to control work? How is the working class being mobilized?

Who Is in the Working Class?

Disagreement on the composition of the working class reflects differences in sociologists' ideological, methodological, and substantive orientations. Since I cannot impose my definition of the working class on others, this review deals with a wide range of definitions. In my view, classes in industrial societies are composed of occupational groups that share common career and generational mobility patterns (Weber, 1978). Thus, if within or between generations, the majority of workers move in a number of closely related occupations, those occupations belong in the same class. Husbands, wives, and children of nuclear families typically move in a relatively narrow range of occupations. The actual occupations which comprise the classes must be empirically determined (Breiger, 1981).

Research on how occupations cluster to form classes and the demarkation of class boundaries has just begun in sociology. The literature suggests that career and generational mobility are fairly common within and among the following occupational groups: unskilled, semiskilled, and skilled manual occupations; domestic, personal, and professional service occupations; lower sales and office occupations; supervisors of manual and service workers; solo self-employed manual and lower-white-collar occupations (Vanneman, 1977). These occupations constitute about two-thirds of the U.S. labor force. Excluded from the working class are proprietors who have employees, self-employed professionals, professional occupations that require a university degree, managers, administrators, officials, and some technical and upper-white-collar workers.

While most sociologists who write about the working class do not define it, I gather from the imagery of their writing that they are thinking primarily of male manual workers who operate simple machines. This group comprises about 20 percent of the labor force or 30 percent of the working class as I define it. The group appoximates Poulantzas's (1975) definition of a proletariat that is capable of political action. Among Marxists, this is a minimalist conception of the working class. "Maximalists" (Szymanski, 1974; Freedman, 1975) include almost everybody except the big capitalists in the working class. Marxists, who lack consensus on the composition of the working class (Parkin, 1979), face a dilemma: if they cling to Marx's maximalist prediction that the proletariat will grow under capitalism, they must then explain why such a large class has not seized control of the state.

Resolving this dilemma involves specifying relationships among the major occupational strata. Wright (1976) illustrates how Marxists struggle with this problem. He criticizes Poulantzas for overemphasizing the political mission of the proletariat rather than its economic relations to capital. Wright (1979) excludes only large owners and managers from the working class but assigns owners of small firms, the self-employed, supervisors, and autonomous workers to "contradictory" class locations, a situation where ownership, control over production, and control over labor do not converge in the same occupations. By assigning managers to the bourgeoisie and salaried professionals to the proletariat, Wright makes authority as decisive as ownership for determining class relations, a stance perilously close to Dahrendorf's (1959) which Marxists generally disavow (Parkin, 1979:23). For Wright, American workers in contradictory class locations are as numerous as those in the working class, about 46 percent each.

Some sociologists interpret the declining percentage of manufacturing employees as a shrinkage of the working class (Bell, 1973), while others see the growth of clerical, service, and technical employees as its expansion (Braverman, 1974) or as the growth of a "new" working class (Tourraine, 1971). The clerical, service, and technical-professional employees as a group are more numerous and heterogeneous than the traditional working class of manual workers. Sociologists have generally failed to examine how elements of the traditional and "new" working class relate to each other.

With some important exceptions (Breiger, 1981), most sociologists accept Mills's (1956) view that lower sales and office clerks (the salariat) are part of the working class. Most clerks are recruited from manual and lower-white-collar origins and remain clerks most of their lives. Moreover, the earnings, work environment, education, and technology of blue- and white-collar workers are becoming more alike (Gordon, 1972). Many scholars (Braverman, 1974) conclude that the salariat over the years has become more impoverished, deskilled, and disesteemed, but their evidence is speculative. Like today, early clerks did not make managerial and property decisions unless they were destined to inherit the family business (Davies, 1974). While deskilling of many manual occupations can be documented (Wallace and Kalleberg, 1982), this is more difficult to do for clerical occupations. As I have pointed out elsewhere (Form, 1980), most clerks have always done simple copying, figuring, and keeping track of transactions. If anything, these tasks are more complex today and require more education to perform. Although research on clerks has recently increased, its focus rests more on sex than on class stratification (see Glenn and Feldberg, 1977).

The enormous expansion of service occupations also slowed

the shrinkage of the working class. Levison (1974) makes the reasonable claim that, because most service occupations are manual, they are part of the working class. Cleaning, handling food, and taking care of the body have always had low status. The commercialization of these functions has been assigned to women's occupations: waitresses, cooks, domestics, nurses' aides, practical nurses, hairdressers, stewardesses, and nursery school workers. Guarding, police, and fire protection have been assigned to men. The diversification and sex stratification of service occupations have not been examined for their effect on working-class social organization.

Liberals and conservatives (Bell, 1973; Parsons, 1968) have pointed to the growth of complex technical-professional occupations as evidence of middle-class expansion in postindustrial societies. Radicals, however, (Aronowitz, 1973) emphasize that the trivialization, routinization, and deskilling of technical-professional work enlarges the working class and continues the bureaucratic labor process of exploitation. Both liberals and radicals agree that technical-professional workers, unlike clerical and service employees, are important class actors.

After the events of May 1968, French writers (Tourraine, 1971; Gorz, 1973; Mallet, 1975) wrote voluminously about the revolutionary potential of technical-professional workers, a role formerly assigned to the manual proletariat. Reminiscent of Veblen (1921), they wrote that technical workers have the knowledge to run society and, in fact, do run it. Contrary to Veblen's despair that engineers would not run society, French radicals were more optimistic. They reasoned that since technicians know they can run society, and since they are deprived of policy-making, they will become more alienated and more motivated to lead the revolt against capitalism. As members of the "new" working class, technicians, not the traditional proletariat, have the most revolutionary potential (Denitch, 1973). These arguments run contrary to the traditional radical view that capitalism trivializes everybody's work.

Research on this topic in the United States is sparse. Silver's (1979) comparative study of engineers in England, France, and the United States concluded that engineers everywhere think they have a great deal of work authority. Moreover, he found no relationship between the technological setting of their work and their political predispositions. Low-Beer (1978), who interviewed technical employees in two northern Italian electronics firms, concluded that technicians are not a homogeneous stratum in their social origins, work situations, or political dispositions. Their politics are influenced more by their political socialization than by their work.

Only technicians who have working-class origins, identify with the working class, and experience incongruent work situations (e.g., high work involvement but hierarchical supervision) tend to be militant. Aronowitz (1971), in a systematic attack, correctly concluded that the "new working class" theory cannot be universally applied, least of all in the United States. The theory overestimates technological change in industry and fails to differentiate the behavior of technicians, who are a stratum of the working class, from production technocrats, who are not. Unfortunately, he offered no data to support his position.

A few sociologists have excluded some manual workers from the working class. Reminiscent of Marx's distinction between the proletariat and the lumpenproletariat, some writers have separated the lower class from the working class (Van Doorn, 1956; Mayer, 1966). On the basis of subcultural differences, Warner and Lunt (1941) divided America's lowest class into upper-lower and lower-lower. Social psychologists (e.g., Hyman, 1966) later tried to document the socialization process in these class subcultures. In the East, where ethnicity is pervasive, Gans (1962) speculated that class and ethnic cultures may fuse, but he concluded that working-class culture was independent from ethnicity. He too, however, distinguished a lower class from the working class, the lower having a female-dominated family structure.

Lipset (1960) hypothesized that the working class could be identified by an authoritarian subculture, but this position was quickly rejected by liberals (Lipsitz, 1965), who insisted that the working class is no more or no less bigoted than other classes (Hamilton, 1972). Other sociologists thought that the working class is split generationally and that its youth are more inclined to change things. Shostak (1971), however, demonstrated diversity among working-class youths: some are rebellious, others accommodate to their status, and still others (achievers) are oriented toward the middle class. *Work in America* (U.S. HEW, 1973), a governmental study, also concluded that the working class is culturally split by generations. Compared to their elders, the young are overeducated for their jobs, have higher economic expectations, demand more work autonomy and freedom, are less satisfied with routine work, and are becoming more militant. These conclusions were widely criticized for ignoring the available evidence (Form, 1974). Wright and Hamilton's (1979) analysis of the national Quality of Employment Survey found no evidence that age, education, and job satisfaction were related. Even young, college-educated, blue-collar workers were as satisfied with their jobs as were their co-workers.

These almost random efforts to identify the working class by cultural features or to exclude disreputable elements from it (Matza, 1971) came virtually to naught. Glenn and Alston (1968) examined twenty-three national polls to distinguish the cultures of occupational groups but found high disagreement among laborers, semiskilled, and skilled workers. Sociologists gave up the search for working-class culture, but social historians took up the task.

One residue from these efforts to locate the "true" working class was an implied consensus that it was stratified. Workers with regular employment and stable family life comprise the "old" working class; the remaining (poor, blacks, old, welfare groups, migrants) constitute the "new" working class (Miller, 1964). This new-poor-low-subclass is not considered disreputable, unreliable, or unusual in any way, but simply a product of monopoly capitalism (Morgan, 1981). Leggett (1968), Blauner (1972), Oppenheimer (1974), and other Marxists believe that blacks constitute an internal colony or a subproletariat in capitalist America. Nyden (1979) considers Appalachian miners in the same position. Almquist and Wehrle-Einhorn (1978) place black women at the bottom; still others, Mexican migrants. Whichever group is designated as below the working class, this split between the two is considered larger than that between the working- and the middle class (Wilensky, 1966).

Is the Working Class Becoming Deskilled?

Two prominent theories of industrialization come to different conclusions on working-class formation and its political mobilization because they disagree as to whether industrial workers tend to become deskilled over time. In the first, capitalist competition stimulates efficient production which in turn encourages occupational specialization and the mechanization of simple jobs. This process reduces the number of low-skilled jobs and increases the demand for highly trained skilled, technical, and professional occupations. A post-industrial society emerges that increasingly calls for work autonomy and opportunities to innovate (Foote, 1953; Parsons, 1968; Bell, 1973). Class formation does not figure in this script because society's main concern is to plan and facilitate cooperation among specialized occupations. How this cooperation is organized is not made clear, perhaps along corporatist lines as envisioned by Durkheim (1964).

Braverman (1974) and other Marxists strongly challenge this view and assert that capitalists, in pursuit of profits, rationalize production, push specialization, and deskill labor. The degradation of skills increases job dissatisfaction and work alienation. The rising educational requirements of new occupations simply represent a form of credentialism that hides and justifies capitalism's high unemployment rates. Historically, management seeks to deprive workers of their skills in order to monopolize them. In time, all manual, clerical, and professional work is deskilled and dehumanized. Eventually, workers recognize their exploitation and revolt.

The crucial question is whether the working class is being deskilled. This historical question deserves a historical analysis, but such studies are rare. If the working class includes manual, clerical, technical, and even professional workers, research must consider skill changes in all of these occupations. Most studies focus on manual occupations that are being deskilled (Noble, 1979) but rarely study new occupations or occupations that are becoming more complex.

Census data on long-term occupational trends may point to increasing rather than decreasing occupational complexity (Form, 1980). The decline of unskilled and the rise in semiskilled manual labor has been amply documented. The growth of the service sector calls for occupations that require more education. Thus, the decline in personal and domestic service work has been accompanied by an increase in public service (police, firemen, health aides) and other jobs (flight attendants, hairdressers, and cooks) with relatively high occupational complexity scores (Miller, et al., 1980). The expansion of female labor force participation has been largely a shift from unpaid domestic labor to clerical work that requires more training and skill. Even today's routine office jobs require more training than most manual skilled jobs (Smith and Snow, 1976). Braverman and others err in equating routine work and unskilled labor.

Contrary to collective wisdom, the percentage of skilled manual workers in the working class has risen since 1900. This eighty-year trend undoubtedly antedates the twentieth century. The persistence of contrary beliefs reflects errors in the interpretation of census data prior to 1900 and mythologies about skilled work in the preindustrial and early industrial periods. Contrary to Braverman's arguments, skilled workers were more overrepresented in earlier than in recent censuses (see Chapter 5).

What was the distribution of skills like in nineteenth-century cities, the era of early industrialization? In twelve occupational reconstructions of such cities, I (1980:152) observed that artisans and skilled workers comprised from 25 to 50 percent of the recorded labor force, and unskilled laborers and servants made up 25 to 54 percent. All of these studies omitted women and children who worked for their room and board, unpaid family workers, transients, vagabonds, and the unemployed, thus overestimating the proportion of skilled in the labor force. If the omitted workers were included in the labor force, the proportion of skilled workers in early industrial cities would be about the same or smaller than in today's cities.

More's (1980) landmark study of changes in the English working class focuses on the critical period of rapid industrialization (1870–1914), the period of alleged deskilling and growth of industrial unions. He analyzed 440 biographies of unskilled, semiskilled, and skilled workers who started to work in the Edwardian period. Testing the hypothesis proposed by radical theorists (skilled jobs are simply social constructions promoted by the skilled to protect their interests), More (1980) found that the impact of mechanization on skill varied by industry. Marx's analysis of skill dilution in textiles was correct, but that industry was not typical. Skill requirements increased, for example, in metal manufacturing, chemistry, electricity, gas, maintenance services, and other industries. The joining of skilled and less-skilled workers in industrial unions resulted not from the erosion of craft workers' skills but from the gradual accumulation of skills on the part of the increasingly educated semiskilled workers.

Only two studies have measured recent trends in the complexity of the entire occupational structure, both based on samples of occupations in the *Dictionary of Occupational Titles* (DOT) for 1965 and 1977. Spenner (1979) found that work with data, people, and things had become slightly more complex in all occupational and industrial sectors. Rumberger (1981), working with the same DOT data for general educational development (GED) of occupations (a good measure of skill complexity), found: (1) higher skill requirements resulting from interoccupation shifts in employment, (2) an increase in skill for intraoccupational shifts in employment, (3) an increase in skill requirements of individual jobs at the middle-class level, all resulting in (4) a net increase in percentage of jobs in the upper-middle range of skills. Linking his data with a 1940–50 study of GED shifts, Rumberger found steady increases in the skill levels of jobs in the U.S. from 1940–76.

Is Work Discontent Increasing?

Put simply, Marx's theory of class formation is a concatenation of causes that increase worker discontent. Capitalist industrialization increasingly separates workers from the products of their labor (objective alienation) and leads to deskilling. These conditions foster subjective work alienation and discontent that, in turn, lead to class action to change work organization and capitalist society. For the theory to be supported, historical data must show that each stage of development preceded the next. No one can deny that a growing percentage of the labor force does not own the means of production (Marx, 1967) nor the means of administration, violence, and services (Weber, 1978). On such grounds, objective alienation is increasing in all capitalist and socialist industrial societies. Whether this form of alienation precedes or accompanies deskilling is unknown. I have found no compelling evidence to support the hypothesis that working-class occupations have become progressively deskilled since the industrial revolution. The hypothesis that deskilling has increased subjective alienation therefore cannot be accepted; however, work alienation and discontent can result from other causes, a subject worthy of examination.

Authors use the concept of alienation in so many different senses that Lee (1972) thinks it has no core meaning. Most scholars, however, accept Seeman's (1959) typology of alienation as including normlessness (anomie), powerlessness, social alienation (isolation), and self-estrangement. The critical question is whether technological change increases any type of alienation. The evidence is mixed, and recent research casts doubt about technology's effects on any type of alienation (Seeman, 1975; Form, 1976a, ch. 11; Shepard, 1977). Even if technological explanations were accepted, most studies confirm Blauner's (1964) thesis that alienation is lower among workers in the fastest changing and technologically most advanced industries. Assuming that automation will grow, work alienation actually may decrease (Hull, Friedman, and Rogers 1982). Longitudinal research on this question is still scanty.

Perhaps measures of alienation do not reflect workers' job satisfaction. While no necessary theoretical relationship exists between work alienation and job satisfaction (Braverman, 1975:20), an empirical relation usually appears (Shepard, 1977). Work routinization could increase job dissatisfaction as well as alienation. The mountain of research on job satisfaction cannot be reviewed here, but a few conclusions about it are pertinent. First, from the earliest research to the present, most workers everywhere have reported job satisfaction (Hamilton and Wright, 1982; Thurman, 1977). Second, over time, fluctuations in job satisfaction are small and differences within occupations are larger than among them (Jencks, 1972:247). Third, although evidence is conflicting, Shepard's (1977) literature review convinced him that workers in more complex jobs are somewhat more satisfied than those in routine jobs (Gruenberg, 1980).

Fourth, survey questions can be manipulated to vary the proportion of employees reporting dissatisfaction (see Sheppard and Herrick, 1972).

Two explanations have been offered to discredit data supporting widespread job satisfaction. Dubin (1956) found that work satisfaction is not a central life interest of the working class; Goldthorpe and colleagues (1969) found that workers with an instrumental orientation toward work seek high-paying, low-skilled jobs. Both explanations fit Marx's theory of alienation, but that theory assumes a view of human nature that makes job satisfaction inherently more important than family consumption, and other types of satisfaction (Gruenberg, 1980), a position that has not been empirically demonstrated.

Who Is Winning the Class Battle to Control Work?

Almost no empirical studies have examined the link between struggles to control work and class grievances, class consciousness, class socialization, and class mobilization. Since some sociologists (Clawson, 1980) claim that the labor-management struggle over work control is a form of class conflict, I will review the research. The sizable literature on work control can be divided into three stages: pre–World War II, the industrial sociology era (1945–65), and the subsequent era dominated by Marxist sociology.

Prior to World War II, study of shop-floor conflict was dominated by students of labor economics, management, and journalism. While this literature cannot be reviewed here, two studies developed ideas that are still being pursued today. In 1926, Barnett, a labor economist, published *Chapters on Machinery and Labor.* Barnett studied the historical effect of technological change on occupational skill, wages, and union organization in four industries. He found that some technological changes affected occupational skills positively, raised wages, and helped the unions prosper, while other changes destroyed skills, lowered wages, and weakened unions. Barnett concluded that no easy generalizations are possible in this complex area. Few sociological studies match Barnett's work in its historical, comparative, and holistic (economic, social, and organization) approach to technological change.

Mathewson's (1931) participant observation of restriction of production among unorganized workers in several industries was an insightful study of shop-floor conflict. He examined co-worker pressures to restrict production, boss-ordered restrictions, the impact of wage levels and unemployment on workers' restrictive practices, conflict between workers and time-study officials over quotas, and grievances and ideologies that managers and workers develop over restrictive practices. He observed that workers' restriction of production is a rational tradition of self-protection that arises in response to management exploitation and duplicity, that workers' tactics are more ingenious than management's, and that scientific management cannot change the balance of power at work. Mathewson concluded that shop-floor conflict is a structural feature of industry, and that workers give management not their best but only an expedient performance.

Industrial sociology emerged in response to an idea proposed by Elton Mayo (1945) and his Harvard colleagues in the 1930s and 1940s: management had to respond to the informal social organization of factory workers. Irked by being scooped by students of business, industrial sociologists attacked the Harvard school as being pro-business and anti-labor, as having a clinical bias, and as ignoring the impact of class, community, and society on the social life of workers (see the bibliography in Landsberg, 1950). Scientific management, human relations practices, management education, and industrial psychology were criticized in great detail (see, for example, Mills, 1948a; Bendix, 1956; Knowles, 1955). Ideological analysis of managerial practices is an important legacy of this generation of sociologists (Karsh, 1968).

To correct the deficiencies of the Harvard school, sociologists published numerous studies of social life in the factory, union, office, mine, shop, government, prison, hospital, military, restaurant, bank, and railroad (see bibliography in Miller and Form, 1980:26–37). Most of these studies focused on the informal organization of workers inside and outside the work place. Although informal organization as a concept has fallen into disuse, or disrepute, the concept helped students describe a great deal of working-class culture and behavior. Scholars of all persuasions (Moore, 1951; Roy, 1952; Gouldner, 1954; Friedmann, 1955; Homans, 1961) agreed that the main function of informal organization is to control the work process by disciplining workers, manipulating management, and articulating external organizations (union, party) to plant-work issues.

Many of these studies examined worker responses to new technology and new managerial practices. I summarize two of the best contributions. Sayles (1963) observed several work groups in different industries over a period of time. He noted that groups differed in the number of grievances they generated, the number of spontaneous outbursts against management, their internal cohesion, labor union participation, and performance evaluation by management. Reminiscent of Barnett (1926), Sayles created a behavioral typology of four groups: apathetic groups (low use of pressure tactics, undefined leadership, internal disunity, suppressed discontent); erratic groups (easily inflamed, episodic pressure tactics, volatile relations with management, centralized leadership, active in union); strategic groups (continuous monitoring of work, well-planned grievances, high unity, sustained union participation, good production records); conservative groups (restrained pressure on management, moderate unity, fluctuation in union and grievance participation). These groups differ in their occupational composition, the way that technology organizes their work, and the way that work groups behave. For example, assembly lines contain workers who performed different routine tasks. They conform to the apathetic type. Isolated groups of skilled workers tend to be strategic. In short, technology, work group structure, union participation, and work-group behavior toward management are highly related.

Lupton (1963), in a participant observation study reminiscent of Mathewson (1931), observed restriction of production in garment and transformer factories. He noted that cohesive work groups did not always necessarily try to control or restrict production. Informal groups in the garment factory were not coterminous with production groups and did not control production. In the transformer factory, cohesive informal groups and production groups coincided and controlled production. Lupton concluded that differences in the external markets of the two industries explain the behavior of the work groups. In the garment factory, management set work quotas, and workers, irrespective of their solidarity, met the quotas because the industry was very competitive and workers realized they could not get higher wages. In contrast, the transformer industry was highly cartelized. It had a complicated wage-determination process that workers manipulated by restricting production. Management responded by price fixing. The Sayles and Lupton studies together present a high point in the analysis of worker-management struggles: work-group behavior varies according to variations in the occupational-technological work process and the market situation of industries.

Marxists have added a sizable literature on the class struggle to control production. Marx thought that the self-interest of employers drove them to rationalize production by increasing the division of labor, introducing new machines, and increasing the exploitation of labor. Braverman (1974) sought to update Marx by describing how monopoly capitalism, by adopting Taylor's scientific management, further divided and degraded labor's skills. Marglin (1974) offered a different explanation that was quickly accepted by the neo-Marxists.

He claimed that in Britain's early textile mills, managers divided and deskilled labor not to increase efficiency but to control workers. The factories could have been just as efficiently run with skilled labor, but that would have left the workers in control of production. Deskilling was a capitalist drive to monopolize control of production, expropriate workers' skills, and concentrate them in management's hands. Contrary to Marx's dictum, the social relations of production determined the forces of production.

Stone (1974) "replicated" Marglin's findings in a historical study of the American steel industry, and Clawson (1980) did the same in a wide range of British industries. Both studies expanded neo-Marxist organizational theory (Heydebrand, 1973), which holds that bureaucracies with many units and many levels of authority central-ize bourgeois power and split the proletariat (see Form, 1980, for an evaluation of this thesis). This power theory of management control over the work process is as evolutionary as Marx's theory of techno-logical determinism, but more pessimistic. In both theories, capital relentlessly divides and degrades labor. Worker resistance, as revealed by studies of industrial sociologists, has little room in Braverman's and Marglin's scenarios. Attempting to embrace both theories, Aronowitz (1973) argues that technological change did reduce skills, but "skilled" workers (in name only) were retained by management to divide the working class in the shop. Management created need-less "training" programs to instill a false ideology of skill in some workers. These workers, who generally captured union offices, cooperated with management to institute detailed job classification and seniority schemes designed to perpetuate wage inequality and split the working class. Aronowitz offers no data to support his position.

Burawoy (1978) accuses Braverman of being a romantic utopian who lacks an historical or comparative sense. Burawoy hypothe-sizes that workers' tactics to control work change with the stage of economic and labor union development. Thus, serfs could readily observe the amount of their labor or production that lords expropri-ated, but in impersonal capitalist markets, workers cannot readily measure the amount of surplus labor expropriation. In fact, capital-ism depends on its ability to obscure the expropriation of surplus labor value. Burawoy (1979) replicated Roy's (1952) early study of restriction of production in a firm that had shifted its market situa-tion from one of competition to one of near monopoly. He noted that work control struggles shifted from the factory floor to the bargaining table. "Struggles" on the plant floor were games that management contrived to secure worker consent and involvement in rule-making.

Work was not continually degraded, as Braverman had insisted. Workers successfully restricted production, and obtained seniority and other rights, while capital secured and obscured surplus labor value. Although Burawoy's observations are plausible, the observation that capital secures surplus value is hardly news to most workers; unions easily learn about company profits by consulting their financial reports.

The most sophisticated Marxist interpretation of the labor process is that of Edwards (1979) who showed that different stages of capitalism have produced different types of technologies, markets, and class struggles. In the first stage of small capitalist enterprises, workers confronted the personal authority of owners. With the growth of large-scale mechanical industry, the assembly line or technology controlled workers' behavior. In today's automated industries and white-collar organizations that have complex occupational structures, rules and bureaucratic control are dominant. All three types of organizations, control mechanisms, and workers' resistance patterns survive in today's economy and parallel the stratification of the working class. The under-class in the periphery confronts personal owner control, the proletariat in the core economy confronts technological control, while professionals and holders of primary jobs in large organizations confront bureaucratic control.

How Is the Working Class Being Mobilized?

Class theories are particularly weak in their inability to explain how the working class mobilizes on its own behalf. Marxist theory causally links technological relations to worker alienation, which, in turn, is linked to class action. General sociological or "spillover" theory directly links social relations at work to social and political relations in the wider society. What is the evidence for either theory?

In Marx's theory, technological change leads to skill degradation of work that results in worker alienation from capitalist society, which, in turn, leads to proletarian class action. We have already examined the technology-skill degradation link and the technology-work alienation link and found little evidence to support them. Thus, it is unnecessary to investigate other causal links; nevertheless, sociologists continue to study other linkages, especially those between technology, work, and societal alienation. Shepard's (1977) review of this literature reports mixed results, but most recent studies show no strong or consistent relationship between technological relations, work alienation, and societal alienation.

Seeman's (1971) work is decisive. In ten studies dealing with different social strata in various countries, Seeman found no correlation between alienation from labor and various measures of societal alienation, including hostility, punitiveness, political knowledge, voting, political disengagement, low self-esteem, status striving, leisure pursuits, and other variables. Though most of these variables were related to a sense of powerlessness, powerlessness was not highly related to work alienation.

An alternative explanation of class action would link the technology-work alienation nexus to class consciousness, the necessary precursor of class action (Mann, 1973). Ollman (1970) outlines nine steps in the class mobilization process and concludes that workers' hatred of capitalism, as an element of class consciousness, is a crucial step that is lacking in the United States. Lockwood (1981) agrees with Ollman that the weakest link in Marxist analysis is how the working class gets socially organized. Lockwood thinks that a theory of class action must precede a theory of class structure, the reverse of Marx's approach. Unfortunately, sociologists would rather speculate about this topic than conduct empirical research on it. Ironically, we know more about working-class mobilization in France (Tilly, 1978) than in the United States.

The "spillover" sociological explanation of class action derives from Durkheim's theory that social relations at work carry over into the community and society. As in Marxist theory, this process applies not only to the formation of labor unions but also to the formation of leisure, special-interest, political, and class organizations. One advantage of spillover vis-à-vis alienation theory is that spillover theory does not insist that class action will eventually flow from work relationships. Indeed, the theory explains the absence of class action when work organization is bereft of social bonds. But the theory does not specify the amount and type of work relations that are needed to facilitate or inhibit various types of non-work social action. Very few researchers have measured technical and/or social relations at work and traced them into non-work arenas. Studies of organizational efforts by labor unions and parties to build upon work organizations are equally rare.

Industrial sociologists (Sayles, 1963; Blauner, 1964; Meissner, 1969) have shown that worker interaction and informal organization are highly conditioned by technology and work flow. Industries and occupations differ widely in the quantity and quality of interactional opportunities they offer workers. The data reveal that the more workers interact at work, the more they interact in the community. I have argued (Form, 1976a:183) that for working-class movements to arise, workers must participate in formal organizations that extend beyond friendships, family visiting, and neighborhood contacts. The more that work and labor union ties carry over into community organizations, the more class movements are possible. Thus, political (class-oriented) unionism is most successful when union activists also participate in community organizations. I found that this organizational-linking function applied only to a small minority of auto workers in the four countries I studied. In the United States, the activists who linked work groups, union, community, and political organizations were not an effective avant garde because they lacked a coherent ideology and ideological fervor.

Kornblum's (1974) magnificent study of blue-collar steel workers in South Chicago documented the complex network of relations that is needed to produce class-oriented politics. He traced multi-ethnic, work-group relations into the ethnic neighborhoods, unions, and the local Democratic party. He uniquely demonstrated how external national organizations (ethnic, political, labor union) inhibit and/or promote working-class political solidarity in ethnically divided groups. More such studies are needed.

If the working class were politically united, the Democratic party would always remain in power. The research task is to explain why this is not the case. Instead, most researchers have tried to explain why the Socialist party did not succeed in the United States (see the bibliography in Lipset, 1977). This persistent fascination with the history of a small political party perhaps says more about the ideology of scholars than about the working class. After World War II, when worker incomes were improving, the hypothesis was proposed that affluence was making workers more middle class and conservative (Mayer, 1956). Hamilton (1972) and others quickly showed that this was not the case, but these studies did not explain why such a large part of the working class could not be relied upon to vote consistently for the Democratic party.

From the hundreds of voting studies, a few conclusions may be drawn about working-class party loyalty. Converse (1976), studying trends in party voting since the 1950s, concluded that party loyalty has been quite stable; however, five Republican presidential victories from 1952 to 1980 suggest something less than consistent working-class support for the Democrats. Pomper's (1975) review of voting trends convinced him that, though people are aware of ideological party differences, they shift their party support. Only the blacks remain cynical, liberal, and consistently ideological in their politics. Lipset (1981) explains this instability in party loyalty as pointing to a world decline in class voting since World War II and to the emergence of a new Left whose interests differ from those of the old Left.

Since the working class is not solidly loyal to the Democratic party, research should concentrate on class political segmentation. Ra's (1978) longitudinal studies showed that union membership increases voter turnout and support for Democrats. Union members are consistently more class-conscious, liberal, and dissatisfied with their economic situation. But Wilson (1979) found that the AFL- -CIO's Committee on Political Education (COPE) increased voter turnout of both union and non-union workers. Harwood's (1982) careful 1950–80 review of local and national studies of union member voting convinced him that union members' identification with the Democratic party is decreasing, and that they are not becoming more liberal politically.

Since the working class is split by income, union membership, skill, industry, ethnicity, race, sex, and region, political preferences should reflect these splits. Hamilton's (1972) comprehensive voting study found that economic differences did not explain workers' politics, but some differences appeared among skill groups. My analysis of six elections (Form, 1976b) showed that voting participation of skilled workers was consistently higher than that of the less skilled, an observation verified by Pomper (1975) and the U.S. Bureau of the Census (1978a). I also found that the skilled changed party vote and party identification more often than did the less skilled (Form, 1976b).

If the working class has an organizational voice, it is the labor union. Arnold Weber (1963) discovered that conflict between craft and unskilled workers did not disappear in industrial unions, and that conflict between craft and industrial unions declined only a little after the AFL-CIO merger. Aronowitz (1973) claims that craft workers captured the main offices of industrial unions in order to advance their own interests. Wilensky (1975) found that the upper working class opposes the expansion of the welfare state more than the lower part. Survey data assembled from Yankelovich, Gallup, Roper, SRC, and other polls by Heldman and Knight (1980) showed that splits between officers and union members on social and political issues were greater than splits between union and nonunion members. Harwood's (1982) and my 1960–80 survey of union political research (Ch. 9) verified deep cleavages between officers and rank and file on using union dues for campaigns, public employee bargaining, open housing, school busing, welfare reform, voting for union-backed candidates, and union issues such as common situs picketing, the closed shop, guaranteed annual wage, and repeal of the Taft-Hartley Act. Union officers clearly are more liberal and interested in working-class welfare than are union members. Blume's (1970) study of union locals provides persuasive evidence that their members see their officers' liberalism as a prerogative of office.

Conclusions

Sociologists disagree on who to include in the working class. Poulantzas (1975) includes only a fifth of the labor force, and Wright (1976) places as many in contradictory class positions as in the working class. Although clerical, service sector, and technical occupations now outnumber manufacturing employees, most studies continue to focus on the male minority in manufacturing. While clerical, service, and technical occupations have expanded the working class, the connections among these groups are virtually unexplored. Research on working-class culture has not helped define the class's upper boundary but has separated out an under-class. Even though sociologists continue to discover "new" working-class segments (the poor, women, technicians, intellectuals), they neglect to examine the ties among these groups and the ties between the new and old working class. Students of the women's movement, the black revolt, white-collar unionization, and poor people's protests have not examined how these movements affect working-class solidarity.

When historical data are examined, the evidence does not support the idea that skill degradation is making the class more homogeneous. Studies of occupational trends, intensive studies of workers in different historical epochs, historical reconstruction of urban occupational structures, and studies of recent trends in occupational complexity all point to increasing skill differentiation in the working class. Even though too much insufferably mindless labor persists in American society and even though many individual occupations are being deskilled, these conditions do not provide factual support for the skill-degradation and class-homogenization hypotheses.

Research fails to support a causal link between technological change and increasing working-class alienation. When job dissatisfaction is considered, again, the evidence does not show widespread or increasing dissatisfaction. Nonetheless, many sociologists believe (see the bibliography in Hamilton and Wright, 1982) that massive alienation and job dissatisfaction are increasing. This misreading of the data must be traced to ideological bias (Hamilton and Wright, 1982). Hatred of machines and bureaucracy on the part of many sociologists leads them to project their feelings onto the working class (Roberts, 1978) even though the evidence shows that most workers like their machines and are not disturbed by working in bureaucracies (Mueller, et al., 1969; Form, 1976b; Hull, Friedman, and Rogers, 1982; Form and McMillen, 1983). Professors probably underestimate the complexity of low-skilled jobs and workers' ingenuity to make them satisfying and/or bearable (Kusterer, 1978).

How much progress has been made in the analysis of class struggles to control work? Barnett's (1926) early analysis remains significant because its broad scope included technology, the union, management, and economic market factors. Mathewson's (1931) descriptions are unique in including management collusion in restrictive production practices. The ideological analyses of managerial philosophies by industrial sociologists in the 1950s and 1960s remain unsurpassed, and their analyses of informal organizations as mechanisms of worker control remain solid contributions.

Some recent neo-Marxist studies of work conflict are naive rediscoveries of ancient ideas (Rubin, 1976; Pfeffer, 1979). Braverman's (1974) influential study was a not step forward, and virtually all of his ideas have been reformulated by Marxists and non-Marxists alike (Braverman Symposium, 1978). Neo-Marxists have reemphasized the importance of property in the determination of income and class relations. But class exploitation and class control were widely recognized by the older generation of industrial sociologists, many of whom were or are Marxists who abandoned the Marxist lexicon for plain English. By widening their view of workplace conflict to include historical, comparative, technological, and organizational factors, the new generation of Marxists has abandoned much of early Marxist theory to arrive at observations much like those of the first generation of industrial sociologists. Both generations emphasize the interplay of technological, organizational, and market factors, and both conclude that neither competitive nor monopoly capitalists have monopolized control of the labor process.

Marxists and non-Marxists suffer some common disabilities. Both have concentrated on men in manufacturing whereas the growing area of conflict is in the office and store where women workers predominate (Baxandall, et al., 1976). Both have seen management as monolithic and not subject to internal disagreements (Moore, 1951). Both have focused on occupations that encountered deskilling and ignored old and new occupations that increased their skill and autonomy. Both have ignored situations where labor and management have been forced to cooperate even against their wishes.

Finally, both have failed to link issues of work control to class issues outside the enterprise.

The weakest part of working-class theory deals with class mobilization. Marxist-alienation theory has not advanced our understanding of class mobilization, and sociological spillover theory is still at a primitive stage. Two questions need attention. The first, the extent to which different occupations, unions, and industries generate class linkages to non-work organizations; second, the process by which community class organizations activate local work groups. In this two-way process, the union should be critical because it is supposed to link work groups to class party-politics. A systematic treatment of union politics cannot ignore the conflicting interests of government and industry unions, craft and industrial unions, individual international unions and the Washington AFL-CIO, and unions inside and outside of the AFL-CIO. An informed sociology of the working class must examine both conflict among unions and conflict among parts of the working class.

Such a research program must immediately consider two problems. First, only a minority of the working class is unionized and, second, industrial unions encounter difficulty activating their members because they lack meaningful occupational bonds (Calhoun, 1982). Developing class-consciousness is less important than developing class organizations. Skilled workers normally form cohesive work groups, and they understand the need to act collectively inside and outside of the work place. To organize other, less skilled workers politically is not easy given their social heterogeneity. Sociologists need to develop a theory of how a segmented and stratified working class can develop bonds strong enough to enable it to act in its self-interest.

Research Questions

It is easy to criticize the shortcomings of research on the American working class as I have done, but it is another matter to come up with something better. In this study, I have tried to prevent my hopes for the working class from interfering with my observations on what is happening to it. At this stage of American history, it appears that the working class is more divided than organized; therefore, it makes more sense to concentrate on its divisions and to probe their magnitude rather than search for the hoped-for underlying unity.

These chapters do not examine the full range of issues raised in the above literature review, nor do they examine all the cleavages within the working class; however, I believe I have addressed its main economic, status, and political divisions. The incomplete coverage is partly the result of my desire to report on my own research wherever possible. Unfortunately, all my studies in the past decade do not fit into a neat pattern because I kept changing my views of the working class and its problems. Nevertheless, I hope that a modicum of consistency runs through my work.

I have always thought that workers are concerned more about their earnings than anything else, and that their beliefs are heavily influenced by the industry in which they work and its technology. Therefore, I first consider class earnings differences that are based on occupational and industrial status. Second, since most workers see the union as an economic rather than as a social or political instrument, I next examine the impact of union membership on the major economic and social divisions of the working class. Then I examine three major elite groups (foremen, self-employed manual workers, and craft workers) to discover how their earnings are determined and whether their economic situation bears on their social status and politics.

I divide the lower half of the working class into three strata: nonskilled (unskilled and semiskilled) employees who work in high-wage industries, nonskilled employees who work in low-wage industries, and the marginally employed. Since the social and political bonds of workers in these three strata are tenuous, I concentrate more on their pattern of earnings. Here the influence of labor unions is important, and I explore its impact on workers with different ascriptive characteristics. The last chapter in this section explores how men and women are technologically stratified in the labor force.

The inability of the American working class to unite politically has attracted much scholarly attention, and I devote three chapters to the problem. The first deals with the extent that American workers in different strata develop a consistent ideology of economic conflict that is independent of their political beliefs. The second examines the extent to which union officers speak to the economic and political views of their diversified membership. The third attempts to measure the amount of political consensus among the segments of the working class.

My limited experience with European working classes suggests that their cleavages parallel those found in the American working class. I test out my ideas on the French working class which allegedly is more homogeneous, more politically mobilized, and more united than the American. I expose some mythologies about national differences in working classes and raise some important questions, which I attempt to answer in the final chapter that deals with the future of the American working class.

2

Economic Cleavages

Introduction

This book contends that the American working class is divided along several lines, and that these divisions prevent concerted social and political action. In this chapter, I propose a division of the working class that is generally useful for several research purposes. Ideally, the proposed divisions should be more or less durable and important, from both the point of view of subclass members and from the point of view of scholars who do research on the working class. I start with the assumption that any division in the working class must first be based on consistent earnings differences. These lead to important behavioral effects when they are based on markets that are organized along different lines. The carry-over or lack of carry-over of market relations to non-work arenas affects the possibility of social action. Therefore, most of this chapter examines the question whether the earnings differences among the proposed five strata of the working class are statistically significant and important. After a rather elaborate exhibition of data on earnings and social status differences, I compare the five strata scheme to divisions of the working class proposed by other scholars.

The working class was shaped by the industrial revolution. With few exceptions (Michels, 1959; Bauman, 1972), scholars have emphasized the homogenizing impact of industrialization on it. Thus, while Marx (1967:628–39) recognized the existence of "lazarous layers" of the proletariat, he predicted that mechanization would meld them into a homogeneous class of machine tenders. Many scholars have since elaborated this theme of homogenization (Carr-

---

An earlier version of this chapter was co-authored with George Putnam.

Saunders and Jones, 1937; Warner and Low, 1947; Friedmann, 1955; Kuczynski, 1971; Stone, 1974; Braverman, 1974). Even orthodox economists agree that the rising educational levels of workers have increased their uniformity and job substitutability (Gunter, 1964). Some students (Marglin, 1974; Noble, 1979) now predict that automation will further erode skills and create a homogeneous class of meter watchers.

Most social scientists have also accepted the thesis that class homogenization heightens class awareness and leads to the formation of working-class parties. Sombart (1906) and subsequent scholars (see Lipset's bibliography, 1977) explained why this did not happen in the United States as a result of the action of countervailing forces such as the absence of a feudal tradition, the escape valve of the frontier, rapid economic growth, high wages, and ethnic and religious diversity. Although some of these conditions have changed (e.g., disappearance of the frontier, decline in economic growth, slowing of immigration, the declining significance of religion), a genuine labor party has not materialized, possibly because new working-class cleavages have emerged.[1]

Important variations in the economic experiences of workers still divide the U.S. working class. In some industries the wage ratio between skilled and unskilled labor has not declined in a century (Ozanne, 1962). Contrary to conventional wisdom, the relative size of the skilled aristocracy of labor has not declined in over eighty years. The labor movement, far from equalizing working-class earnings, has split workers into secure and insecure strata (Rees, 1976:92–99; Kahn, 1978, 1980). Changes in the economy have so segmented labor markets that earnings inequities have widened (Averitt, 1968; Bluestone, 1970; Doeringer and Piore, 1971; Freedman, 1976). Business, government, and welfare policies have spawned a permanent under-class of semi-employed workers (Piven and Cloward, 1971; O'Connor, 1973). Selective tracking of students in schools has barred some working-class youth from upward mobility (Miller and Rein, 1966; Berg, 1969; Bowles, 1972). Ascriptively based labor markets have perpetuated working-class inequality along racial, ethnic, sex, and age lines (Webb, 1891; Brissenden, 1929; Breckenridge, 1933; Woofter, 1933; Drake and Cayton, 1945; Oppenheimer, 1970; Bonacich, 1972; Stolzenberg, 1975). Finally, a dominant ideology has justified these economic inequalities with a rhetoric of equal opportunity, merit, and individual responsibility (Huber and Form, 1973).

Despite evidence of structurally based economic inequality within the working class, relatively few scholars have systematically examined the impact of this inequality on the social and political behavior of the class.[2] Some scholars avoid such an analysis because they consider conflict between capital and labor to be more important than conflict within the working class (e.g., Braverman, 1974). Other students neglect the study of intraclass inequalities because they think that economic and status differences result from individual and not stratal experiences (e.g., Sewell and Hauser, 1975).

The five-fold division of the working class that I propose is based on three factors which, when combined, reflect differences in property, occupational skill, and economic power of the employment sector. This structural approach to dividing the working class must be compared against the most prevalent individual approaches that divide the class solely on the basis of the workers' individual skills. If the stratal or structural approach is as powerful as three alternative individual approaches in explaining earnings, then the stratal approach should be selected for research because it offers the greater promise of also explaining stratal social and political behavior. That is, noneconomic behavior can be explained better if we have knowledge about organizational ties in the labor market.

For this research, the working class is composed of all workers in all non-farm manual and service jobs that are listed in the U.S. census. Farm laborers and tenants are excluded because their earnings are difficult to estimate and because they interact little with other manual and service employees. Although most office and sales clerks resemble manual workers economically, I decided to omit them from this study because two-fifths are secondary workers in families whose other earners include owners, managers, and professionals. Further, chief earners in blue- and white-collar families do not exhibit common patterns of generational mobility, a typical feature of social class membership (Weber, 1978; Baron, 1980; Breiger, 1981).[3] The omission of white-collar employees from this study is a conservative approach that works against the major hypothesis, that a heterogeneous working class is composed of several hierarchical fragments; adding white-collar workers would only increase working-class heterogeneity. The inclusion of foremen in the working class is questionable, and that issue will be taken up in Chapter 3.

Dividing the Working Class

Scholars differ on how they should divide the working class. Marx thought that traditional artisans (the aristocrats of labor) and the lumpenproletariat were temporary vestiges of an earlier economy, and that only the industrial proletariat would survive in mature capitalism. This prediction failed to materialize because capitalism spawned new types of skilled, technical, and service-manual occupations (More, 1970). Lynd and Lynd (1937:460) retained Marx's divisions, but they did not consider how new industries might alter class fragmentation. On the basis of their associational patterns, social status, and subcultures, Warner and Lunt (1941) divided workers into lower-middle, upper-lower, and lower-lower social classes, but the Warner school slighted the economic and political basis of class membership (Mills, 1942). Reiss (1961) and Blau and Duncan (1967) convinced a host of sociologists to reject the idea of discrete classes altogether in favor of locating individuals according to their rank on *continua* of income, education, and occupational prestige. Shostak (1969), like many others, simply divided the working class into skilled, semiskilled, and unskilled employees as defined by the U.S. Bureau of the Census, but he omitted service employees, most of whom are manual workers (Levison, 1974). Moreover, while Conk (1978) offered little quantitative evidence, she attacked the census skill classification as arbitrary and class-biased.

Although all of these stratal divisions are useful for some research purposes, a classification is needed that is both theoretically cogent and useful for a wide range of research tasks. The sociological tradition of Weber (Parsons and Smelser, 1965:146–56) and Stinchcombe (1965:164–71) emphasizes that differences in the social and economic organization of labor market affect workers' life chances, property, earnings, and unemployment. Markets vary in the organizational strength of their component occupations, the economic strength of their industries, and the social status of their workers. The intersections or matchings of the occupational, industrial, and status dimensions of markets should point to divisions of the working class along economic lines (Granovetter, 1981:25). Each dimension is now briefly elaborated.

The organizational strength of occupations is reflected in their work autonomy, social cohesion, and extent of unionization. Work autonomy or work control is higher for self-employed workers (Kalleberg and Griffin, 1978), but it also rises with the skill level of occupations (Blauner, 1964; Spaeth, 1979). Autonomy and control are also high in occupations such as crafts that recruit and train their own members. Social cohesion in occupations flourishes where managers are least able to routinize work (Edwards, 1979), thus permitting workers to move about, socialize, and organize (Sayles, 1964). Social cohesion among low-skilled workers is facilitated when large numbers are crowded in restricted quarters (Form, 1976a:100 passim). Labor unions, as formal organizations, try to foster social cohesion by limiting management's power to control work. Understandably, unions are more successful where workers are already informally organized and control work. Thus, unions typically organize skilled workers more easily than they do the less skilled. In sum, occupations vary in their organizational strength; some have all three sources of strength (autonomy, cohesion, and unionization), but others have fewer or none (Form, 1976b).

The economic strength of industries, along with their associated organizational characteristics, also influences employee life chances. We used Averitt's (1968) crude dichotomy of economic "core" and "periphery" industries because this classification highlights important economic and organizational attributes (Gordon, 1972). Industries in the core sector generally are large, capital intensive, and profitable because they tend to operate in oligopolistic markets (Doeringer and Piore, 1971), while industries in the periphery are typically smaller, labor intensive, and less profitable because they operate in competitive markets. Although the core-periphery distinction is less adequate for research that considers the entire industrial and occupational structure (Hodson, 1983; Tolbert, et al., 1980), it is more useful in pointing to earnings distinctions in the working class. Thus, firms in the core sector generally pay low-skilled workers a higher wage and provide them with more secure jobs than do firms in the periphery (Cain, 1976:1237).[4] Skilled workers, because of their short supply, greater social solidarity, and high unionization, can command higher wages in any sector (Douty, 1961). When low-skilled manual employees are heavily concentrated in relatively few core firms, their unionization is relatively easy, and management is forced to pay higher wages and fringe benefits. The dispersion of workers in many small firms in the periphery makes their unionization difficult, further enabling employers to pay lower wages and fringe benefits (Freeman, 1980; Lord and Falk, 1982). Even without unions, core industry firms pay low-skilled workers relatively high wages because the industries need a dependable source of labor to meet their long-term production and investment targets (Roomkin and Sommers, 1974; O'Connor, 1973:44).

The third factor that affects workers' markets is their social status. Groups that have status advantages by virtue of their sex, race, ethnicity, age, or other ascriptive attributes tend to enter self-employment or the skilled trades, gain preferential access into core industry firms, and obtain the protection of strong unions. Workers with ascriptive disadvantages (women, blacks, others) either receive less formal education, less vocational training, less union protection, or less socialization to become reliable workers (Bibb and Form, 1977). Lacking personal networks into good paying firms, they take the left-over and low-paying jobs in the economic periphery (Granovetter, 1981).

The above discussion points to several related criteria that stratify workers: whether or not they exercise work autonomy on the basis of their property (self-employed vs. employee) or skill; whether or not they achieve social cohesion through their occupational socialization (crafts) and/or unionization; whether or not they find employment in economically strong sectors (core or periphery); and whether or not their ascribed statuses are favorably rewarded in society. The task now is to propose a limited number of strata and to justify them on the basis of the above criteria. Later, factual evidence is examined for its support of the divisions of the working class. This theoretical approach is preferred over letting the data speak for themselves by using such statistical techniques as factor or discriminant analysis.

I decided to divide U.S. manual workers into five major divisions: self-employed; skilled or craft employees; nonskilled (semiskilled and unskilled) employees in the core sector of the economy; nonskilled (semiskilled and unskilled) workers in the peripheral sector; and the marginally employed who work fewer than twenty-seven weeks a year. Foremen are sometimes included in the working class because some scholars do not consider them part of management. I do not include foremen in the present analysis, but in Chapter 3 I examine the evidence of whether their social and economic characteristics are closer to the middle or working class. In terms of the criteria used to stratify the working class, foremen resemble the skilled more than other strata.

In Marxist theory, self-employed manual workers are not in the working class because they work for themselves. With respect to their life chances and their career and generational mobility (Breiger, 1981), however, they are in the same class as other manual workers. The available evidence clearly shows (see Chapter 4) that the self-employed often earn wages in addition to profits and become manual employees when they fail in business. For purposes of this research, the critical factor is that the self-employed are manual workers.

As suggested above, the five working-class strata differ in their labor market resources. Thus, the resources of the self-employed are work autonomy, property ownership (tools, equipment, materials), above average occupational skills, as well as favored ascriptive status (being male, white, and native-born). The skilled also have (a) above average work autonomy and work control, (b) social solidarity derived from common training, work in tightly-knit groups, and labor union membership, (c) high social status as the aristocrats of labor, and (d) favored ascriptive status (male, white, native-born). Nonskilled (semiskilled and unskilled) employees in core sector industries, lacking autonomy, work control, and high social status, derive their market power primarily from their union's ability to extract concessions from employers and from their male social status. The nonskilled in the periphery sector lack work autonomy, work control, and union protection. They often suffer from negatively evaluated ascriptive status (being female, black, foreign-born, young). They have but one advantage over the marginally employed; they are higher in the labor queue because of full-time participation in the labor market.

Four Hypotheses

We can now investigate four hypotheses to determine the empirical validity of these contentions. First, other things being equal, self-employment provides greater economic returns than does wage labor. Second, the semiskilled more closely resemble the unskilled than the skilled in their wage determination, thereby suggesting that the main skill break is between the skilled and the remaining unskilled. Third, the economic strength of industries better differentiates earnings of nonskilled than of skilled because the skilled have other sources of occupational power. The second and third hypotheses, if supported, would justify separating the skilled as a separate stratum and ignoring skill divisions between the semi- and unskilled in favor of their sector (core or periphery) of employment. Fourth, the five working-class strata provide as much power to predict earnings as models based on continua of occupational complexity, such as those furnished by the census and the *Dictionary of Occupational Titles*. If the four hypotheses are supported, the stratal model is selected because it is more useful for research on social and political class cleavages.

In the following section, I compare the five earnings models in great detail. Readers may prefer to skip the statistical analyses and go directly to a discussion of the results beginning on page forty-four.

The data source for this research is the county file, 1/1,000 Public Use Sample of the 1970 United States census. The census divides manual workers into three skill levels: craft and kindred workers as skilled, machine and transport operatives as semiskilled, and laborers as unskilled. We removed foreman from the skilled category because they perform little manual labor. Although the census does not divide service occupations into manual and non-manual, most of them are heavily manual in content: chambermaids, janitors, cooks, waiters, practical nurses, barbers, guards, hairdressers, firefighters, police officers, housekeepers, porters, attendants, lay midwives, flight attendants, and dental assistants (Parker, 1972; Levison, 1974). I decided to include all service occupations in the working class. These service occupations comprise almost 35 percent of blue-collar workers as defined by the census or 26 percent of the working class as defined in this study. This working class comprises about half of the total labor force.

Since the census does not classify service occupations by skill, I allocated them into skilled, semi-, and unskilled groups. On the basis of a factor analysis of forty-four occupational attributes provided by the fourth edition of the *Dictionary of Occupational Titles* (DOT), Miller and colleagues (1980, Table F-2) calculated the occupational substantive complexity scores of all occupations in the census. Most crafts or skilled occupations had complexity scores of 3.5 and above, and most unskilled occupations scored below 2.4. I placed service occupations with scores of 3.5 or above in the skilled category, occupations with scores of 2.4 to 3.4 in the semi-skilled, and occupations with scores below 2.4 in the unskilled category.[5]

The dependent variable is the natural log of annual earnings for 1969. This variable was logged to transform a skewed distribution into a symmetrical one. Earnings were coded in hundreds of dollars. Those who did not work in the previous year or who earned no income or a negative income were removed from the sample to minimize core-periphery differences (Hauser, 1980). Only income from self-employment, wages, and salaries was used. Earnings from self-employment were increased by a factor of 30 percent because studies by the Internal Revenue Service reveal that profits are underreported to the census by at least that amount (U.S. Department of the Treasury, 1979).[6]

The remaining variables were ascriptive worker characteristics (sex, race, marital status), human capital characteristics (education, skill, occupational complexity, work experience), extent of labor market participation (hours and weeks worked), and industry strength (core and periphery).[7]

Model 1 of the working class separates workers into five discrete strata: the self-employed; the skilled; the nonskilled (semi- and unskilled) workers in core sector industries (hereafter simply referred to as core workers); the nonskilled in periphery industries (here-after simply referred to as periphery workers); and the marginally employed— those who work fewer than twenty-seven weeks a year. Models 2–4 each contain different continuous measures of skill, and sector is treated as a separate variable. Model 2 uses three skill grades as described in the census: skilled, semiskilled, and unskilled. Model 3 ranks workers on five *DOT* continua of occupational com-plexity (see below). Model 4 is based on scores of two skill factors derived from the *DOT* continuous variables used in Model 3.

I digress to explain the *DOT* scores and factors in models 3 and 4. Despite its shortcomings, the *DOT* contains the best data on occupational complexity because its measures are based, in part at least, on direct observation of workers' functions (Cain and Treiman, 1981).[8] Five unambiguous *DOT* indicators of occupational complex-ity were selected and merged with the census data. Three indica-tors deal with complexity of manipulating DATA, PEOPLE, and THINGS on the job. GED (general educational development) and SVP (specific vocational preparation) respectively measure the education and vocational training required to achieve acceptable work efficiency. "GED includes aspects of formal and informal education that con-tribute to the worker's reasoning development, the ability to follow instructions, and the use of language and mathematical skills. SVP includes training acquired in a school, work, military, institutional, or vocational environment but excludes schooling without specific vocational content" (Miller, et al., 1980:29).

Model 4 includes two skill factors derived from a factor analy-sis of the five *DOT* occupational complexity variables. The remaining DOT variables were not used because the twenty-six that measure aptitudes, temperament, and interests are psychological attributes that do not bear directly on occupational complexity. Five variables that cover physical demands of jobs are quite unreliable (Cain and Treiman, 1981:262), and the six working conditions variables do not measure occupational complexity. In the ensuing discussion, the reader should remember the direction of occupational complexity scores (see n. 7).

In deriving the two skill factors, one should note that the correlations among DATA, GED, and SVP are high (above .80), and the remaining correlations are moderate (between .16 and .37). The initial factor mix suggested two factors, the first being more impor-tant because its eigenvalues explained 81 percent of the variance and the second, 19 percent. The factors were then rotated orthogonally using the varimax procedure. The pattern of loadings is clear. Since GED and SVP have large positive loadings (.88 and .98 respectively), and DATA a large negative one (−.83), high educational background, high specific vocational training, and handling of complex data go together.[9] I call this complexity factor "skill." The pattern of loadings on the second factor is less clear. PEOPLE has the highest positive loading (.77), followed by THINGS (.40) and DATA (.33) with smaller positive loadings; GED has a moderately high negative loading (−.35) and SVP, a small negative one (−.04). Since this factor loads heavily on PEOPLE and moderately high on THINGS, I call it, "sociotechnical complexity." This type of skill is found in many women's service occupations, especially in the health area (McLaughlin, 1978).

Profit and Wages

I hypothesized that self-employment would generate higher earnings than would wage labor, and that the two groups would differ in their social characteristics. The self-employed comprise only 5 percent of the manual labor force, but they enjoy economic, human capital, labor market, and social status advantages over employees (Table 2.1). Not surprisingly, the self-employed annually earn 63 percent more than do employees; the former own houses of higher value and suffer considerably less unemployment. Self-employed workers are older than employees; most of them are married white males living with their spouses. They have more work experience and more formal and vocational education than employees. These favored ascriptive and human capital characteristics translate into more hours of work and less unemployment.

Although descriptive analysis shows that the self-employed have a distinct earnings advantage over employees, regression analysis tells us whether this holds when other variables that affect earnings are controlled. Data in Table 2.2 reveal that the self-employed enjoy a nine percent earnings advantage over employees even when ascriptive, human capital and market participation variables are controlled. A separate regression analysis in Chapter 4 reveals that ascriptive factors (being male, white, and married) and hours worked account for relatively more of self-employed earnings, while skill level and weeks worked account for more of employees' earnings. The higher variance (R^2) of earnings explained for employees (.55) than for self-employed (.36) suggests that the latter's market is less structured and regulated. Altogether, these data support the decision to keep the self-employed as a separate stratum. The question now is whether the skilled should be kept as a stratum of employees separate from the rest of semi- and unskilled workers who are divided by sector of employment (core and periphery) rather than skill.

Table 2.1. Social and Economic Characteristics of Self-Employed, Employees, and Three Skill Groups (percent unless specified)

Variables	Self-Employed	Employees			
		Total	Skilled	Semi-skilled	Unskilled
Av. annual earnings ($)	8,844[a]	5,570	7,237	5,475	3,245
House value > $12,500	71	64	69	50	49
Gross monthly rent ($)	122	107	116	105	103
Unemployed	2	5	4	6	6
Completed high school	47	46	55	42	40
Work experience (av. yrs.)	26	19	21	19	18
Vocational training	42	26	40	21	20
Specific voc. prep. ≥ 6 mos.	71	41	98	17	0
Hours worked ≥ 40	76	73	81	77	58
Weeks worked ≥ 50	70	61	70	63	50
Male	82	70	84	68	55
Chief earner	79	67	80	65	52
Married w/spouse	84	69	79	72	53
Age (av. years)	46	39	41	39	38
White	92	84	91	85	76
Size	5	95	31	36	28

[a]Uncorrected, $7,328.
Data source: Public Use Sample, U.S. Census, 1970, 1/1,000 County File.

Skill and Industrial Sector

Employees are often divided into three rather than two skill grades: skilled, semiskilled, and unskilled. Although the three grade scheme serves some research purposes well, I argue that (1) all three skill grades do not differ equally in their economic and social characteristics, (2) a more appropriate classification dichotomizes labor earnings into skilled and nonskilled (semi- and unskilled combined) groups, and (3) the sector of employment economically and socially stratifies the nonskilled more than does degree of skill.

Data in Table 2.1 show that the skill levels are about equally distant in their earnings but that the two lower levels are more alike in their unemployment and property values. Also, for the human capital characteristics of education, specific vocational preparation, and work experience, the unskilled and the semiskilled are closer together, while the semiskilled resemble the skilled more in the extent of labor market participation. More of the skilled are ascriptively

Table 2.2. Regression of the Natural Log of Annual Earnings on Social, Economic, and Stratal Characteristics of the Working Class

Variables[a]	B	beta	B	beta
D–Skilled			.344	.167
D–Semiskilled			.268	.129
Self-employed/employee	.093	.020		
Skill level	.163	.130		
Education	.034	.098	.035	.100
Vocational training	.096	.043	.111	.049
Experience	.007	.110	.008	.116
Sector	.280	.140	.265	.133
Hours worked	.256	.397	.104	.177
Weeks worked	.106	.180	.255	.395
Sex	.345	.156	.352	.159
Marital status	.265	.121	.261	.119
Race	.115	.041	.112	.040
Constant	.698		.816	
N	33,564		33,564	
Adjusted R^2	.602		.604	

Data source: Public Use Sample, U.S. Census, 1970, 1/1,000 County File.
[a]All significant below .001.

advantaged (being males, white, chief earners, married, and older), but here the skill levels are about equally apart from each other. In short, though the semi- and unskilled are more alike than the skilled and semiskilled, the three-fold gradation of skill does not accurately and systematically depict the divisions of the working class.

An alternative method for examining the utility of the threefold versus the twofold skill division is regression analysis. A dummy variable was created for each of the three skill levels, and the unskilled were excluded from the regression. The semiskilled and unskilled should be combined into a nonskilled category where the unstandardized regression coefficient for the semiskilled dummy variable is less than that for the skilled and also approaching zero. The first condition is met in Table 2.2 because the unstandardized coefficient for the semiskilled is smaller than for the skilled in the prediction of earnings; however, the coefficient for the semiskilled does not approach zero. Overall, the data suggest that although the semiskilled and unskilled are not identical in their characteristics, they are closely allied.

The second task is to assess the importance of sector of employment for the earnings of the skilled and nonskilled groups. Students of a dual economy disagree on the sector importance of skills. Those who emphasize internal labor markets in core industries (e.g., Doerlinger and Piore, 1971) believe that workers may have few skills when first hired, but that they are later developed in company training programs. Small increments of job skills are planned and each new job in the promotion ladder requires considerable time to master. Management therefore, recruits employees who have the greatest learning potentials, i.e., workers with more education, vocational training, and general ability. Researchers in the radical tradition (e.g., Blackburn and Mann, 1979:280) insist that most workers in both sectors have few skills and that most jobs can be learned quickly, perhaps within a week or two at most. Others believe that the decisive break is between skilled and all other labor (Cain, 1976). The research tasks then are to (a) classify industries into sectors, (b) ascertain their importance for distinguishing earnings within the skilled and nonskilled strata, and (c) determine the extent to which sector interacts with skill to predict earnings.

The assignment of industries to sectors followed a scheme first developed by Bibb and Form (1977) and later refined by Bibb (1981). Using the census three-digit industrial code, Bibb (1981) reasoned that the industrial organization, market structure, market concentration, and economic performance of industries create conditions that differentially affect employee earnings, unemployment, unionization, fringe benefits, and working conditions. Bibb developed seven indicators of industrial economic structure: capital intensity, growth or expansion orientation, intensity of research and development, economic scale, degree of concentration, price behavior, and profits. He then subjected the indicators to discriminant function analysis. All variables attained statistical significance at or below the .05 level as measured by the t-test. Two clusters of industries were clearly separated according to their economic structure, with 93 percent of the industries correctly labeled as falling in the core or the periphery.

Data in Table 2.3 summarize information on the occupational skills of workers in the core and periphery sectors. DOT and other indicators of occupational complexity reveal consistent sector differences. Jobs in the core sector require higher skill as measured by the lower scores in complexity of handling data and things and higher scores in general educational development and specific vocational preparation. Understandably, core sector employees score higher on the skill factor while periphery employees score higher on the sociotechnical factor. Importantly, the training time required for adequate job performance in the core sector is almost twice that of the periphery, a fact that supports the theory that the core sector tends to develop internal labor markets. Workers in the core sector also score higher on physical strength required for their jobs, an attribute associated with male jobs.[10] In short, employees in the core sector have slight advantages over those in the periphery in formal education and vocational training, and they have more complex jobs that require more time to master.[11] Yet, jobs in the periphery have higher prestige scores.

Table 2.3. Occupational Complexity Sector Scores

| | Sector | |
Variables	Core	Periphery
Data complexity	4.03	4.36
People complexity	7.11	7.08
Things complexity	3.78	3.50
General educ. development	3.17	2.92
Specific vocational preparation	4.94	4.12
Skill factor	.23	− .25
Sociotechnical factor	.12	− .12
Training time (months)	20.5	12.3
Strength scale	2.98	2.09
Envir. conditions scale	1.21	.73
Vocational training (%)	29	24

Data source: Public Use Sample, U.S. Census, 1970, 1/1,000 County File, and DOT 4th Ed. Tape.

The next task is to ascertain whether sector of employment stratifies the nonskilled more than the skilled. As expected, data in Table 2.4 reveal that the skilled enjoy higher ascriptive social status, higher levels of human capital, more hours and weeks of work, and higher earnings than the nonskilled. Only in a few instances are sector differences among the skilled as great or greater than those among the nonskilled. Sector differences in sex, race, and chief earner status are almost as large among the skilled as among the nonskilled, but differences are trivial for the skilled in most of the remaining variables and are larger for the nonskilled. The most important advantages that nonskilled core sector workers have over the nonskilled in the periphery are earnings, hours and weeks worked, vocational preparation, and marital status (married). In short, employment sector more powerfully divides nonskilled than skilled workers.

The regression analysis in Table 2.5 adds evidence that sector more powerfully determines earnings among the nonskilled than among the skilled. For the nonskilled, controlling for other variables, members in the core sector earn 32 percent more than periphery sector workers; for the skilled, the difference is 25 percent. The

Table 2.4. Social and Economic Characteristics of Skilled and Nonskilled by Sector (percent unless specified)

Variables	Skilled		Nonskilled	
	Core	Periphery	Core	Periphery
Size	42	58	40	60
Male	97	68	81	50
White	93	89	84	79
Married w/spouse	85	73	76	57
Chief income earner	90	68	74	50
Mean annual earnings ($)	8,384	5,797	6,199	3,406
Mean work experience (yrs.)	22	20	20	17
Completed high school	56	55	44	40
Vocational training	41	40	22	19
Spec. voc. prep. $\geq$ 6 months	98	99	18	5
Hours worked $\geq$ 40	86	75	81	60
Weeks worked $\geq$ 50	72	68	66	52
Mean house value ($)	5,016	4,819	4,285	4,302
Mean gross monthly rent ($)	117	115	107	102
Unemployed	5	3	6	6

Data source: Public Use Sample, U.S. Census, 1970, 1/1,000 County File.

relative ranking of the betas for the non-skilled suggest that, except for sex, weeks, and hours worked, sector provides a stronger independent effect on earnings than do ascriptive and human capital characteristics. For the skilled, the sector effect is surpassed by sex and weeks worked. To determine the extent that sector interacts with skill to predict earnings, a dichotomous skill variable (skilled = 1, nonskilled = 0) was combined with the sector variable (core = 1, periphery = 0) to produce the interaction term. In Table 2.5, the interaction term produced a small but significant negative coefficient, further supporting the contention that sector is more important for nonskilled than skilled workers.

All these data undoubtedly underestimate the impact of sector on the earnings of the nonskilled because they do not consider earnings supplements or fringe benefits which account for 37 percent of total pay. Lord and Falk's (1982) study of the Quality of Employment Survey data for 1972 revealed that differences in benefits between primary (skilled) and secondary (nonskilled) occupations in the monopoly or core sector were small compared to differences in the competitive or periphery sector. This suggests that, compared to the nonskilled, benefits for the skilled were less affected by employment sector.

Unfortunately, historical data on earnings supplements are not

Table 2.5. Regression of Natural Log of Annual Earnings on Social and Economic Characteristics of Workers: Skilled and Nonskilled as Control Variables and Interaction of Skill and Sector

Variables[a]	Skilled		Nonskilled		Interaction Skill/Sector	
	B	beta	B	beta	B	beta
Education	.039	.128	.035	.099	.036	.101
Voc. training	.135	.084	.072	.028	.103	.046
Hours worked	.075	.143	.129	.219	.112	.189
Weeks worked	.239	.378	.265	.426	.260	.403
Experience	.007	.131	.007	.105	.007	.110
Sector	.250	.156	.318	.151	.326	.163
Sex	.444	.200	.337	.157	.358	.162
Marital status	.250	.124	.293	.135	.284	.129
Race	.160	.056	.137	.052	.140	.050
Two skill levels[b]					.210	.102
Skill/sector[c]					−.069	−.028
Constant	1.197		.821		.861	
N	12,358		21,206		33,564	
Adjusted R^2	.484		.583		.594	

[a]All significant below .001.
[b]Dichotomous variable: skilled = 1, nonskilled = 0.
[c]Interaction term (skilled = 1, nonskilled = 0) X sector (core = 1, periphery = 0).
Data source: Public Use Sample, U.S. Census, 1970, 1/1,000 County File.

available for single industries and occupations, but reliable data are available for 1929–70 by broad industry groups (U.S. Bureau of the Census, 1975, Part D:893–904). On the assumption that manual workers proportionately share the earnings supplements of all workers, some tentative conclusions may be drawn. From 1929–70, with the exception of farm workers, employees in service (periphery) industries received the lowest supplements, running from $4 per capita in 1929 to $384 in 1970. In 1970, government (core) employees received 3.8 times the supplements of service workers. Although data are not separated for durable (core) and non-durable (periphery) manufacturing, employees in manufacturing and transportation (core) received three times the supplements of service workers. Workers in none of the core sector industries received less than 2.5 times the supplements of service workers. In 1970, communications and public utilities (core) workers received $1,000 more in benefits than did service workers, while manufacturing and transportation workers received over $800 more. In unionized firms, firms that predominate in the core sector, Freeman (1981) found that fringe benefits averaged 72 cents an hour compared to 29 cents for non-union firms in the periphery. In short, the nonskilled in the core sector have massive earnings advantages over the nonskilled in the periphery.

Working-Class Strata

To this point, the data show that the self-employed differ from employees, that the skilled differ from the nonskilled, and that the nonskilled form two strata on the basis of sector of employment. The distinguishing feature of the self-employed, skilled, and core workers, apart from their higher earnings, is that they are mostly white married males living with their spouses (Table 2.6). In contrast, almost half of the periphery sector and marginally employed are women, and most of them work as operatives in non-durable goods manufacturing and in service jobs. Expectedly, more of the workers in the top three than the bottom two strata are chief earners of their families, were high school graduates, work more hours, suffer less unemployment, earn substantially higher incomes, and own more valuable homes.

Table 2.6. Social and Economic Characteristics of Working-Class Strata (percent unless specified)

Variables	Self-Employed	Skilled	Nonskilled Core	Periphery	Marginally Employed
Size	5	28	24	31	12
Male	82	84	82	56	52
White	92	91	86	78	84
Married w/spouse	84	79	79	64	42
Chief income earner	79	80	79	61	30
Work experience (years)	26	21	21	20	11
Completed high school	47	55	44	42	46
Vocational training	42	40	21	22	18
Spec. voc. prep. ≥ 6 mos.	71	98	20	12	23
Hours worked ≥ 40	76	84	84	71	48
Weeks worked ≥ 50	70	76	71	67	0
Mean annual earnings ($)	8,844	7,237	6,883	4,540	1,442
House value > $12,500	71	69	59	47	63
Mean gross monthly rent ($)	121	115	107	103	106
Unemployed	2	3	5	3	15

Data source: Public Use Sample, U.S. Census, 1970, 1/1,000 County File.

From self-employed to marginally employed, the variables in Table 2.6 change in a consistent direction. Thus, the self-employed not only earn most, but the earnings differences between the strata increase as one moves from the self- to the marginally-employed. Two types of irregularities occur. In some instances the values for the skilled are higher than for the self-employed, and some of the values for the marginally employed are higher than those for periphery workers. For example, a slightly higher percentage of the skilled than self-employed are males, high school graduates, and chief earners of their families. Similarly, a higher percent of the marginally employed than periphery workers are white, not currently married, own property of higher value, and have more specialized vocational preparation. These data generally reflect the greater heterogeneity of the self- and marginally employed and greater homogeneity of skilled and core workers.

So far, the evidence provides some support for the existence of the five strata but not their independence from one another. If the strata are not independent, then they overlap considerably, thereby suggesting that the working class is not segmented and stratified. The correlations among the strata range from $-.43$ to $-.08$, indicating a low amount of commonality. The regression of earnings on the strata, ascriptive, human capital, and market participation variables provide further support (see Table 2.7). Five dummy variables representing each stratum were created, and the periphery stratum dummy was excluded to prevent perfect collinearity. The unstandardized regression coefficients attest that, controlling for all other variables, the skilled and core strata earn the highest incomes relative to periphery workers, followed by the self-employed, while the marginally employed stratum shows a negative coefficient. The standardized beta of each stratum variable indicates the power of its effect on earnings relative to the other variables. The betas reveal not only that the strata are significantly independent of each other, but as a group they affect earnings to a greater extent than any set of variables except sex and labor market participation.

Comparing Four Models of Class Stratification

In creating the working-class strata, we combined skill level and sector to form the nonskilled core and periphery strata. Can we better account for earnings if skill and sector are treated separately? To answer this question, we compared four equations or models that had different terms for skill and sector. The first model combined sector and census skill level to form the two nonskilled strata, while the three remaining models used different measures of skill and

Table 2.7. Regression of Log of Annual Earnings on
Working-Class Strata, Human Capital, Market
Participation, and Ascription Variables

Variables[a]	B	beta
D–Self-employed	.254	.056
D–Skilled	.223	.132
D–Core nonskilled	.295	.116
D–Marginally employed	−.465	−.145
Education	.038	.109
Vocational training	.112	.050
Hours worked	.113	.190
Weeks worked	.174	.271
Experience	.007	.111
Sex	.415	.187
Marital status	.288	.131
Race	.151	.054
Constant	1.219	
N	34,209	
Adjusted R^2	.593	

Data source: Public Use Sample, U.S. Census, 1970, 1/1,000 County
File.
[a]All significant below .001.

retained sector as a separate variable. If little explanatory power for
earnings is lost by combining skill and sector as in model 1, support
for the working-class model is suggested.

Model 1 used the five working-class strata; model 2, the census
classifications of skilled, semiskilled, and unskilled; model 3, the
five DOT occupational complexity variables; model 4, two skill
factors derived from the factor analysis of the DOT occupational
complexity variables. In model 1, the working-class strata are four
dummy variables as in Table 2.7. Note 7 contains the coding for
the census skill categories and the DOT occupational complexity
variables. In model 4, standard deviations for the DOT factors were
used.

All of our models were equally powerful because they each
explained approximately 60 percent of the logs of earnings. Differences among the models were small because their total explained
variances were within 1.6 percent of each other. Although skill was
measured differently in models 2–4, its impact was about the same
in all models. For the census skill measure (model 2), each skill level
raised earnings 17 percent. In model 3, which used the five DOT
occupational complexity variables, specific vocational preparation
by far had the strongest influence: each unit raised earnings about

13 percent. In model 4, each additional standard deviation in the skill factor raised earnings about 11 percent; the sociotechnical factor, 4 percent. Overall, these data support the use of the five-strata model of the working class because it explained earnings as well as alternative models that measure skill and sector separately.

Since 45 percent of periphery employees are women compared to 12 percent in the core sector, a possible criticism of using sector to form the working-class strata is that some women prefer not to work steadily and/or full-time. Consequently their lesser work experience, labor market participation, and lower earnings may not reflect sector "discrimination" but the market's adjustment to women's preferences.[12] If this reasoning is correct, then differences in sector earnings should be trivial for fully committed workers, e.g., the family's chief earner. We pursued this question. About 80 percent of the workers in the three top strata (self-employed, skilled, and nonskilled core) were chief earners compared to 58 percent in the periphery, and 29 percent of the marginally employed. Men consti-tuted 84 percent of chief earners and 41 percent of non-chief earners. Expectedly, chief earners worked more hours and weeks and had more work experience than non-chiefs,[13] and their earnings were 2.6 times those of non-chiefs.

A multiple regression analysis of the earnings of chief earners revealed that sector effects remained substantial: core workers earned about 23 percent more than periphery employees. Nonskilled chief earners in the core sector earned 72 percent more than marginally employed chief earners, controlling for all other effects, while nonskilled chief earners in the periphery sector earned only 47 percent more. A comparison of the regression equations for chief earners and all earners showed that differences in the coefficients were trivial and unsystematic. Thus, earnings differences for non-skilled core and periphery strata are not artifacts of the greater representation of partially committed women in the periphery.

Discussion

In examining working-class earnings, I found that weeks and hours worked, male status, and even marital status for men contributed as heavily to their earnings as did occupational skill, employee sector, and self-employment—the factors that underpin the formation of the five strata. Yet, it makes sense to use the five-stratum framework. Although ascriptive and labor participation factors are important, they do not contribute as much to group action as do occupational skill, employment sector, and self-employment. If sex were used to create strata, this would place some spouses in two-earner families in different strata. That would make for some interesting family fights. Moreover, women workers are only recently beginning to fight collectively for their interests at work. The same reasoning applies to labor market participation as a device for creating strata. Except in rare instances, collective action in the United States is not organized on the basis of number of weeks and hours that employees work. But workers often do act on the basis of their occupational skills, the industry in which they work, and their property—the factors that underly the five strata.

Not surprisingly, the strata differ in the factors that affect their earnings. In a separate regression analysis for each stratum, a comparison of unstandardized coefficients showed that ascriptive characteristics (sex, marital status, and race) are largest for the self-employed, pointing to ascriptive barriers in that stratum. Predictably, for the skilled, the main human capital variables of vocational training and education contribute more heavily to their earnings. Earnings of the marginally employed are also highly influenced by human capital, but, by definition, weeks worked are the most important. Significantly, weeks and hours worked are decisive for periphery workers. Plainly, unemployment accounts for their low earnings, while for many of the marginally employed, part-time work is normal, as for students, the semiretired, some housewives, and others.

In each stratum, with the exception of the marginally employed, the standardized betas for sex ranked first or second in size, pointing to sex stratification in all strata. Surprisingly, race and vocational training betas rank lowest in all strata. For the self-employed and periphery employees, hours worked are of primary importance for earnings, while for the skilled and core workers, it is weeks worked.

Although the five strata stand up rather well with respect to their ability to differentiate groups by economic and social status, I need to justify using this division of the working class instead of others that have been proposed; therefore, I will review some of the more prominent alternative suggestions and compare their strengths against the division that I propose.

Relatively few students have systematically analyzed the earnings of working-class segments. Wright's (1979) important study distinguishes semi-autonomous workers from others because the former have skills that enable them to control the labor process. He included professional, technical, and some craft workers among the semi-autonomous, making the stratum more heterogeneous than that of the manually skilled. Since the skilled resemble other manual workers more than they do professional and technical employees, the skilled should remain a separate category of semi-autonomous workers within the working class. Wright's petty bourgeoisie includes all self-employed workers: farm, professional, white-collar, and manual. His data reveal a very heterogeneous stratum, while my data show that the manual self-employed most closely resemble semi-autonomous skilled workers. But the self-employed should remain a separate stratum because they have more autonomy and property than skilled workers.

Edwards's (1979) working-class fragments somewhat resemble my strata because he separates the traditional proletariat from the working poor along sector lines. The proletariat work in the core sector. Edwards's working poor include employees who have an unstable attachment to the labor force (marginally employed) as well as regularly employed workers in the periphery. The distinction between partially- and fully-committed workers is probably worth preserving. In addition, Edwards identifies a third fraction of the working class as a "middle layer" of professionals, technical, supervisory, and skilled workers who stand between capitalists and managers and the other working-class fractions. Though he does not present detailed earnings data for the occupations in the "middle layer," surely the earnings of the skilled (SK) are nearer those of the nonskilled in the core (the proletariat) than those of the professionals, administrators, and supervisors in the "middle layer." It makes sense, therefore, to consider the skilled as a separate fraction of the working class closer to the traditional proletariat than the "middle layer."

Shostak's (1969) suggestion that the working class be divided into three skill blocs (skilled, semi-, and unskilled) has great appeal because of its simplicity. The utility of his scheme would increase if service workers were included, divided along skill lines, and dispersed among the three skill blocs. The above analysis has shown that Shostak's classification falsely assumes that the two lower skill blocs are independent of each other and homogeneous in their ascriptive, human capital, labor market, and earnings characteristics. Our decision to combine the semi- and unskilled and divide them by employment sector revealed important cleavages along economic and social status lines. Sectors, we found, differentiate employees by size of work organization, union membership, and many other organizational features (Gordon, 1972).

How large, permanent, and important are the five strata of the working class? Annual earnings of the self-employed are more than twice those of workers in the periphery; the skilled earn 77 percent more, and core workers 58 percent more. Equally important are the stratal differences in unemployment. Since skill, sector, and property form the basis of the strata, other indirect evidence about stratal differences may be gleaned from information on how these three variables differentiate workers.

Evidence suggests that social and economic cleavages along skill and sector lines are stable or increasing. Lindert and Williamson (1977) found that on the aggregate level, despite downward fluctuations, skill earnings differentials remained high in the United States from 1850 to 1948, and Schoeplein (1977) showed that differentials have stabilized or increased slightly since World War II. Miller (1966:282, 293) estimated that the lifetime earnings of skilled male workers were 56 percent higher than those of the unskilled, and Carol and Parry (1968:186) found a slightly higher ratio. Finally, census data reveal that the percentage of skilled who worked fifty or more weeks a year increased from 67 percent in 1950 to 75 percent in 1979, while the percentage for laborers remained constant at 50 percent.

Industrial sectors also appear to be stable. Gordon (1972) contends that unemployment and underemployment are consistently lower in core than in periphery sector industries. Cullen (1956) showed that the interindustry wage structure remained constant between 1899 and 1950, and Miller's (1966:265) national data revealed that skill differentials in the industries we assigned to the core and periphery sectors remained constant or increased between 1939 and 1959. Stinchcombe's (1979) intensive study of occupational and industrial mobility in Norway showed that skilled workers in competitive industries that they dominated (e.g., construction) and skilled workers in oligopolistic industries earned increasingly higher incomes over the years than did employees in competitive free markets and low-skill industries. Since most workers do not significantly improve their occupational skills after age 30 (Blau and Duncan, 1967:49), since earnings differentials between skill groups increase with experience, since sector wage disparities remain constant or grow over time, and since unemployment differentials between skill levels remain constant or grow (U.S. census, 1973),[14] stratal economic inequalities probably are stable or increase over the lifetime of workers.

To what extent do the working-class strata form classes or class segments? In Marxist theory, the five strata could be considered fractions of the working class. In Max Weber's (1978) framework, a social class is that totality of class situations within which individual and generational mobility is easy and typical.[15] Unfortunately, satisfactory generational and career mobility data are not available for all five strata; however, data for skill levels and sectors provide clues to what may be going on. As early as 1937, Davidson and Anderson noted that sons of skilled workers inherited their father's occupations more than sons of any other occupational group. Rogoff's (1953:57) Indianapolis study discovered that in 1910 and 1940 sons of skilled workers were less likely to leave their fathers' occupation than were sons of most other workers. Glass and Hall (1954:182) found that skilled workers in England and Wales inherited their fathers' occupations more than did other sons.

Blau and Duncan's (1967:31) national study of male occupational mobility found less change among skilled workers than among those in other occupations except for professionals, proprietors, and managers. The same finding was reported in Featherman and Hauser's (1978:56) replication of the Blau and Duncan study. Moreover, all of the above studies found that skilled workers' children experienced more upward and less downward mobility than did children of other manual workers. Though many of the stratal differences were small, they appeared to be constant and ubiquitous. Thus, relatively more of the wives of craft than other manual workers have white-collar origins (Blau and Duncan, 1967b:348). Two to three times the percentage of skilled than other manual workers' children enter universities (*Chronicle*, 1982). Skilled workers associate more with each other off the job than do members of other manual groups (Mackenzie, 1973; Form, 1976b). Such data suggest a basis for differentiating the skilled as a social class. The sparse comparable data for the self-employed suggest they resemble the skilled (Chapter 4). Perhaps both strata should be considered as social class segments of the aristocracy of labor.

The remaining strata (core, periphery, and marginally employed workers) probably are class segments rather than social classes. The above analysis showed that core and periphery sector workers differed in their ascriptive and labor market participation characteristics. Since some two-earner families have one spouse employed in the core and the other in the periphery, it makes little sense to split families along sector lines. According to the 1970 PUS sample, 62 percent of the husbands and 20 percent of the wives work in the core sector. These husbands have higher earnings and more steady employment than do husbands in the periphery sector. Only 28 percent of women who head families work in the core compared to 50 percent of men who head one-earner families. Expectedly, the men have higher earnings. Thus, other things being equal, for both one- and two-earner families, having one spouse employed in the core sector gives that family a noticeable earnings advantage.

Do employment sectors stratify workers into quasi-permanent groups? Can the advantages of core sector employment, for example, be intergenerationally transmitted? Harrison (1974), reviewing the literature on poverty, discrimination, and unemployment, concluded that sector inequalities are transmitted intergenerationally through the school system which socializes children of core and periphery workers differently. Children of core sector workers are taught habits of work regularity and responsibility and are steered toward core sector jobs, while the reverse happens to children of periphery employees. Tolbert (1982) analyzed generational sector mobility with data that combined the Blau and Duncan (1967) study and Featherman and Hauser's (1978) replication. Tolbert used Breiger's (1981) eight occupational classes. Although Breiger's definition of strata (classes) and sector do not exactly match those used in this study, there are similarities. Tolbert found evidence supporting dual labor-market theory. Not only did the majority of men remain in their father's sector, but most of the small intersector mobility was from periphery to core. For craft, manufacturing, and service occupations, sector placement was clearly influenced by father's employment sector. Moreover, the mobility patterns of workers in craft and manufacturing firms in the core were similar, while patterns in the periphery were more disparate. Because the data deal exclusively with male workers, they probably underestimate sector inheritance among nonskilled workers.[16] In short, the evidence suggests that nonskilled workers in the core and periphery strata may have nascent social-class characteristics with respect to career and generational mobility.

Data in this chapter are not sturdy enough to draw firm conclusions about the marginally employed, probably because the group includes several types of low-employment workers: e.g., high school drop outs, college students, housewives working part-time, and the semiretired. The limited evidence on the perennially poor and unemployed suggests that their condition is not generationally transmitted and thus they do not form an under-class in Weber's terms (Matza and Miller, 1976). A better method of identifying the marginally employed is called for. Perhaps they should be defined as fully committed workers with very low earnings or heads of families who are persistently underemployed.

In summary, a comparison of the five working-class strata with other schemes that divide the class suggests that our strata are more readily identifiable in terms of their economic and social status characteristics. The biggest division in the class is between the upper three and the lower two strata. The self-employed and skilled are quite alike, and they have nascent social-class characteristics. The skilled and core workers are more alike economically than in social status, while core and periphery workers are quite distinct along both dimensions. The marginally employed are insufficiently differentiated from periphery workers in this analysis, but maintaining their separate identity is important.

The most important sociological question is, does the economic and social segmentation of the working class have important behavioral and political consequences? Current evidence is contradictory (Hamilton, 1972; Pomper, 1975) partly because of inadequacies and/or variations in the definition of working-class divisions. Clearly, the next task is to investigate the extent to which the strata differ in their social cohesion, labor union membership, ethnic affiliation, and voting behavior. In the subsequent chapters I attempt this task. Before that, I examine the economic and social status characteristics of each stratum in detail.

Notes

1. Lipset (1977) proposes an alternative "Marxist" interpretation. The U.S. is the most advanced industrial country in the world and, therefore, its working class is the most highly developed. As other countries industrialize, their working classes will increasingly resemble the U.S. experience.

2. Mills (1956) and Hamilton (1972) are important exceptions. This study parallels Mills's (1956) *White Collar*, which demonstrates the economic, status, and political heterogeneity of the middle class.

3. Manual workers represent a wider status span than most people think. In the Duncan, SEI, a laborer in a textile mill was ranked 1 and a locomotive engineer 73—above clergymen, electrician, forester, nurse, photographer, surveyor, floor manager, and boat pilot (Hall, 1969:280). In 1970, the railroad engineer earned a higher median income than did professional workers, accountants, biological scientists, teachers, draftsmen, editors and reporters, and electrical technicians. The SEI range for manual workers is larger than that of any major occupational family in the census.

4. The depression of the early 1980s cast some doubt on this generalization (Schervish, 1981). Heavy industries (auto, steel) seemed to suffer more unemployment than some service industries, but the wage differentials remained as wide as ever.

5. The classification has a downward bias, probably classifying more semiskilled service workers as unskilled than vice versa.

6. The Treasury study found that the lower the occupational level, the higher the percentage of earnings not reported. I found (Chapter 4) that almost one-tenth of manual proprietors are incorporated, list themselves as

their own employees, and probably report only wages in the census. Also, the value of their homes and property exceeds that of employees (Table 2.1). My non-systematic interviews and observations suggest that, on the average, the self-employed report less than half of their earnings to public agencies. Therefore the 30 percent added to their census earnings is an extremely conservative estimate.

7. Economists see human capital as assets that increase workers' productivity, but from a stratification perspective, human capital represents stratal advantages that help workers maintain or improve their life chances (see Haworth and Reuther, 1978). The scoring for these variables follows: sex: females = 0, males = 1; race: nonwhites = 0, whites = 1; marital status: not married = 0, married = 1; education, number of years completed; skill level: skilled = 3, semiskilled = 2, unskilled = 1; sector of employment: core = 1, periphery = 0; hours worked per week: fewer than 15 = 0, 15–29 = 1, 30–34 = 2, 35–39 = 3, 40 = 4, 41–48 = 5, 49–59 = 6, 60 and over = 7. For weeks worked: 13 or fewer = 0, 14–26 = 1, 27–39 = 2, 40–47 = 3, 48–49 = 4, 50–52 = 5. Years of experience was measured differently for the sexes. For males, age–education–6 years; for females, .75 × (age–education–6 years) (Parnes, 1976). For the strata, a series of dummy variables was used in which each stratum = 1 and the residual = 0. The DOT occupational complexity variables from high to low are handling DATA (0–6), PEOPLE (0–8), THINGS (0–7); low to high, GED (1–6), SVP (1–9) (Miller, et al., 1980:165). Earnings were predicted using structural equations and ordinary least squares.

8. I am grateful to Donald J. Treiman for providing the DOT tape for the fourth edition that corrected the earlier edition's bias of underestimating the complexity of those occupations predominantly filled by women.

9. The loading for PEOPLE, −.11 and THINGS, −.14.

10. Fortunately, Miller and colleagues (1980) coded DOT occupations and industries according to the U.S. census codes. Periphery employees generally scored higher in temperament traits dealing with feelings, influencing people, doing repetitive work, performing under stress, changing tasks, as well as intelligence, verbal, numerical, spatial, form, and clerical aptitudes. Core workers had higher scores for interest in data, scientific, and abstract activities as well as for tasks that involve machine and tangible production.

11. These periods of time are much longer than those reported by Blackburn and Mann (1979), suggesting that researchers may underestimate the complexity of manual work (see Kusterer, 1978).

12. In 1976, 1,700,000 women were working part-time because they could not find full-time jobs (Barrett, 1979:67).

13. Chief and non-chief earners had about the same levels of education. About 19 percent of the chiefs worked fewer than 40 hours a week, compared to 46 percent of non-chiefs; 21 percent of chiefs worked fewer than 48 weeks compared to 53 percent of non-chiefs; chiefs had 22.7 years of work experience; non-chiefs, 14.4.

14. Schervish (1981) found higher rates of unemployment in the oligopolistic sector, but he omitted government workers and did not control for sex, skill, and holding part-time jobs.

15. Using Blau and Duncan's (1967) occupational categories, Breiger (1981) found eight classes, three of which were manual: semi-autonomous skilled workers, manufacturing workers, and an "archaic" class of service employees, operatives, and laborers.

16. Blackburn and Mann (1979) studied a sample of nonskilled male manual workers in a British city who were employed primarily in the core sector. They found that jobs differed according to desirable working conditions, career potentiality, long-term earnings, ethnicity, and other characteristics. They concluded that the privileged and disprivileged were not separate social classes because they did not differ in occupational inheritance and because labor market careers could not be predicted on the basis of worker characteristics. In short, core nonskilled workers formed a single stratum.

3

Foremen: Between Labor Aristocracy and Management

I did not consider foremen in the previous chapter dealing with the divisions of the working class because foremen are not manual workers. Scholars clearly disagree as to whether foremen belong to the middle class or the working class, and students of industrial organization disagree whether they are part of management, part of labor, in between, some of both, and so on. Where foremen belong depends on the researcher's theoretical orientation to stratification and the problem being considered. In the previous chapter, I indicated that I was inclined to take a Weberian approach to class definition. That approach stresses occupational mobility within and between generations as crucial in the class designation of occupations. Pools of occupations wherein mobility is easy and typical within and between generations tend to define class boundaries. "Easy" and "typical" are statistical ideas, but we have no easy way of deciding what exact probabilities to use to define them. The literature does reveal that mobility among manual occupations is more typical than mobility across the blue- and white-collar line. Therefore, there is no contradiction between thinking of the working class as heavily manual in occupational composition and defining class in mobility probability terms. In the case of foremen, the evidence that I will review suggests that they are bound in the same occupational mobility pool as other manual workers, but they do not perform manual labor. They are white-collar supervisory workers by any definition, but their social origins, social destinations, daily interaction patterns, and other attributes may place them close to the working class. Therefore, their relations to manual workers deserve careful study because, along with others, they may influence working-class destiny.

Since only 8 percent of first-line supervisors of manual workers are women, this chapter focuses primarily on male foremen. In this chapter, I first trace the evolution of the foremen's functions. Second, I examine variability in the intensity of supervision they exert over skilled and nonskilled workers in different industrial and technological situations. Third, I analyze the foremen's social and economic characteristics to ascertain how closely foremen resemble two other labor elites, the skilled and self-employed. In a subsequent chapter I compare the political dispositions of the three elites to gauge their influence on the political behavior of other manual workers.

Unfortunately, no national study of U.S. foremen systematically compares their economic, social status, and political characteristics with other manual and white-collar workers. The data I use are derived from the U.S. census which includes foremen in the same occupational family as craft workers. This inclusion makes historical sense. Traditionally, employers promoted their most skilled and trusted workers to be foremen because they needed supervisors with technical competence and ability to get along with other workers. Even in some of today's small shops the distinction between foremen and other employees is statistical rather than categorical. There the foreman works alongside other workers and supervises or consults with them as needed. In some shops such occasions are so rare that employers designate the most knowledgeable worker as the leading hand and dispense with the foreman's position altogether.

Historical Background

The origin of the craft-supervisor can be traced to preindustrial times when the owner of a shop performed all the tasks: hired apprentices and workers, supervised their training, organized the work, bought the materials, dealt with customers, and did the most complicated work. Indeed, from the beginning of the industrial revolution until late in the nineteenth century, some enterprises were simply clusters of independent shops organized under one roof by the owners (Clawson, 1980). They subcontracted work out to masters and their crews in the shop. Out of a lump sum paid to the masters, the latter bought materials, organized production, and paid their crews; the surplus was profit. This petty bourgeoisie artisan-master model of work organization survives today only in small family-owned enterprises.

With the growth of industry in the nineteenth century, supervision of production was gradually removed from the artisan subcontractor and transferred to an employee called the foreman. In other situations, where the owners of enterprises supervised their workers, a rapidly expanding labor force compelled them to name one of their foremost workers to do the overseeing. Transferring supervision from the subcontractor to the foreman or subdividing the owner's functions into general supervision and immediate supervision of workers were part of a movement that concentrated control of the enterprise in the hands of the owner-capitalist (Clawson, 1980). In both situations, however, the foreman still had the power to hire, train, supervise, promote, and fire workers. Together, the foreman and owner planned the organization of work in the shop, introduced technological changes, reorganized production, and did other tasks. In enterprises that eventually became gigantic and very complex, the functions of the foreman became increasingly restricted, bureaucratized, and routinized. Most of the American literature since the 1950s focuses on this theme, assuming that it describes the typical case (Zaleznik, 1951; Harvey, 1971).

The evolution of the foreman's position is described as stripping him of his functions and assigning them to staff specialists (Miller and Form, 1980:343 ff.). Hiring and promoting were increasingly assigned to the personnel department. The right to fire workers was restricted by the union contract. Settling important grievances was shifted to higher levels of management and the union. Judging the quality of production was assigned to the inspection division. Efficiency of production was monitored by the financial division. Decisions to introduce new machines were transferred to the engineering department, and so on. The foreman's functions were reduced to implementing the decisions of others, providing them with detailed information, calling in experts when something went wrong, and monitoring but not controlling work. Both management and the union came to see the foreman as a worried but much needed busybody who was not very powerful. He was not really a manager, but neither was he a worker. Management demanded his loyalty but gave him little power, and the unions challenged the little authority he had. Having to placate union, management, and the workers, the foreman was early characterized as the master and victim of doubletalk (Roethlisberger, 1946).

Today, U.S. unions do not accept the foreman as a worker although in most western European countries the foreman is often unionized and belongs to the same union as the workers he supervises (Hill, 1976:136). Most U.S. labor union contracts forbid the foreman to engage in productive labor. In 1959, the Wagner Labor Act defined foremen as employees who were entitled to legal protection to form unions. A few such unions were formed, but strong protests by business and changes in the personnel of the National Labor Relations Board led to decisions that defined foremen as supervisors and not entitled to legal protection to form unions. In 1947, the Supreme Court overruled these decisions, but in the same year Congress passed the Taft-Hartley Act that specifically excluded foremen and supervisors from the legal protection to form unions (Gregory, 1949:347).

These legal and contractual restrictions do not describe the foreman's actual functions and stratal location in many enterprises. Many foremen in construction, for example, are members of craft unions. They do not hover over their workers and they see themselves primarily as craft workers, not supervisors (Sable, 1982:83–92). In departments where all workers perform semiskilled tasks, foremen may press workers hard to produce more and thus increase the tension and social distance between management and workers. Foremen vary widely in their functions and social status. Some are strong supervisors and others are weak; some are socially close to their workers, others are distant. Unfortunately, research is scanty on variations in foremen's functions, social status, and class membership.

The debate about whether foremen are part of labor or management is clarified when their functions are analyzed according to the technology of their work organizations and the occupational complexity of their work crews (Perrow, 1970:21). In shops that have a high percentage of skilled workers, foreman-worker interaction is probably high, because, as Blau (1968) observed, complex occupations call for more consultation between workers and supervisors. These work groups are typically small because their members need to consult frequently. Where foremen and workers have similar occupational backgrounds and share technical knowledge, they respect one another and social distance between them is low. In large enterprises, where production is highly mechanized and routinized, and the proportion of semi- and unskilled to skilled workers is high, work groups under one supervisor tend to be large because supervision is built into the flow of work, as in the assembly line, or in the design of a machine, as in a preset punch press (Edwards, 1979, Ch. 7; Mueller, 1969). Where foremen put pressure on workers to increase productivity rather than to ensure high quality work, tension and social distance between them and the workers probably increase (Sayles, 1963:13–18). Even here, the foreman's position may vary. Thus, Charters (1952) found that in a unionized automobile factory that had a strong and aggressive union, only 47 percent of the foremen agreed that they were "men in the middle" between management and workers; the remainder felt no strain or conflict.

Unfortunately, representative data are not available for the full range of technologies, sizes of work groups, their occupational composition, and the social and economic characteristics of their workers and foremen. The problem is further complicated by unclear definitions as to who is a foreman. In the census, foremen are workers who so identify themselves to census enumerators. Most of these probably supervise manual workers, but some manual service workers (firemen, hospital attendants, waitresses) have bosses who are called supervisors, chiefs, and even managers. The paucity of research on the organizational setting of the foreman's work and the absence of representative data on their social backgrounds and current attributes (Dunkerly, 1975) forced me to rely almost exclusively on data derived from the Public Use Sample of the U.S. census used in the previous chapter.

Industry, Occupation, and Supervisory Intensity

Census trends reveal that foremen are supervising fewer and fewer workers. In 1940, one foreman supervised 37 manual-service workers; in 1950, 29 workers; in 1970, 22. During this interval, the foremen category increased more rapidly than did any other major manual occupational family. This trend partially reflected a response to the increasing skill level of the labor force, i.e., a decline in the proportion of unskilled laborers, an increase in semiskilled operatives, transport operatives, and skilled workers (Featherman and Hauser, 1978:56). The growing number of service workers in small enterprises and the greater push for production undoubtedly also stimulated the growth of the foremen category.

According to the 1970 census, the ratio of foremen to manual workers was about 18:1; when service workers were added to the manual, the ratio was 24:1.[1] Although only 5 to 7 percent of workers are foremen, depending on the base used, the total number of workers supervised is small enough for foremen to know them individually. Using the number of non-service manual workers as the base,[2] the foreman intensity ratio (number of workers per foreman) varies considerably by industry (Table 3.1). Foremen typically supervise about 20 workers in manufacturing, transportation and communication, and professional service industries. They supervise many fewer (about 11) in mining, primary ferrous, aircraft, fabricated metals, and chemical industries. Above average ratios hold for construction (24) and retail trade (30).[3] Industries in the core sector of the economy generally have fewer workers per foreman than do industries in the periphery. This situation reflects the more complex technology found in core industries, larger proportions of skilled workers, and more highly developed internal labor markets. Foremen supervise many more workers in textiles, apparel, and non-durable goods industries in the periphery because these industries have a much larger proportion of nonskilled workers. The pattern of more foremen per skilled worker holds for all industries except construction and printing, where the ratio of foremen to skilled worker is low. Apparently, autonomous craft workers in those industries need little supervision, whereas skilled workers in manufacturing and mining require more supervision and consultation. We can conclude that when foremen supervise few workers, they tend to be skilled males; when they supervise many workers, they tend to be nonskilled females.

Table 3.1. Foremen Intensity Ratios for Skilled, Nonskilled, and Manual Workers, Exclusive of Service Workers[a]

Industries	Skilled Foremen	Nonskilled Foremen	Manual Foremen
Mining	2.9	7.1	11.0
Construction	16.0	6.7	23.7
Manufacturing	4.6	13.7	19.3
Primary ferrous	4.2	5.9	11.1
Fabricated metals	3.2	7.4	11.6
Machinery	4.2	7.7	12.8
Electric machinery	2.4	9.4	12.8
Motor vehicles	4.5	9.6	15.1
Aircraft	4.1	4.8	9.9
Chemicals	1.7	4.7	7.3
Furniture	3.7	8.5	13.2
Food	2.0	10.6	13.6
Textiles	1.6	11.5	14.1
Apparel	1.8	21.2	23.5
Printing	9.0	3.7	13.9
Other nondurables	3.5	17.3	21.8
Transportation	6.5	11.5	19.0
Public administration	6.8	6.7	14.6
Wholesale trade	2.6	9.4	13.0
Retail trade	10.0	20.2	30.2
Professional service	8.9	10.3	20.2

[a]Includes both men and women workers and supervisors.
Data source: U.S. Bureau of the Census, 1972. Subject Reports. PC(2) 7C.

Social and Economic Characteristics

Representative national studies of foremen fail to describe their social and economic characteristics. Census data suggest that movement in and out of the occupation is fairly high. In 1970, only 56 percent of foremen were in that occupation five years earlier. Of the remaining 44 percent, 31 percent had been blue-collar workers and 13 percent, white-collar. Case studies (Dunkerly, 1975; Hill, 1976) suggest that most foremen have blue-collar backgrounds and that they resemble blue-collar employees more than they do white-collar. During 1965–70, most foremen remained in the same industry. About 90 percent of the foremen in mining, construction, manufacturing, transportation-communication-utilities, and government (all core industries) indicated in 1970 that they worked in the same industry five years earlier. Between 70 and 80 percent of foremen in other industries, mostly in the periphery, were employed in the same industries five years earlier.

The idea that foremen are highly educated workers with white-collar backgrounds who are temporarily assigned to first-line supervision prior to careers in higher management receives little support. Data based on four combined presidential election surveys (Table 3.2) show that foremen were reared in socioeconomic circumstances only slightly better than those of other manual workers. For example, 74 percent of foremen's fathers were manual workers compared to 82 percent for nonskilled core workers. Also, a slightly higher percentage of foremen had fathers who were foremen, but fewer were high school graduates. Overall, the foremen resemble the self-employed and skilled in their social background. Compared to the nonskilled, the three groups had slightly higher proportion of fathers who were high school graduates, white-collar, or skilled workers.

Census data in Table 3.3 reveal that in race, work experience, and rate of unemployment, the three elite occupational groups resemble each other closely. Although the differences are small, foremen are slightly more privileged than are the two other elite groups: a larger percent are males, married, chief earners in their families, and high school graduates. Although fewer of the foremen had vocational training, they had more specific vocational preparation in their jobs; 90 percent had more than two years. All these advantages resulted in higher earnings and a higher rate of home ownership. Foremen annually earned almost $1,700 more than the skilled workers and $1,000 more than the self-employed. These earning advantages derived in part from foremen's greater concentration in the higher paying core industries and more full-time and year-around employment.

Table 3.2. Socioeconomic Characteristics of Fathers of Strata[a] (percent)

	Fathers					
Strata of sons	Education > 11 Years	White-collar	Foremen	Self-employed	Skilled	Non-skilled
Nonmanual	48	48	4	7	20	22
Foremen	24	26	7	8	29	30
Self-employed	26	21	2	18	25	26
Skilled	32	24	4	9	29	33
Nonskilled core	20	18	4	8	22	49
Nonskilled periphery	29	22	4	8	22	43
Marginally employed	35	30	3	9	20	37
Total N	8,518	2,832	314	626	1,713	2,366

[a]p of X^2 of original tables < .01.
Data source: General Social Survey, presidential elections surveys: 1968–80.

Table 3.3. Social and Economic Characteristics of Three Aristocracies of Labor and the Nonskilled (percent)

Variables	Foremen	Self-employed	Skilled	Nonskilled
Annual earnings (mean $)	9,902	8,844	7,237	4,660
House value over $12,500	77	71	69	58
Age (mean years)	45	45	41	45
Male	93	83	84	63
White	96	92	91	81
Married with spouse	90	84	79	64
Chief earner	92	79	80	61
Completed high school	61	47	55	37
Vocational training	34	42	40	20
Spec. voc. prep. > 6 months	100	71	98	10
Experience (mean years)	24	26	21	19
Hours worked (40+)	92	76	81	70
Weeks worked (50–2)	87	70	70	57
Unemployed	2	2	4	6
Core sector employment	65	36	58	40
Same occup. level 5 years ago	56	69	84	95
Percent of total	4	5	29	63
N	1,505	1,884	11,698	25,844

Data source: Public Use Sample, U.S. Census, 1970, 1/1,000 County File.

The mean annual earnings of 1970 foremen were three times those of unskilled laborers, 37 percent more than the skilled, and 12 percent more than the self-employed. These differences are smaller than those found in European industrial countries, both capitalist and non-capitalist (Brown, 1977:41, 47), yet the foreman's earnings advantage in the United States appears to be large enough to challenge the idea that manual workers are not attracted to the job. Contrary to collective wisdom, the earnings advantage of foremen over manual workers is increasing. In 1940, the mean annual earnings of male foremen were exactly twice those of laborers; by 1980, the advantage had increased another 56 percent.

Understandably, foremen's earnings differ by their industry of employment, race, sex, and other characteristics. For example, foremen in mining, construction, and transportation-communication-utilities earned 60 percent more than those in service industries. Core industry foremen earned 22 percent more on the average than those in periphery industries. This sector advantage is about half of the sector advantage (42 percent) enjoyed by skilled workers. Thus, periphery employers must pay their foremen salaries that are closer to those paid in the core. The earnings gap between foremen and unskilled labor is higher in the periphery probably because unskilled periphery workers are paid much less and their unemployment rate is higher.

A multiple regression analysis of foremen's earnings clarifies the sources of their earnings advantage. Controlling for the main factors that affect earnings (education, vocational training, experience, hours worked, weeks worked, sector, race, sex, and marital status), foremen earned 65 percent more than the marginally employed and at least 50 percent more than workers in other strata. Separate regression analyses for the skilled, the nonskilled strata, and the foremen revealed an important difference: for the foremen, the standardized beta for education was the largest of nine variables in the equation, whereas it ranked fifth and seventh respectively in the equations for skilled and nonskilled workers. Betas for weeks worked and sex ranked high for all three groups and race ranked low. Apart from education, the beta patterns for foremen and skilled were similar, but the explained variance for foremen was only .26 compared to .48 for the skilled and .58 for the nonskilled. The unstandardized betas for the skilled and nonskilled were larger than those of the foremen for all variables except education and race, which were larger for foremen. This suggests that personal qualities not captured by the variables in our analysis contribute importantly in management's calculus to reward foremen, most notably the extra reward for supervisory status and responsibility.

Finally, the regression results for foremen reveal that they earned 22 percent higher incomes in the core than in the periphery. The standardized beta for sector ranked fourth in size after education, weeks worked, and sex. In a separate analysis of earnings by sector, the variance explained for foremen in the core was only 18 percent compared to 33 percent in the periphery. The standardized beta for education again ranked highest in the core, but only fourth in the periphery, behind race, weeks worked, and sex. Race ranked last of seven variables in the core. This pattern suggests that black foremen in the periphery, who probably supervise other blacks, get paid poorly compared to white foremen, but particularism along race and sex lines is much less important in the core, while education as a status or human capital variable is crucial.

Conclusions

A review of the U.S. literature on foremen suggests that it over-emphasizes their marginality in industry and their ambiguous social status. The data I examined suggest that foremen vary considerably in their work situation, especially in the number of workers they supervise and their occupational composition. Clearly, a large proportion of foremen have interesting jobs that call for considerable interaction with skilled workers. As Moore (1982) suggests, supervisors enjoy much more work autonomy and variety than most employees. Foremen enjoy a slight social status advantage over the other aristocrats of labour while earning significantly higher incomes. The main distinguishing feature about foremen is their higher education and its importance for their jobs.

Whether foremen have had more advantages in their social backgrounds than other blue-collar workers is unclear. My analysis of national surveys suggests that they have (see Chapter 10). Hill's (1976) study of ninety-three foremen in London's docks may not be representative, but his findings confirm my speculations. Hill's foremen came from blue-collar backgrounds and had worked in blue-collar jobs most of their lives. Although they had considerable authority over other workers and suffered little ambiguity about their job responsibilities, they did not see themselves as leaders or managers. Moreover, they agreed with their workers that unions are necessary but they did not want unions to engage in politics. Although foremen had higher occupational aspirations than did workers, their children did not achieve more upward mobility than the children of the workers they supervised. However, compared to their workers, foremen associated more with other foremen and with white-collar workers. This partly reflected the higher socioeconomic status of neighborhoods in which foremen lived. Finally, though foremen were more favorable to the Labour than Conservative party, they were more conservative than their workers. In short, foremen appeared to be another aristocracy of labor. In Chapter 10, I examine the extent to which U.S. foremen differ politically from the other aristocrats of labor and other manual workers, but, in the meantime, I agree with Wright (1979) that foremen are not securely in the middle class, although they lean a bit more than manual workers toward a middle-class view of the world.[4]

Two additional sources of data bear on the class location of foremen: their social class identification and their economic ideology. The most recent survey on social class identification is a national study by Jackman and Jackman (1983). They asked respondents to assign a number of occupations to various social classes. For present purposes, it is sufficient to compare two occupational groups: foremen and plumbers and carpenters. About 40 percent of the respondents placed foremen and the two skilled occupations in the working class. The same proportion placed the skilled in the middle class, but slightly more (48 percent) placed the foremen in that class (p. 26). Slightly more than half of the working-class respondents placed plumbers and carpenters in the working class, and slightly fewer placed the foremen in the same class. Middle-class respondents reversed the pattern: slightly more than half placed the foremen in the middle class, and slightly less placed the skilled in that class. These data suggest that the population as a whole almost equally splits the class location of both foremen and skilled occupations, and that differences in class placement by working- and middle-class rankers is trivial.

In Chapter 8, I discuss differences in the economic ideology of three classes (professional-administrative, clerical, and manual) and five strata of the working class. Here I briefly examine the question as to whether foremen's economic ideology more closely resembles that of the other classes or the working class. Again, it is instructive to compare the ideology of foremen and the skilled stratum. In the fifty-four ideological beliefs, about half of the foremen's beliefs were closer to the working than other classes, compared to 70 percent for the skilled.

A closer examination of the content of the beliefs reveals a complex pattern. The foremen resembled the manual workers more in their beliefs about pay dissatisfaction and support for rewarding group rather than individual productivity. The strata resembled each other also in beliefs that the income gap between rich and poor is increasing and that the government should limit the profits of private business. Foremen resembled the professional-administrative group more in the belief that earnings should not be influenced by the social responsibilities and needs of workers, that the present earnings of corporations are fair, that taxes are worst for the middle class, and that supervisory responsibility should be rewarded more than skill. The two groups were also more alike in their compassion for disprivileged groups such as Spanish-speaking workers, blacks, and welfare clients, while more of the working class respondents thought these groups receive more money than they deserve. Finally, foremen and the professional-administrative stratum were more alike in their opposition to governmental guarantees for jobs, free health care for all, and free education for children of the needy.

These findings are hard to generalize about because the differences between the classes were often small and sometimes contradictory. The foremen resembled the working class more in their beliefs that workers receive less money than they deserve, that unionized workers receive the money they deserve, that workers suffer more from inflation and related economic beliefs. Foremen were less punitive than workers toward the economic disprivileged, a feature they shared with the professional-administrative class. But overall, in their economic ideology, foremen displayed a more conservative drift than did the working class.

The conclusions of the chapter suggest that foremen are working class in their social origin and in their present economic and social status. Most of the population ranks their occupational prestige at about the same level as other highly skilled occupations, e.g., toolmakers, typesetters, airplane mechanics, and telephone linemen. Both working- and middle class are almost evenly split in assigning foremen and skilled workers to the working and middle class. In economic ideology, although foremen share many beliefs with the working class, they tend to be more conservative and believe that their supervisory skill is undervalued both by manual workers and management. In short, foremen are meshed into the working class, are more conservative in some respects, and are more liberal in others. Therefore, the relationship between foremen and workers must be investigated further.

Notes

1. In manufacturing, the 1940 and 1970 figures were twenty-eight and twenty workers respectively.
2. This base is more reliable than one that includes service workers

because their supervisors are sometimes referred to as chiefs, nurses, and even managers. The greatest and only important differences in the two bases appear in public administration, retail sales, and professional service industries which contain large proportions of service workers.

3. The foremen intensity ratios do not exactly agree because they were derived from two sources: the Census Bureau publications and the PUS tapes.

4. From an intensive search of the British and U.S. literature, Dunkerly (1975) concluded that both working- and middle-class types of foremen exist, but he did not speculate on their proportions. His study also confirms that foremen have been stereotyped as "men in the middle" and that their functions vary enormously according to the technology and organization of the work group.

4

Self-Employed Manual Workers: Petty Bourgeoisie or Working Class?

Despite two centuries of proletarianization of American labor, 40 percent of blue-collar workers in 1976 revealed that they aspired to go into business for themselves (Schlozman and Verba, 1979:158). Although this figure is down from 70 percent in 1939, it is still impressively high. Therefore, the failure of American scholars to study manual proprietors is puzzling. Perhaps, unlike Europe, traditional artisan occupations such as the local butcher and baker have practically disappeared in the United States. Moreover, the self-employed worker is hardly considered to be in business by the U.S. Small Business Administration, which defines small business as firms with fewer than 250 employees. In Europe, the economic survival of artisans, usually defined as manual workers who hire fewer than 10 employees, is an important political issue and the topic of a substantial literature (Zarca, 1977).

Perhaps American sociologists think that artisans are not a part of the working class and that they are too few to merit serious attention. Wright and Perrone (1977) and others define artisans as petty bourgeoisie because they own their means of production (tools and materials), but they do not control the labor of others. Yet many artisans do control the labor of their families, and artisans often hire other workers on a temporary basis. Many artisans also become employees only to become artisans again. It may be simplistic to place artisans outside of the working class just because they own their own tools and intermittently work for themselves. Artisans may be part of the working class in terms of their earnings, type of work, social origins, class identification, occupational mobility, and other social attributes. The resolution of this question is the purpose of this chapter.

Chinoy (1955) convinced many sociologists that manual workers who seek self-employment are pursuing an impossible dream; yet almost two million non-farm manual workers are self-employed and, contrary to popular belief, their numbers are growing (Ray, 1975; Fain, 1980). Excluding self-employed professionals, manual proprietors now almost equal white-collar proprietors (U.S. Bureau of the Census, 1970:Table 225).

Perhaps because they comprise only 5 percent of manual workers, scholars have ignored the possible political importance of the manually self-employed. Yet farmers, who constitute only three percent of the labor force, have considerable political influence. Although artisans clearly do not approach farmers in their level of political influence, artisans may have more effect than their numbers suggest. Because attaining self-employment signifies upward mobility in the United States, the survival of manual proprietors may function to keep entrepreneurial aspirations alive in the working class. A fifth of all manual workers have been self-employed at one time or another, and two-thirds have thought about making it on their own. Manual proprietors sometimes employ family members or neighbors temporarily, suggesting the possibility that the majority of workers may have, at one time or another, worked for manual proprietors (Lipset and Bendix, 1951:103).

In this chapter, I compare the economic and social status characteristics of manual proprietors and employees and assess whether the differences could manifest themselves in politics. Since I cannot determine whether social and economic cleavages cause political fragmentation, I try to ascertain which of three theories about the causal relationship has greatest plausibility.

Three Theories

Three theories address the question as to whether proprietors and employees are in the same social, economic, and political stratum. First, among the several conflicting Marxist views (Parkin, 1979), the dominant one holds that manual proprietors are not in the working class; they are petty bourgeoisie or small employers because they own their businesses and sometimes supervise employees. In either case, they differ from the skilled aristocrats of labor who are employees and often belong to labor unions. As capitalism matures, manual proprietors experience increasing economic difficulties as they sink into the proletariat (Wright, 1979:156). Because they must work longer and harder to remain independent, they pay the penalty of increasingly lower incomes. In the desperate effort to differentiate themselves from employees, proprietors become conservative or even reactionary in their politics (Mills, 1956:52; Bechhofer and Elliott, 1976).

The second theory, a traditional economic view (Machlup, 1967), holds that mature capitalism provides small proprietors good economic opportunities because the economy needs services that big business cannot efficiently perform. In these niches, the returns to even small amounts of risk capital and hard work exceed wages which are constrained by collective bargaining agreements and the presence of surplus labor. Moreover, artisans develop more specialized skills than do factory and service employees who perform the routinized work of factories and large-scale enterprises. Since capitalism rewards people according to their real and human capital investments, proprietors earn more money than do employees and therefore become more conservative politically.

The third theory held by some sociologists (e.g., Hamilton, 1975) claims that some class theories are myths; possession of small amounts of property does not differentiate proprietors from employees. Artisans do not own much property and consider self-employment as just another way to make a living (Mayer and Goldstein, 1964). Further, artisans emerge out of the working class and, when they fail in business, return to it (Mackenzie, 1973). Experience, vocational training, skill, education, race, and sex determine the earnings of proprietors much as these factors determine wages (see Kalleberg and Griffin, 1978). Since the two groups are virtually identical socially and economically, their politics will not differ. Moreover, ownership status does not affect manual proprietors' attitudes toward capitalism (Berg and Rogers, 1964).

In short, these three views differ in their economic and political forecasts. The first predicts that proprietors earn relatively less than employees, the second predicts higher incomes, and the third predicts no difference. Both the Marxist and the traditional economic position predict, for different reasons, that proprietors will be more conservative politically than employees, while some sociologists predict no differences.

The adequacy of these theories can be determined by systematically comparing proprietors' and employees' social, economic, and political attributes. Although this is the aim of this chapter, my own view is that all three theories probably attribute more homogeneity to proprietors and employees than actually exists. I now elaborate this position and present a rationale for some expected findings.

Class, Status, and Political Differentiation

Except in the strict definitional sense, the manually self-employed may not constitute a single Marxian class. In fact, using the term "proprietor" may be a misnomer. Although a few proprietors may own a considerable amount of property in the form of large trucks, earth-moving equipment, and so on, many more (e.g., gardeners and dressmakers) own little more than their labor which they may sell at a wage-like rate. Earnings may be quite high for a house builder who exploits his family's labor and occasionally hires a few helpers, or earnings may be at poverty level for the trash hauler who works episodically. To my knowledge, no research is available on the total value of property held by manual proprietors.

Social science imagery of the self-employed may be distorted by visions of frequent failures of mama and papa retail stores (Bunzel, 1962). Inexperience, undercapitalization, and competition from chain stores makes the survival of family-run retail enterprises highly precarious. But many manual proprietors, unlike shop keepers, have mastered complex skills that are in high demand. Automobile mechanics, carpenters, electricians, and other craft workers, depending on market conditions, shift back and forth from self-employment to wage labor in order to maximize their earnings. Isolated communities, needing specialized services but unable to provide large markets, enable solo proprietors to earn comfortable incomes, e.g., mechanics who repair farm equipment and workers who provide services for vacationers. On the other hand, employees who have no skills sometimes turn to self-employment when they become unemployed and often earn less than do wage workers (Ray, 1975). Since economic and social status are correlated, proprietors may exhibit more socioeconomic diversity than do employees. Thus, more artisans may be white, male, older, and better educated than skilled employees, and more unskilled proprietors may be female, black, young, and poorly educated than unskilled employees.

Politics are not highly fragmented in the United States, so the politics of the self-employed and employees cannot differ radically. If artisans are more affluent than skilled workers, of higher social status, and live in smaller communities, artisans should be more conservative (vote Republican), more independent (shift party allegiance), and more involved (vote regularly) in politics. In short, at the unskilled level, proprietors and employees may be politically indistinguishable; at the semiskilled level, factory operatives, because they live in large cities and belong to labor unions, may be more liberal; at the skilled level, artisans may be more conservative.

The data for this chapter were derived from the county files of the 1–1000, 5 percent Public Use Sample of the 1970 U.S. Census of Population. All the manual proprietors (1,884) and employees (35,529) in the file comprise the study population. The political data were derived by combining three national election surveys (1968, 1970, 1972) of the University of Michigan's Survey Research Center.

Social Profiles of Proprietors and Employees

The census reveals that about 5 percent of all manual (including manual-service) workers are self-employed.[1] Almost one-half are craft or skilled workers, one-quarter (mostly unskilled) are in service occupations, and the remainder are semiskilled, transport operatives, or unskilled laborers (see Table 4.1). More than one-fifth of all men in each of the following occupations are self-employed: tailors and upholsterers, masons, painters and paper hangers, cabinet makers, radio and television repairers, laundry and drycleaning operatives, and personal service workers. Female self-employed constitute over one-quarter each of dressmakers and seamstresses outside of factories, hairdressers and cosmetologists, and personal service workers.[2]

Self-employed women are crowded into fewer occupations than are men. More than two-thirds of the women work in 5 of the 41 occupations listed in the sample: hairdressers and cosmetologists, dressmakers and seamstresses, cooks, child caretakers, and other service workers. For men, the five most numerous occupations among the 123 listed are: carpenters, automobile mechanics, barbers, truck drivers, and painters and paperhangers.[3] Over 100,000, or 9.2 percent of all proprietors, are legally incorporated and list themselves as their own employees. Ninety percent are men whose skills roughly parallel those of other proprietors.

Though the data are not shown here, proprietors in the skilled and service trades, who together make up three-quarters of all the self-employed, differ little in age and education, but the skilled earn about $2,500 more annually. Proprietors in the skilled trades are disproportionately male, white, married, incorporated, less vocationally trained, and work more hours a week; service proprietors are disproportionately female, black, married, unincorporated, have more vocational training, and work fewer hours a week (see Table 4.1).

Proprietors comprise a higher status group than employees because a larger percent of proprietors are white, male, married, older, better educated, and better trained vocationally.[4] Almost one-half of the self-employed, compared to one-quarter of the

Table 4.1. Social and Economic Characteristics of Manual Proprietors and
Employees, 1970 (percent)[a]

Characteristics	Proprietors	Employees
Total number (in thousands)	1,884	35,529
Female	17.6	29.5
Nonwhite	7.8	15.4
Spanish surname	10.8	15.6
Age (mean)	45.9	39.1
Experience (years)	26.3	19.3
Married	84.4	69.5
Husband-wife family	90.7	88.3
Highest grade attended (mean)	12.3	12.3
Vocational training	41.8	26.4
Training time (mean months)	23.5	15.8
Skill groups		
Craft	47.0	28.0
Operatives	11.2	28.0
Transportation operatives	8.3	8.1
Laborers	7.1	9.2
Service workers	26.5	26.7
Worked 40 hours or more last week	76.3	73.5
Worked 50 or more weeks last year	77.6	68.5
Incorporated	10.5	2.8
Core industry employment	36.3	46.5
Same occup. level five years ago [b]	85.3	69.1
Rural residence	35.0	26.0
SVP (mean)	5.5	4.5
Unemployed	1.6	5.2
Annual earnings (mean)	$8,844	$5,572
Value of property > $20,000	25.4	17.6
Gross monthly rent	$122	$107

[a]Excludes those not in the labor force and those making no income in 1969.
[b]Self-employed five years ago: 69.5%.
Data source: Public Use Sample, U.S. Census, 1970, 1/1,000 County File.

employees, are skilled workers while considerably more of the
employees are semiskilled operatives. Proprietors and employees
are equally distributed among transport operatives, laborers, and
service workers. At all skill levels, proprietors are older than are
employees, more highly educated, and generally earn higher annual
incomes. More of the proprietors also live in small communities (see
Table 4.2).

While direct evidence on job stability is unavailable, data in
Table 4.1 reveal that more of the proprietors than employees were in
the same occupation five years earlier, 84 and 70 percent respectively.
Contrary to popular belief concerning the high rate of small busi-

Table 4.2. Mean Annual Earnings, Education, and Age Composition of Manual Proprietors and Employees

Occupational Groups	Earnings ($)		Education[a]		Age	
	Proprietors	Employees	Proprietors	Employees	Proprietors	Employees
Craft	10,098	7,998	12.3	12.7	46.0	40.5
Transport operatives	10,503	6,589	12.1	12.3	46.3	38.9
Operatives	8,291	5,345	12.2	12.1	46.1	38.7
Laborers	8,350	4,495	11.4	11.7	41.8	35.5
Service	6,466	3,318	12.6	12.3	46.7	39.6
Totals	8,844	5,737	12.3	12.3	45.9	39.1

[a]Highest grade attended
Data source: Public Use Sample, U.S. Census, 1970, 1/1000 County File.

ness failure, 70 percent of the proprietors reported that they were self-employed five years earlier. Data were not available on economic losses that proprietors suffered when they became employees. If their business investments had been small, becoming employees may not have represented great loss; for some, the shift could even have represented a gain (Ray, 1975).

Losing a business may be compared to becoming unemployed. In 1972, 15 percent of all male employees suffered at least one period of unemployment that lasted an average of five weeks (U.S. Bureau of Labor Statistics, 1972). Over a five-year period, for workers 20 to 25 years old, this rate could represent six months of unemployment. Even the most stable employees (men over forty-five years of age) suffered one spell of unemployment every four or five years that lasted seven weeks (Hall, 1972). Although the economic effects of unemployment are cushioned by social insurance payments, one cannot conclude that losses suffered from losing a business are greater than becoming unemployed. Though the above data suggest that the self-employed are more affluent than are employees, only a multivariate analysis of earnings can resolve the issue.

Reliability of Earnings Data

Wages and salaries overwhelmingly represent the sources of employees' earnings, while many self-employed workers receive both profits and wages. The first problem in comparing earnings is to assess the reliability of earnings data. Herriot and Spiers (1975:31) matched almost 70,000 individual wage and salary reports from the Current Population Survey (CPS) with reports from the Internal

Revenue Service (IRS) and found that CPS earnings data averaged 98 percent of the IRS average. Bielby and Hauser (1977:275), who compared data from the CPS and the Survey of Occupational Change in a Generation II, concluded that census wage earnings are among the most accurately measured data in survey research. A U.S. Bureau of the Census (1979) study that compared incomes reported to it, to the Social Security Administration, and to the Bureau of Economic Analysis concluded that the underreporting of wage earnings is very low (under 3 percent), and that census data are highly reliable and valid. The study also found that non-farm self-employment earnings reported to the census were 30 percent lower on the average than those reported to other agencies. The U.S. Department of the Treasury also carefully studied 50,000 income tax returns in 1973 in order to gauge compliance with tax laws. It concluded that proprietors reported between 60 to 64 percent of their earnings to the IRS. This percentage was relatively constant across the earnings spectrum, but it increased somewhat toward the bottom (U.S. Department of the Treasury, 1979).

The exact earnings of manual proprietors are probably unknown even to themselves. Most do not keep accurate records nor do they untangle all family and business receipts and expenditures. Incorporated proprietors probably underreport their earnings even more than do the unincorporated. Since the reason for incorporating is to pay lower taxes, at least the costs of incorporation must be saved: $300–600 initially and $100–200 annually to file reports and renew licenses. Part of the family's expenses (telephone, automobile, utilities, rent, taxes) can be assigned to the corporation. Tax rates on corporate earnings are lower than on wages, so proprietors assign themselves relatively low wages. Even without taking hidden earnings into account, census data show that blue-collar incorporated proprietors report mean annual earnings that exceed those of the unincorporated by $3,000.

Though the census does not provide data on the value of business property, most proprietors invest more in their tools and materials than do most employees. Home ownership, an indirect indicator of wealth, is reported by the census. Though the rate (56 percent) of home ownership is about the same for proprietors and employees, the value of proprietors' homes is 16 percent higher.[5] I conducted a multiple regression analysis of house value with the following variables in the equation: employment status (proprietors or employee) of the chief earner, earnings of respondent, earnings of other family members (mostly the spouse), and age, sex, skill level, and residence (metropolitan or non-metropolitan) of the chief earner.[6] These variables accounted for 20 percent of the variance in property value. The unstandardized partial regression coefficients estimated that the impact of proprietary status is $815, a sizable amount in view of the mean home values: proprietors ($5,208), employees ($4,481). However, the standardized betas demonstrate that spouses' earnings, respondent's earnings, and residence each contribute more to house value than does employment status.

In short, manual proprietors probably own more property than do employees. Census data accurately reflect employee earnings, while they underestimate proprietors' earnings by at least 30 percent. The distribution of proprietors' earnings, however, appears to be accurate. Therefore, when their earnings are treated as the dependent variable in multiple regression equations, the relative magnitude of the betas is not changed by using census data because the distribution of earnings is altered by a constant percentage. When treated as an independent variable, earnings must be increased by a conservative 30 percent. Although census earnings are reported by skill level, I divided both operatives (semiskilled) and laborers (unskilled) into two groups. Transportation and other semiskilled operatives are reported separately because their earnings vary considerably (see Table 4.2). The great majority of service workers are unskilled, and they are reported separately from laborers because of the large earnings gap between the two groups.

The Structure of Earnings Inequality

The census reports proprietors' earnings in both wages and profits. About 70 percent of the self-employed reported only profits, 20 percent (including the incorporated who list themselves as their own employees) reported only wages, and 10 percent both wages and profits.[7] About 80 percent of male and 33 percent of female proprietors were the chief income recipients of their families. Although some proprietors undoubtedly used unpaid family labor, the value of that labor is difficult to assess. Unpaid manual workers numbered 4.8 percent of all manual proprietors. Since 61 percent of unpaid family workers were women, compared to 18 percent for the proprietors, obviously relatively more women than men were unpaid. Unpaid workers also had lower occupational skills than did proprietors (U.S. Bureau of the Census, 1970:Table 225).[8] These data suggest that most manual proprietors do not have the help of unpaid family workers, and that the aggregate value of their unpaid family labor does not exceed 4 percent of their earnings.

An Earnings Determination Model

In the multiple regression equation, workers' characteristics that affect earnings were grouped into four categories (Brown, 1977): (1) occupational competence or human capital (skill, experience, education, vocational training), (2) social status (marital status, sex, and race), (3) labor market participation (weeks and hours worked), and (4) capital investment.[9] I assumed that incorporated proprietors invested more capital in their business than did the non-incorporated and that employees in the core sector of the economy worked in more capital intensive industries than did employees in the peripheral sector.

In this analysis, annual earnings, as the dependent variable, included only profits and wages. The natural log of earnings was used to normalize the distribution and reduce kurtosis. Logging permitted me to interpret the unstandardized partial regression coefficients in straightforward percentage terms (Cook, 1979). The zero-order correlations among the independent variables revealed somewhat higher correlations for wage workers than for proprietors. Sex, hours worked, weeks worked, marital status, and skill were highly correlated with earnings for both populations while race, education, vocational training, and age had lower correlations.

Data in Table 4.1 show a mean income for proprietors of $8,844 and $5,572 for employees, a difference of $2,272. I regressed annual earnings on the variables in the model, including type of employment (proprietor or employee). I increased the profit contribution of proprietors' earnings by 30 percent. The model accounted for 60 percent of the variance in earnings (see Table 2.2). Controlling for all other variables, self-employment earnings exceeded those of employees by at least 9 percent, a significant difference.

A separate regression analysis of the earnings of proprietors and employees appears in Table 4.3. Here the census earnings for proprietors are used because raising them by a constant percentage does not change the size of the partial regression coefficients. For both proprietors and employees, all coefficients in the equation are statistically significant beyond the .01 level. The independent variables explain more of the variance of employees' (.645) than proprietors' (.341) earnings. For employees, duration of employment (weeks worked), chief earner status, hours worked, skill level, and sector of employment, in declining order, contribute most to earnings; for proprietors, chief earner status, sex, hours worked, skill level, and marital status contribute in declining order. However, F tests between two unstandardized partial regression coefficients (Cohen,

1978:473) revealed that the only statistically significant differences between the two groups were weeks worked, skill, and vocational training. Weeks worked and skill contributed more to employee earnings while vocational training contributed more to self-employment earnings. Employees who worked fifty or more weeks earned 24 percent more than those who worked less time; for proprietors, the parallel situation produced a 5 percent advantage. Each level of skill raised employee and proprietors' earnings 17 percent; vocational training raised employees' earnings about 10 percent and proprietors, 6 percent.

Table 4.3. Regression of Annual Earnings on Social and Economic Characteristics of Self-Employed and Employees

Variables[a]	Self-employed			Employees		
	B	SE	beta	B	SE	beta
Experience	−.007	.002	−.102	.005	.000	.075
Skill	.170	.514	.137	.169	.008	.135
Incorp./sector	.029[b]	.056	.010	.257	.007	.130
Race	.248	.071	.071	.124	.010	.044
Marital status	.344	.055	.129	.263	.008	.121
Weeks	.049[b]	.020	.053	.237	.003	.375
Chief earner	.759	.053	.328	.390	.009	.183
Voc. training	.061[b]	.039	.033	.100	.008	.044
Hours worked	.072	.010	.159	.095	.002	.163
Education	.025	.007	.079	.033	.001	.090
Sex	.409	.058	.168	.211	.009	.097
Spec. voc. prep.	−.029[b]	.024	−.043	−.011[b]	.004	−.018
Constant	1.740	N = 1,647		.752	N = 30,312	
Adjusted R^2	.341			.645		

[a]$p < .000$ [b]$p > .05$
Data source: Public Use Sample, U.S. Census, 1970, 1/1,000 County File.

Although the data are not presented here, an analysis of subgroups of proprietors and employees reveals consistently greater earnings inequality among employees. The earnings gap between core and periphery employees is much larger than that between incorporated and non-incorporated proprietors, and the earnings spread between skilled and unskilled employees is greater than that between skilled and unskilled proprietors.[10] White male proprietors received higher earnings than did white male employees, regardless of skill level. A separate multiple regression analysis of earnings for each skill level, sex, and race showed that proprietors work in a more homogeneous labor market than do employees because employee markets are more differentiated by skill and sex. In short, the analyses support the earlier finding that proprietors comprise a more homogeneous, a more affluent, and a higher status group. The question now is whether the economic and status differences manifest themselves politically.

Occupational Politics

Both Marxists and traditional economists assert that proprietors are more conservative than employees, while some sociologists hypothesize no differences. To obtain a sufficiently large sample of manual proprietors, I aggregated the 1968, 1970, and 1972 national election surveys of the Survey Research Center of the University of Michigan. Though only 108 manual proprietors appeared, they closely resembled the skill composition of those in the census Public Use Sample used in this study. The survey data relevant to this study are present and past party identification, past voting behavior, intention to vote, and social-class identification. Voting Republican or Independent in the past, identifying oneself as a Republican or Independent voter, regularity in voting, and identifying with the upper working class or middle class are interpreted as conservative orientations (Campbell, et al., 1964:67–68).

Data in Table 4.4 show small differences between proprietors and employees, but proprietors tend to be more conservative. Slightly more of them identified with the Republican party, voted Republican or Independent in the past, voted in past elections, intended to vote in the forthcoming election, and identified with the upper working class.

Though the responses to these political items varied by skill level, those of self-employed laborers and service workers seemed inconsistent with their occupational status. Compared to employees at the same skill level, proprietors were consistently more conservative. More of them identified themselves as Republicans, voted Republican or Independent in the past, voted regularly, and identified with the middle class. Such data suggest that perhaps proprietary status may have a conservative effect independent of skill level. This turned out to be the case. No statistically significant differences appeared among the proprietory skill groups in response to these questions, but differences appeared among employees. More of the skilled employees identified with the upper working class, the middle class, and the Republican party, and had independent politics. More of the skilled split their party votes in the past, voted in the past, and intended to vote in the future. Thus, the political profile of skilled employees resembled that of proprietors. Not only

Table 4.4. Political Party, Voting, and Social-Class Identification for Proprietors and Employees

Item	Proprietor		Employees	
Present party identification				
Percent Republican (p < .12)	32	(108)[a]	24	(1,722)
Past party identification				
Percent always Republican (p < .10)	16	(94)[a]	10	(1,305)
Voting				
Percent not voting in last congressional election (p < .13)	41	(93)	47	(1,419)
Percent intending to vote in next presidential election (p < .28)	82	(79)	76	(1,261)
Social class (p. < .21)				
Percent middle class	26		26	
Percent upper-working class	13		10	
Percent working class	61		65	
Total	100		100	
Number of cases		(108)		(1,700)

[a]The number of cases on which the percentage is based is given in parentheses.
Data source: Survey Research Center, University of Michigan, Surveys for 1968, 1970, and 1972 national elections.

were employees more politically split than proprietors, but both skilled employees and proprietors seemed politically removed from employees with lesser skills.

Since the politics of employees and proprietors seemed to reflect differences in their social backgrounds, I ran separate multiple regression equations for each, using as dependent variables present and past party preference, intention to vote, and class identification. The independent variables are those commonly used in studies of group politics: age, race, union membership, religion, region of residence, rural-urban residence, skill level, home ownership, education, and income.[11]

Data in Table 4.5 show that more independent variables attained statistical significance for employees than for proprietors, and that fewer variables explained more variance in the politics of proprietors. Again, these data point to greater political homogeneity of the self-employed. Only the social class and party identification of proprietors were affected by their backgrounds, while all four political variables of employees were influenced. The middle-class identification of proprietors was robustly affected by having higher income, and being older or Catholic. Their Republican party identification was influenced only by having higher income and being white. For employees, higher social-class identification was moderately influenced by income but weakly by being white, by education, and by urban residence (see Table 4.5). Their Republican party identification was influenced by white ethnicity, non-South residence, being Protestant, non-union status, and being younger. A similar constellation of variables plus home ownership and urban residence affected their past party identification and their intention to vote. None of these findings is surprising.

Although the above analysis would be improved by including more political variables and a larger sample of proprietors (see Chapter 9), certain patterns are clear. For employees, race had a persistent effect on all four dependent variables; religion, income, and house ownership affected three; and urban residence and union membership, two (present and past party identification). Race exerted a much stronger influence on the past and present party preferences of proprietors while income strongly affected their class and party identification. In short, the data pointed to some racial and income cleavage among proprietors, with high income workers strongly identifying with the middle class and the Republican party, and blacks identifying with the Democratic party. Income might have had an even stronger effect if it had been reported more accurately. Altogether, employees appeared to be more politically fragmented than proprietors along racial, religious, and property (house ownership) lines, but employee splits did not appear to be as deep because the variances explained were lower.

Conclusions

None of the three theories (Marxist, classical economic, or independent sociological) accurately portrays the stratal position of manual proprietors. The classical economic position best predicts their economic status, while the independent sociological position best predicts their politics. The preliminary political analysis reveals that proprietors are more conservative than the bulk of the working class, i.e., the semi- and unskilled workers. Since proprietors appear to be economically upwardly mobile (Lipset and Bendix, 1959:179), the Marxist thesis that they are conservative because they are being proletarianized is not supported. Therefore, if one theory must be selected for its ability to predict *both* economic and political positions, the traditional economic approach appears to be the strongest.

Although artisans and employees are not distinct strata, artisans have important social status and economic advantages. More of them are better educated, white, male, married, rural, and of

Table 4.5. Standardized Partial Regression Coefficients of Manual Proprietors and Employees for Social Class and Political Variables

Variables	Class identification		Party identification		Past party identification		Intend to vote	
	Proprietors	Employees	Proprietors	Employees	Proprietors	Employees	Proprietors	Employees
Age	.348[b]	.039	.201	−.090[b]	.100	.024	−.020	.144
Race	−.013	.096[b]	.414[d]	.294[d]	.422[d]	.288[d]	.015	−.118[d]
Union	—	−.046	—	−.100[d]	—	−.060[d]	—	.036
Religion	.252[b]	−.032	−.124	−.109[d]	−.203	−.123[d]	.244	.074[a]
Region	.058	.015	.085	.109[d]	.266	−.065	.132	.046
Skill	.126	−.022	−.167	−.011	−.043	−.047	.094	.027
House ownership	.023	.014	−.107	.035	−.089	.065[a]	−.049	.114[c]
Rural-urban residence	.103	.083[b]	−.012	−.040	−.049	−.060[a]	.047	−.058[a]
Education	.148	.088[b]	−.087	.036	−.019	.038	.207	.135[d]
Income	.415[c]	.156[d]	.257[a]	−.050	.066	.031	−.079	.061
N	96	1,472	96	1,483	83	1,142	64	1,079
R²	.264	.061	.265	.127	.331	.128	.129	.058

[a]p = < .06. [b]p = < .01. [c]p = < .001. [d]p = < .0001.
Data source: Survey Research Center, University of Michigan, Surveys for 1968, 1970, and 1972 national elections.

native stock. Proprietors have more human capital (skills, education, training), more capital and property, higher earnings, and more ability to control their work. The suggestion that proprietors are more economically, socially, and politically heterogeneous than employees was not supported by the data. On the contrary, while skilled employees resemble artisans in many ways, nonskilled proprietors rank higher socially and economically than do comparable employees. Moreover, earnings of proprietors are more influenced by their social status (race, age, marital status, and sex), while market factors, such as skill level and duration of unemployment, more directly affect employee earnings.

A multiple regression analysis revealed that proprietors' earnings are higher than those of employees' even after controlling for important variables. Therefore, the claim that proprietors earn more because they work longer hours must be rejected. On the contrary, their higher earnings probably reflect their more favorable societal niche. Proprietors can exploit their higher social status, use family labor profitably, accumulate more property, and pay relatively lower taxes. These advantages help explain why they have more life and work satisfaction than do employees (Kalleberg and Griffin, 1978). In short, the evidence suggests that mature capitalism has not eroded all the advantages of petty bourgeois status.

More data are needed before we can determine whether the social status and earnings advantages of proprietors have distinct political effects (see Chapter 9). Although proprietors are not much more conservative than employees, all the signs point to more conservatism. Proprietors with different skills have similar political profiles, while employees with different skills have different politics. This suggests that the economic and social homogeneity of the proprietors produces greater political consensus.

I am not certain that these stratal differences affect political drifts of the working class. There are not enough proprietors to block working-class political consensus, but along with other groups, they can exert an unstabilizing influence. Thus, the politics of skilled employees resembled those of proprietors more than those of other employees. The politics of foremen resemble those of manual proprietors and skilled employees.

Manual proprietors, craft employees, and foremen constitute three groups that remain sociologically marginal to the main body of semiskilled, unskilled, and service employees. Five percent of all manual workers are proprietors, 20 percent are craft employees, and 5 percent are foremen. Compared to the main body of the working class, these three groups (amounting to 30 percent of the total) are more affluent, have higher social status, are politically more active, conservative, and independent. Later I examine the possible influence that these three groups, singly or combined, have on the politics of nonskilled employees. If their influence is considerable, we can begin to understand why a viable working-class political party has not flourished in the United States.

Notes

1. Since most service occupations are unambiguously manual, they were included in the study. Workers who own no tools or equipment and work for a wage (e.g., domestics) were excluded from the self-employed.

2. Over 10 percent of the following male occupations were self-employed: carpenters, grading machine operatives, other construction craftsmen, air conditioning repairmen, other craft workers, laundry and dry cleaning operatives, taxicab drivers, and other specified laborers.

3. The five next most numerous occupations were: gardeners, bartenders, masons, hairdressers, and allocated craft workers. For women: semiskilled operatives, barbers, practical nurses, waitresses, and decorators. The ten most populous male occupations included almost half of the men, and the ten for women included 96 percent of all women.

4. An estimated 360,000 manual proprietors are in the labor reserve; i.e., people who have worked some time during the last ten years. Over one-third are sixty-five years or older, and many supplement their retirement income by working. Rones (1978) reported that in 1968, 68 percent of the self-employed who were new beneficiaries of Social Security payments (retired) were still working compared to 32 percent of wage and salary workers. Compared to employees, more of the proprietors in the labor reserve were older, women, not living with a spouse, and previously employed in unskilled and service occupations. Compared to the employed, more of the labor reserve were women, married, and previously employed in retail trade and in unskilled and service occupations. Proprietors in the labor reserve were seventeen years older than ex-employees, better educated, more likely to be males, living without a spouse, and receiving $1,000 more in mean annual income. The labor reserve is not included in this research.

5. For both, the value was higher for craft than for other groups.

6. See n. 9 for the variable codes.

7. For employees, 1.4 percent reported making profits.

8. Obviously, all unpaid family labor at each skill level cannot be assigned to the same skill of proprietors. Skilled proprietors probably have unpaid family members working at lower skill levels, and some manual proprietors have white-collar unpaid family workers to care for their books and telephone calls.

9. The variables in the equation and their coding follows: earnings, none to $50,000 and over, in dollars; sex: female = 0, male = 1; race:

nonwhite = 0, white = 1; marital status: not married = 0, married = 1; for proprietors: not incorporated = 0, incorporated = 1; sector for employees: periphery = 0, core = 1; weeks worked: fewer than 50 = 0, 50 or more weeks = 1; skill level: unskilled and service = 0, semiskilled including transport operatives = 1, skilled = 2; hours worked weekly: fewer than 40 = 0, 40 or more = 1; education in years; vocational training: no = 0, yes = 1; experience: for males, age–education–6, and for females (age–education–6) × .75; employment type: proprietors = 0, employees = 1.

10. The difference between the highest and lowest earnings of the skill groups was $5,538 for incorporated proprietors, $3,700 for the unincorporated, and $2,434 between employees in core and periphery industries.

11. The coding of the variables follows: age, in years; income in dollars; education, in years; religion: non-Catholic = 0, Catholic = 1; community: rural = 0, non-rural = 1; sex: female = 0, male = 1; region: South = 0, non-South = 1; union membership: no = 0, yes = 1; race: nonwhite = 0, white = 1; skill: service and laborer = 1, transport and other operatives = 2, craft = 3; house ownership: no = 0, yes = 1. For the dependent variables; class identification: working = 1, upper-working = 2, middle = 3, upper-middle = 4; party identification: strong Democrat = 1, weak Democrat = 2, independent Democrat = 3, independent = 4, independent Republican = 5, weak Republican = 6, strong Republican = 7; intend to vote: no = 0, yes = 1.

5

Skilled Workers: A Stratum for Itself

Most American social scientists have considered the major societal cleavage to be that between the working class and the middle class. Those who wanted the working class to embrace socialism worried that skilled workers, as the aristocrats of labor, might become middle-class and forever seal off the realization of a socialist America. Therefore, many students asked whether skilled workers resembled the lowest segment of the middle class (clerical workers) more than they did nonskilled manual workers (Hamilton, 1964; Glenn and Alston, 1968; Vanneman, 1977; Jackman and Jackman, 1983). This overriding concern about the manual- and white-collar split diverted attention from the persistent cleavages among manual workers.

The uncritical acceptance of three ideas blinded many social scientists to the importance of working-class cleavages. First, many believed that the mechanization of industry had reduced the need for skilled and unskilled work, thereby making the working class a homogeneous body of semiskilled workers. Second, scholars believed that the rising levels of compulsory education created a flexible pool of workers who could be trained rapidly to fill skill demands, thereby reducing wage inequality and creating an economically homogeneous working class. Third, scholars believed that the rise of industrial unions had severed skilled workers' control over labor unions and shifted the balance of power to the nonskilled. This chapter challenges these three beliefs and proposes the idea that the most important social, economic, and political split in the working class is that between the skilled and the nonskilled.

It is difficult to explain the persistence of the three ideas in the face of the known history of the American labor movement. Its major historians (Commons, et al., 1918; Perlman and Taft, 1935) have shown that skilled workers led the labor movement from its very inception, and that they used it to serve their special interests. Bridenbaugh (1950) found this tendency even in colonial times. Even in cases where early unions were organized along industrial lines, recent evidence shows that the skilled were able to maintain a separate existence to advance their own ends. Thus, Conell and Voss's (1982) study of the Knights of Labor showed that over half of its locals were comprised of skilled workers and only a few were dominated by semiskilled and unskilled workers. The history of the AFL clearly shows that the skilled were able to protect their interests often at the expense of the nonskilled. Additionally, Aronowitz (1973) advanced the thesis that skilled workers organized the industrial CIO unions but made sure to protect and advance their own interests. To be sure, other historians (Hardman, 1959) have taken the view that the less skilled did manage to share power and influence with the skilled.

European scholars have also studied the role of skilled workers in working-class movements. Lenin (1943:92) early condemned them as self-serving conservatives who sabotaged working-class solidarity. Bakunin (1971) also saw skilled workers as semi-bourgeois, upwardly mobile aspirants who were the least radical element of the working class. Thompson's (1963) detailed study of the origins of the British working class documented the drive of early artisans to maintain their cultural community in the face of industrial change. Only Bauman (1972) formally addressed the problem of how working-class cleavages persisted and changed during the growth of the British labor movement. He demonstrated that skilled workers were an occupational society at the beginning of the industrial revolution, that from 1850 to 1890 they formed craft unions that sought respectability and legitimacy, and that they became an elite sector of the mass labor movement between 1890 and 1924. Since then, British skilled workers have maintained a special identity in the large industrial unions (Bulmer, 1975; Currie, 1979:36; Hall and Miller, 1975).

Only Michels (1959:292) has offered a systematic theory of how skilled workers become a subclass even in socialist unions and parties. He insisted that most workers want to become petty bourgeois, but only the skilled have sufficient social solidarity to pursue their special interests in the union and community. Their economic and working-condition advantages, which accumulate over time, transform them into a veritable social class distinguished from the nonskilled. The skilled do not feel obliged to exhibit solidarity with unorganized workers even when both groups are unemployed. When the skilled become the officers of unions and parties, they seek to expand their advantages over the nonskilled and the unorganized; thus, they even transform a revolutionary social movement into a set of special-interest organizations.

In an extensive review of the European and American literature, Sable (1982) summarizes the basis of the skilled worker's independence. Importantly, the skilled can perform almost all jobs in an enterprise, from unskilled labor to the most technical engineering tasks. The skilled typically perform all these jobs without undue protest because they accept hierarchy and rules as the natural order of things. The world view of the skilled is based on the belief that their technical prowess constitutes the bedrock of work organization, and that their apprenticeship and work experience are unique in the working class. Whatever their preparation, skilled workers realize that they can never know everything about materials and work techniques, and that they partly depend on other skilled workers for specialized knowledge that is learned through long experience. In this way, group pride in work is communally based, and these communal standards are used to judge all other workers. The skilled do not feel threatened by engineers who, they think, lack intimate knowledge of the techniques of production, service, and repair. The skilled also maintain their distance from the nonskilled who, they think, lack the qualifications to learn a skill. The normal response of the skilled is to maintain a separate identity in their work politics. They respond as a community both to the opportunity to expand their knowledge and skills, and to challenges by others to dilute their traditional skills.

The Decline of Skill Stratification?

The prevailing social science view is that most manual workers in preindustrial societies were skilled artisans whose representation in the labor force declined with the mechanization of industry. The decline of workers in manufacturing and construction and the shift of workers into the service sector of the economy further accelerated the decline of the skilled. These changes led to a homogenization of working-class skills and wages. Such a trend led, in turn, to a more self-conscious working class disposed to act in its economic and political self-interest. All these ideas bear re-examination.

Demythologizing the Past

As suggested above, social scientists believe that most workers in pre- and early industrial societies were artisans and that most manual employees in mature industrial societies are semiskilled operatives. They conclude that skilled work in the labor force is declining. In their historical analysis, they compare past occupational structures that were largely made up of manual workers to current structures in which manual workers are a bare majority. It is not meaningful to compare only the manual workers in two eras to decide the question of skill dilution in the entire labor force. Since current occupational structures are more complex than were earlier ones, one can conclude that skills have not been diluted. It is theoretically possible to have a structure with many complex occupations that altogether contain relatively few incumbents while a few low-skilled occupations contain the bulk of the labor force (Smith and Snow, 1976). This possibility seems unlikely today because professional and clerical occupations are much more numerous than in the past, and their work also appears to be more complex. But the question I pose here is narrower: how do the skills of manual workers in pre- and early industrial societies compare to those in late industrial society?

In an early study, Mumford (1930:122) estimated that casual beggars in 1684 Paris made up 25 percent of the population. Later studies of the occupational structures of eighteenth- and nineteenth-century cities reveal that most urban manual workers were not skilled. In twelve readily available studies of that era, artisans and skilled workers comprised from 26 to 54 percent of the labor force while laborers, servants, and unskilled workers comprised from 25 to 50 percent (see Table 5.1). Reconstructing occupational structures is difficult and arduous, and we should applaud historians for their efforts. Yet all their studies undercounted low-skilled workers and overestimated the skilled. Most studies counted only male heads of households and omitted younger family members (who probably held the least skilled jobs), employed women (mostly unskilled industrial workers and domestics), women and children who worked for their board and room, unpaid family workers, transients, and unemployed. I estimate that these studies missed from 15 to 40 percent of the low-skilled manual workers.

Knapp (1976), reviewing the literature of eighteenth-century European cities, found that the urban poor were unregistered and undetected unless they came into contact with a record-keeping agency such as the police or a charity hospital. The unemployed, transients, vagabonds, and criminals comprised from 15 to 33 percent of the population of European capital cities.

Though the precise skill composition of the working class of late mediaeval, renaissance, and early industrial cities is unknown,

Table 5.1. Manual Skills in Preindustrial and Early Industrial Cities

Source	Observation Date	Low-Skilled Percent	Skilled Percent	Observation
Aminzade (1977)	Toulouse, 1840	60	40	For working class
Beier (1978)	London, 1548–1694	33–50	25	Unemployed 20%
Foner (1976)	Philadephia, 1771	50		Poor 25%
Garden (1975)	Lyon, 1791	52	20	Excludes most female workers
Geruson and McGrath (1977)	U.S. cities, 1910	31	38	
Hirsch (1978)	Newark, 1800–1860	24	54[a]	Omitted women, 20% employed
Knapp (1976)	Continental Europe, 1850	50	50	For working class only
Main (1966)	Pre-Revolution America	40		
Moch (1979)	Nîmes, 1906	41	25	Sample of households
Thernstrom (1964)	Newburyport, 1850	25	50	Women, unemployed omitted
Tilly (1977)	Milan, 1880	40		Census omits episodic female employment
Tyree and Smith (1978)	Philadelphia, 1789	29	37	Male heads only

[a]Crafts overcounted by U.S. Census; 20 to 50 percent of "craft workers" were not skilled.

we do know that the majority of the bourgeois and working class were not members of guilds where the crafts were concentrated. A careful reading of the literature on guilds leads to three important conclusions. First, the *ideal* version of the skill ladder of apprentice, journeyman, and master as including *most* workers existed (if it did at all) for only a brief period. Second, the main function of the guild system was to restrict the supply of skilled workers so that local monopolies could be preserved. Third, most of what is known about guilds deals with their decline and their abuses. In short, most scholars of the early guild system painted an ideal version of it and most social scientists today still cling to that version.

In the idealized version, a master worked with two journeymen and two apprentices. After an apprenticeship of about seven years, apprentices became journeymen; when they had perfected their skills, they became masters and employed other journeymen and apprentices. Obviously, in such a system, the supply of craft workers would expand rapidly. Every seven years two apprentices would become journeymen and every four to six years, two journeymen would become masters. Unfortunately, the local market for high-quality goods was limited to the petty bourgeoisie and the aristocratic classes. Furniture, silverware, and other goods were passed on to succeeding generations. Long before the commercial and industrial revolutions appeared, the guild system was in trouble (Pirenne, 1934).

To apply the current terminology, the guild system was the very embodiment of over-certification. Its main purposes were to monopolize the local market for the masters, to limit the supply of skilled workers, and to exploit journeymen and apprentices by extending their training and delaying their certification. Journeying removed trained workers from the local labor market and provided cheap skilled labor to masters in other markets. The years spent in journeying far exceeded the time needed to perfect skills. By the end of the seventeenth century, examinations for attaining the master's status were so expensive that only a small minority could afford them.

Prolonged apprenticeship was restricted to children of privileged families as early as the fourteenth century (Pirenne, 1934), and apprentice training was needlessly long. Older boys could be trained in three or four years, but they were acquired at a younger age to provide the master with an inexpensive pool of unskilled labor. The need for this type of labor was high. Before the invention of modern machines, as much as nine-tenths of shop work was unskilled. In cabinet making, for example, apprentices spent years doing little else than sanding wood, rubbing surfaces smooth, sweeping the floor, running errands for workers, and even taking care of the master's children (Knapp, 1976:41). Even before the advent of capitalism and powered machines, most work was unskilled, dull, repetitious, and easy to learn.

By the eighteenth century, parents began to pay masters to accept their children as apprentices (Garden, 1975:207); even this practice did not assure that apprentices would become masters because the system had become stratified. Children of masters could expect to become masters by inheritance, but others could only rarely do so. As the number of journeymen grew, they organized associations to break the monopolies of the masters. Thus, even before the industrial revolution, conflict between the certified skilled and the non-certified was common (Dobson, 1980). In the United States, the apprenticeship system never became widespread. In some eastern cities where it did take hold, journeymen often left the local labor market and later abandoned their occupations. The average age for attaining master's status in 1830 in Newark was 40 years (Hirsch, 1978). More typically, skills were learned informally outside of the organized trades. Understandably, much of the hand-produced articles of the nineteenth century that survives today (furniture, tinware, glass dishes) is of poor quality and not the product of skilled workers.

When trades were brought into pre–Civil War factories, an attempt was made to preserve the apprenticeship system, but the trades quickly became stratified. Women and foreigners were typically pushed into low-skilled jobs that they never left (North and Weissert, 1973). For example, in 1869, unskilled women in Newark factories comprised 34 percent of the shoemakers and 50 percent of the hatters (Hirsch, 1978), yet the census reported them as regular shoemakers and hatters, implying they were skilled.

Industrial and Occupational Trends in the United States

Let us examine Census Bureau data for information on changing skill requirements. Skilled workers have been traditionally concentrated in manufacturing and construction, but since the turn of the century the proportion of workers in these two sectors has changed somewhat. The high point in manufacturing employment was 36 percent in 1950; in 1980 as in 1900, manufacturing employed one-quarter of the labor force. Construction employment has been stable since 1900, fluctuating between 4 and 6 percent. The proportion of skilled workers in the labor force also has been constant since 1920: about 13 percent. Since 1940, the percentage of skilled in manufacturing has held steady, at 20 percent, and the percentage in construction has declined slightly (see Table 5.2). Today, in three sectors, the skilled are more highly represented than in manufacturing: 22 percent in transportation-communication-utilities; 25 percent in mining, and 50 percent in construction. More important, from 1940 to 1980, the representation of the skilled has increased in mining, transportation, trade, government, and agriculture. In short, the skilled are holding their own in manufacturing, declining slowly in construction, and increasing in most other industrial sectors of the economy. These trends buttress Dahrendorf's (1959:49) claim that early manufacturing homogenized skills, early twentieth-century industrialization expanded the ranks of the semiskilled, and the rising complex technology after 1950 expanded the skilled.

Census evidence dealing with the changing skills of manual workers is confusing because of changes in occupational classifica-

Table 5.2. Percent Craft Workers and Foremen by Industry Group, 1940–80

Industry Group	1940	1950	1960	1970	1980
Manufacturing	19	20	20	20	20
Construction	59	57	53	56	55
Mining	13	17	22	25	25
Transportation, etc.	17	21	21	22	21
Wholesale and retail trade	5	6	7	9	8
Government	4	8	8	7	6
Finance	2	2	2	2	2
Service	6	9	7	6	5
Agriculture	—[a]	—[a]	1	2	2

[a]Less than 1 percent.
Data source: U.S. Bureau of the Census, Population Reports, 1940–80.

tions. Scholars, however, have worked hard to make the data comparable since 1900 (U.S. Bureau of the Census, 1975, Series D). I attempted to reconstruct the skill profiles of U.S. manual workers from the censuses of 1870–1980 (see Table 5.3). The most striking trend is the slow rise in the proportion of skilled male workers since 1900 and the rapid decline in unskilled male labor. For women, the proportions of skilled, semiskilled operatives, and laborers remained stable, but the number of service workers increased relatively as domestic work declined. Since occupational classifications were made relatively consistent after 1900, we can conclude, contrary to received wisdom, that skilled manual work did not decline for over eighty years. Braverman (1974) insists that semiskilled work, which has increased, is not more complex than unskilled labor. If he is correct, the important distinction is that between skilled and all other manual labor. The evidence still points to relatively little change in over eighty years. To sustain his position, Braverman had to prove that today's skilled workers are less skilled than they used to be. His attempt was not convincing.

The second conclusion to draw from Table 5.3 is that the census classification of occupations changed drastically after 1890. From 1870 to 1890, about 60 percent of males were classified as being in the crafts, but in 1900, only 31 percent. A similar 30 percent decline also occurred for women workers. Since the occupational classification is more accurate and consistent after 1900 than before, we must conclude, contrary to Braverman, that the percentage of skilled workers before the turn of the century was vastly overestimated. This conclusion is supported by data for women workers. Both conservative and radical scholars agree that women have been traditionally barred from the skilled trades, yet over

Table 5.3. Distribution of Manual Workers by Skill and Sex, 1870–1980 (percent)

Year[a]	Craft		Operatives		Laborers		Service		Private Household		Total	
	M	F	M	F	M	F	M	F	M	F	M	F
1870	61	45	27	13	5	1	5	37	3	5	101	101
1880	60	38	27	28	7	1	4	27	3	6	101	100
1890	58	31	30	25	4	1	8	35	1	8	101	100
1900	31	2	25	38	36	4	7	11	1	45	100	100
1910	31	3	28	39	32	3	8	14	1	41	100	100
1920	34	3	30	42	29	5	7	17	—	33	100	101
1930	32	2	31	37	27	3	9	21	—	37	99	100
1940	30	2	35	38	23	2	11	22	1	36	100	100
1950	35	3	38	46	16	2	11	29	—	20	100	100
1960	37	3	38	14	14	1	11	34	—	20	100	99
1970	38	5	35	38	12	3	15	44	—	10	100	100
1980	39	5	31	32	13	4	16	51	—	8	101	100

[a]Data for 1870–90 from Edwards (1943), tables 9 and 10. Specific trades and occupations were classified as craft workers, while operatives and laborers were entered as separate categories. Data for 1900–1970 from U.S. Bureau of the Census (1975:Series D, 182–232); for 1980, U.S. Bureau of the Census, Population Reports.

one-third of women workers were classified as being in the crafts prior to 1900, but only 2 to 5 percent since then (see Table 5.3). One must conclude that women were not skilled prior to 1900, and that social scientists have perpetuated a skill degradation myth based on questionable data in the pre- and early industrial eras. Only recently have scholars demonstrated that skill upgrading occurs perhaps as often as skill downgrading (More, 1980; Geschwender and Levine, 1983; Spenner, 1979), but upgrading has been traditionally ignored.

Are Skill Pay Differentials Being Equalized?

Many economists have argued that industrialization pushes the wages of skilled and unskilled workers closer together, thus increasing income equality in the working class (Ober, 1948; Kerr et al., 1970:252). In much of the less developed world, skilled workers allegedly receive three and four times the wages of unskilled laborers, while in advanced industrial countries, the skilled typically receive only 20 to 30 percent more. Changing market conditions in the more advanced economies account for declining wage differentials: the supply of skilled labor increases with rising levels of general and technical education, employees are easily trained and upgraded on the job, and labor unions push to equalize wages, especially during inflationary periods (ILO, 1956:25–27). Within given labor markets, the skilled/unskilled wage differential varies with economic conditions. In periods of high unemployment, the skilled replace the unskilled because the skilled can perform a wider range of jobs and, though wages decline, skill differentials tend to widen. During periods of inflation and full employment, all labor is scarce and wage differentials tend to decline (Reder, 1955).

Let us now examine the evidence. I know of no study of skilled/unskilled wage ratios across industries in nations at different levels of economic development. Data in Table 5.4 are derived mostly from case studies of different industries in various countries. The lowest ratio (1.1) is for Austria's construction industry, and the highest (4.0) for factories in Poland (Wesolowski, 1969) and India (Lambert, 1963). Although countries at lower levels of economic development report higher ratios than do industrialized countries, wide variations exist in both socialist and non-socialist countries. Table 5.5 presents data for workers in printing and construction in forty countries. The ratios in the less developed countries tend to be higher than in the Western industrial countries, and they are more alike in construction than in printing, perhaps reflecting the simpler and more uniform technology of construction. Moreover, large variations in the ratios are reported in printing in countries at similar levels of economic development. Thus, no wage differences by skill are reported for Puerto Rico and Greece (unbelievable), while wide differences are reported for Chile and Mexico. In short, economists are probably correct in the general observation that wage differentials diminish with economic development, but many other factors obviously affect the ratio, such as the ideology of equality, the racial composition of the labor force, the power of employers, government policy, and other factors.

The case for low and diminishing wage differentials between the skilled and the unskilled in the United States is not conclusive. Most economists claim the ratio is between 1.2 and 1.3 and declining as in other advanced industrial societies. One obvious source of earnings data is the United States census since 1940. Economists do not like to use this source because the categories are too broad (Scoville, 1972:17–44); they prefer data on hourly wage rates for specific industries, particularly construction (Ober, 1948; Douty, 1953; Gustman and Segal, 1974). Schoeplein (1977) notes that employment in construction is subject to violent fluctuations and that wage rates vary widely between the unionized and nonunionized sectors. Census data have some obvious advantages: they are inclusive, they report actual earnings, they are longitudinal, and they are most accurate in the manual sector where skill differences are clearly

Table 5.4. Wage Ratios (Skilled/Unskilled) of Countries by Level of
Economic Development

Country	Source	Industry	Ratios	Date	Per Capita GNP[a]
India	Lambert (1963)	4 factories, Poona	2.0–4.0	1957	73
China	Giles (1975)	Factory workers	3.0	1974	73
Yugoslavia	Kolaja (1965)	1 factory	2.0–3.0	1959	265
Japan	Taira (1970)	Construction	1.5+	1945–66	306
Cuba	Zeitlin (1967)	Industrial nat. sample	2.5	1962	431
Poland	Wesolowski (1969)	Manual workers	1.15–4.00	1963	475
Argentina	BLS (1966)	All occupations B.A.	1.23	1965	490
Italy	Rothbaum (1957)	Wage workers	1.25	1952–53	516
USSR	CIA (1963)	Wage workers	1.37	1928–61	600
USSR	Geiger (1969)	Machine, Leningrad	1.22	1965	600
Austria	ILO (1974)	Construction	1.1	1973	670
France	Rothbaum (1957)	Wage workers	1.23	1952–53	943
Britain	Hunter and Robertson (1969)	Engineering, industrial	1.42	1967	1189
USA	Rothbaum (1957)	Wage workers	1.37	1952–53	2577

[a]Russett, et al. (1963).

specified (Scoville, 1972:108). But the basic reason why census data
are better than hourly data is that people spend their annual incomes;
they do not spend a wage rate. High wages and high unemployment
can result in poverty.

The annual earnings ratio of male craft workers to those of
unskilled laborers was 1.47 in 1940 and it increased to 1.96 in 1980.[1]
These ratios are not only higher than those provided by economists,
but the ratios are increasing rather than decreasing. Moreover, the
ratios underestimate the actual situation because the lower earnings of apprentices are included with those of craft workers;
additionally, the omission of women in the ratio deflates it because
unskilled women workers earn much lower wages than do unskilled
men. Also, census takers rely on the occupational titles provided by
informants, some of whom report higher status titles than their jobs

Table 5.5. Skill Pay Differentials in Printing and Construction by Country or City [a]

City and Country	Per Capital GNP[b]	Printing (1957)[c]	Construction[d]
Africa			
Elizabethville, Belgian Congo	92	2.27	1.09
Accra, Ghana	172	1.99	1.82
Sierra Leone	—	2.65	1.59
Kartoum, Sudan	60	2.14	2.29
Dar-es-Salaam, Tanganyika	61	3.16	2.04
Capetown, South Africa	395	2.02	3.39
Americas			
Anchorage, Alaska	2577	2.40	1.12
New York, U.S.	2577	1.17	1.24
Buenos Aires, Argentina	490	1.84	1.33
Santiago, Chile	379	4.55	1.70
Jamaica	316	1.84	1.83
Guatemala City, Guatemala	189	1.27	—
Mexico D.F., Mexico	262	3.17	1.49
Puerto Rico	563	1.0	1.70
St. Vincent, West Indies	200	3.95	1.60
Asia			
Taiwan	161	1.48	1.89
Hong Kong	272	2.87	1.38
Bombay, India	73	3.17	—
Tel Aviv, Israel	726	1.45	1.17
Beirut, Lebanon	362	3.36	4.00
Singapore	400	2.60	2.00
Saigon, Vietnam	76	2.70	1.55
Malaya	356	1.74	2.02
Bangkok, Thailand	96	1.46	1.65
Europe			
Austria	670	1.57	1.31
Brussels, Belgium	1196	1.47	1.25
Helsinki, Finland	794	1.36	1.31
West Berlin, Germany	927	1.49	1.05
Athens, Greece	340	1.00	2.32
Hungary	490	1.46	1.43
Dublin, Ireland	550	1.32	1.18
Norway	1130	1.35	1.02
Lisbon, Portugal	224	2.22	1.74
Geneva, Switzerland	1428	1.51	1.23
London, England	1189	1.25	1.13
The Netherlands	836	1.30	1.22
Malta	377	1.40	1.21
Rome, Italy	516	1.54	1.14

Table 5.5. Continued

City and Country	Per Capital GNP[b]	Printing (1957)[c]	Construction[d]
Oceania			
Wellington, New Zealand	1310	1.24	1.09
Sydney, Australia	1316	1.29	1.20

[a]Source of data, ILO (1958).
[b]Russett, et al. (1963).
[c]Ratio of wages of unskilled laborers to machine compositors.
[d]Ratio of wages of carpenters to construction laborers.

warrant. When fringe benefits are taken into account, the earnings of highly skilled workers probably double those of unskilled labor. Hodge and Treiman (1968) report that the skilled own significantly more stocks and bonds than do the unskilled, and Katona (1964) reports a similar advantage in home ownership and life insurance.

The size of the income difference becomes politically important when it is large enough to be worth fighting for and when it inhibits class solidarity. The first difference is easy to specify. In 1980, fully employed skilled males earned a median income that exceeded that of laborers by almost $6,000 (U.S. Bureau of the Census, 1981). In 1980 as in 1970, the earnings of the oldest age cohort (55–64 years) of the skilled were about the same as those of the youngest cohort (25–34 years), while for unskilled labor, its oldest cohort earned considerably less than its youngest (U.S. Bureau of the Census, 1973:Table 1). In a multiple regression analysis of annual earnings, I found that the skilled earned 17 percent more than the nonskilled, controlling for hours and weeks worked, sex, race, marital status, sector of employment, education, and work experience. Sector (core and periphery) differences in earnings were smaller for the skilled than for the non-skilled. The largest earnings gaps between the skilled and non-skilled (circa $3,000) were in public administration and nondurable goods manufacturing. Race differences in earnings were larger among the skilled than the nonskilled in both sectors, and sex differences were greater for whites of both skill levels in the periphery. These figures show the ability of white skilled males to maintain economic distance between themselves and blacks and women, especially in the high-paying industries of both core and periphery.

Finally, Miller (1966:282) reported that the lifetime earnings ratio of all skilled workers is 1.56 that of the unskilled. These large earnings advantages accompanied by an invidious status distinction (skilled vs. unskilled) seem worthy of protection. From 1940 to 1980, the median annual earnings of all skilled workers (including foremen) have also been above those of all clerical workers.

Challenges to the Competitive Model of Skill Stratification

Some economists doubt that competitive market models explain wage differentials between skill levels. Ozanne (1962) examined a century of wage rates in a manufacturing company and found no support for Kerr's hypothesis of narrowing differentials. Ozanne discovered that early unions were dominated by craft workers who widened wage differentials. The Knights of Labor then narrowed them, but succeeding unions widened them again even during prosperous periods. Ozanne concluded that current wage differentials are very carefully controlled by both the union and management. Richard Perlman (1958) analyzed the forces that narrow and widen wage differentials in advanced industrial societies. He concluded that both ideological and economic conditions affect differentials. Thus, Italian and French labor unions are committed to wage equalization and try to move toward that goal by centralizing bargaining especially during inflationary periods. Their success is dubious (see Chapter 11). American unions are not committed to equalization and, contrary to marginal economic theory, have increased wage differentials during periods of full employment, economic depression, and rapid technological change (Schoeplein, 1977).

Mahler (1961) concluded that economic and market conditions have had little effect on wage patterns of large industries that have the following characteristics: are markets for each other, have similar technological and organizational structures, are geographically concentrated, are subject to similar government regulations, and communicate with each other because they bargain with the same unions. This pattern appears most clearly in oligopolistic industries such as steel, automobile, farm machinery, aircraft, rubber, petroleum, electrical equipment, aluminum, copper, shipbuilding, and meat packing. Other economists (Phelps, 1957; Doeringer and Piore, 1971) have proposed market typologies that are based on different economic, organizational, and labor requirements of industries. The economic position of skilled workers is typically recognized in these typologies. Thus, Doeringer and Piore (1971) demonstrated that wage patterns differ in enterprise, craft, and competitive markets. Large enterprises that have internal markets need not respond to community wage patterns because the firms have the resources, training facilities, and traditions necessary to shape their own wage patterns.

Finally, competitive models hypothesize that, because of change in the labor supply, wage differentials decline with inflation and increase during economic depressions. The most careful study of this problem (Schoeplein, 1977) examined the skilled/unskilled wage differential in representative manufacturing and nonmanufacturing industries in sixteen metropolitan areas during the inflationary period of 1952–73. Schoeplein used annual Area Wage Surveys for representative SMSAs gathered by the Bureau of Labor Statistics. He incorporated two improvements in his research design: the elimination of the construction industry because of its volatile wage patterns and the consistent comparison of two occupations (electricians and janitors). Schoeplein's data confirmed my suspicion that the usual ratio reported by economists is too low. He found that a ratio of 1.50 held for manufacturing during the entire period, and that the extent of unemployment did not affect it.

The nonmanufacturing sector hires almost the same number (3.5 million) of skilled workers as does manufacturing. Wage differentials in nonmanufacturing not only widened, particularly after 1965 from 1.7 to 2.0, but they widened even more during periods of inflation and labor scarcity. Thus, in the more unionized manufacturing sector, wages of the unskilled moved up with inflation at the same rate as for the skilled, but in the service sector, the lower unionization of the unskilled had the effect of depressing their relative wages. The higher wages for skilled workers in nonmanufacturing probably resulted from managers raising wages in nonunion shops in anticipation of wage increases in manufacturing (Schoeplein, 1977).

In summary, I examined several predictions of the competitive model that explain wage differentials. I found little evidence of a coherent monotonic trend between a nation's level of economic development and the skilled/unskilled wage ratio. Census data on annual earnings in the United States for the last forty years, an era of rapid technological change, showed that wage differentials have widened rather than narrowed. Case studies of wage patterns conducted by labor economists also challenged the received wisdom. Wage ratios appear to be as strongly conditioned by union strength, union ideology, and union-management decisions as by market conditions. Administered wages in large corporations that have similar structures successfully defy market forces in local community wage structures. Finally, inflation does not equalize wages in manufacturing, and it widens them in nonmanufacturing. The conclusion from these studies is clear: the solidarity of the working class cannot flow from a secular trend toward earnings equalization.

Economic stratification continues in the American working class and it may be increasing in Europe (Archer and Giner, 1971:32).

Conflicts Over Income Differentials

A favored economic interest group typically develops a self-justifying rationale. While craft workers may not possess a distinctive ideology, the literature suggests that they subscribe to a functionalist self-image. They feel they deserve higher pay than the less skilled because the skilled are more capable, perform more important work, and have invested more time, money, and energy to learn their skills (Sable, 1982). This rhetoric is most audible when wage differentials are declining.

The organization to implement this ideology is the union, where it exists, or the informal occupational community where it does not. Where the skilled are a majority or plurality in the union, they usually control it and maintain wage differentials. Even where they are a minority, they sometimes control the union because they typically are its most active members and officers (Tannenbaum and Kahn, 1958:109, Spinrad, 1960; Aronowitz, 1973:157, 181). Arnold Weber (1963) claims that the skilled are most active when they comprise between 15 to 30 percent of the membership because they can control the union only if they are very active and strongly united. Where they are a minority of less than 15 percent, they will experience difficulty in dominating union affairs.

American workers may be divided into three strata: in the highest are those who have high social solidarity and union protection; in the second, those who have little social solidarity but strong union protection; in the third, those who have neither. The skilled are more likely than the unskilled to have both social solidarity and union protection. The solidarity of the skilled partly derives from their greater freedom and autonomy on the job. They can move about, communicate, and organize for their own protection (Blauner, 1964; Form, 1972). Even though they need union help less than other workers, the skilled participate heavily in union affairs and hold most of the local and national offices (Aronowitz, 1973:173). Thus, craft workers supplement the power gained through group solidarity with union influence or control. The semiskilled, especially in mass-production industries, display little work-group solidarity, but when unionized, they develop considerable bargaining power. Even so, a few skilled workers in industrial unions can cause considerable turmoil over the issue of wage differentials, a situation that I later describe in detail. Finally, unskilled workers who are not unionized have the least amount of work-group cohesion (Goode and Fowler, 1949) and union protection. This situation typically exists in economically marginal firms that employ disprivileged groups: blacks, women, Spanish-speaking, the young, sick, and older workers who cannot afford to retire (Miller and Rein, 1966:426–516).

Currently, American skilled workers are more preoccupied with protecting their advantages than with winning new gains. In large industrial unions, they fight to maintain wage differentials. In craft unions, they struggle to prevent blacks and women from learning their jobs. In spite of fair employment and affirmative action legislation, women and blacks have made only small incursions into the skilled trades. Even voluntary programs which labor itself has proposed to integrate blacks and women (Chicago Plan, the Philadelphia Plan, and other hometown plans) have not moved unions, especially in the building trades, to release their control over the apprentice system and other routes into the trades (Marshall, 1968, 1972; Levison, 1974:187).

Little is known about the struggle of skilled workers in ideologically liberal industrial unions to restore wage differentials and keep blacks and women out of their jobs. The United Auto Workers (UAW) may be taken as an example. Widick (1972) and Goode (1976) describe the history of skill and racial stratification in the auto industry. Despite the social solidarity that existed between the races in the early days of the UAW, in forty years the UAW did not become a class-conscious union. Workers became increasingly obsessed with the race issue. Union elections were fought largely along racial lines. Without help from UAW officers, black autoworkers fought to obtain representation on the executive committees. As some blacks won union elections and as management coopted others, whites became more apprehensive about their security. But in the fight to keep their advantages, the skilled were remarkably successful. In 1970, about 65 percent of the manual employees in Detroit's GM plants were black, but 100 percent of the skilled were white. By 1980, blacks increased their representation slightly in the skilled trades.

The craft-industrial union struggle continues in different industries with different outcomes. Thus, while wage differentials in petroleum remained stable for years, they fell from 1.72 to 1.44 in the automobile industry in only three years, 1947–50 (Weber, 1963). In 1966, the skilled won an amendment in the UAW constitution that permitted them to vote separately on contract ratification (Brown, 1967). Later they demanded veto rights over provisions that they considered unsatisfactory. They also protested company practices that permitted production workers to perform some skilled tasks alongside of journeymen. The skilled charged that GM did not pay them the same wages as it paid members of the craft unions; the company failed to respect skill jurisdictions and failed to maintain proper wage differentials with respect to production workers.

The complex issue over whether skilled workers could veto proposed contracts was not satisfactorily resolved; in 1974 the matter was turned over to the UAW Public Review Board for adjudication. Although the board ruled against the skilled trades, the issue did not die. The skilled hired an attorney to fight the decision in the courts. Unsuccessful, they threatened to leave the UAW, form an independent union, or join another. From 1950–59 alone, skilled workers submitted thirty-eight petitions to the National Labor Relations Board to have separate bargaining rights. They also formed the United National Caucus within the UAW to coordinate their activities during national conventions (O'Donnell, 1974; Tillery, 1974). Finally, in 1976, after a long convention fight, the skilled won the right to veto those sections of the contract they found unsatisfactory (UAW Proceedings).

The skilled have been notably successful in keeping women and blacks out of their trades and, in this effort, they have had union support. In the past, some unions had separate bargaining agreements for men and women, but craft unions mainly relied on peer pressure to keep women out. Since most women were unskilled and semiskilled, their complaints rarely received a serious hearing. Cook (1968) and Berquist (1974) concluded that "tokenism" has long been the standard practice in union politics. This is not surprising. Since 1923 the AFL, and later the AFL–CIO, opposed the passage of the Equal Rights Amendment when it was annually introduced in Congress. The most vocal opponents were the skilled trades. In 1973, the AFL–CIO reversed its public stand but took only a few steps to implement its new-found conversion. In March 1974, the Coalition of Labor Union Women (CLUW) was organized to expand women's rights and women's representation within the trade union movement. CLUW had its work cut out. After World War II, as after World War I (Baker, 1925), unions and management successfully reduced women's representation in the skilled trades. Under pressure from the federal government, the percentage of women manual workers in skilled trades increased from 1960 to 1980 from 3 to 9.6 percent, a figure approached during World War II. While the representation of women increased in some occupations (supervision, dental technician, inspector, printer), the goals and timetable requirements of the Office of Federal Contract Compliance did not extend to women in construction trades covered by hometown plans developed in seventy cities and counties, and affirmative action steps toward indenturing minorities by the Bureau of Apprenticeship and Training did not extend to women (Hedges and Bemis, 1974). At first the CLUW could do very little about the problem because it received no financial support from the AFL-CIO. Later some financial support and recognition were given. In contrast, the UAW funded a Director of the Women's Department and the international organization had a women vice-president (Raphael, 1974:32). But even in today's conferences of the CLUW, "sympathetic" male union officers put responsibility for remedying the seniority situation on its victims by asking women what they intend to do about the seniority problem. Although sexism in the labor movement is not limited to the skilled workers, they are more successful than other workers in excluding women from their work. In 1980 only 1.8 percent of all working women were skilled. In contrast, women comprised 11 percent of operatives and 20 percent of service occupations. To conclude: the skilled trades are not only racially but sexually homogeneous.

Political Stratification of the Working Class

Sociological analysis of American politics is complicated by two structural features of its party system: two middle-of-the-road parties and the extraordinarily wide political spectrum of the Democratic party. If parties lean too strongly to support working-class interests, they threaten the stability of their coalitions. Since most of organized labor is strongly committed to the Democratic party, no interest group in the house of labor can, by itself, shift labor's allegiance to the Republican party. The skilled are part of a union coalition which, in turn, is part of a coalition in the Democratic party. Unlike other workers, the skilled make their major gains through factory and union struggles, not in party battles; i.e., they are more effective in shaping the union's internal than external politics. The task here is to examine, in a preliminary way, the extent to which the skilled, compared to other groups, are loyal to the union's attachment to the Democratic party (see Chapter 10).

The most comprehensive American studies of working-class politics are those of Richard Hamilton (1965), who studied the question whether affluence made members of the working class more conservative. Using skill level as an indicator of wealth, he examined the non-South Republican vote in three presidential elections: the 1948 contest between Truman and Dewey, and the

1952 and 1956 contests between Eisenhower and Stevenson. To eliminate contaminating influences of skill-wealth, Hamilton excluded blacks, women, independent artisans, and foremen from the skilled category. He found only negligible differences in the vote of the various skill levels, and concluded that economic differences within the working class do not affect party vote, but sociological factors do: e.g., age, group membership, group pressures, and size of community of residence (see Table 5.6).

Table 5.6. Skill and Politics: Percent Republican,[a] Party Identification, and Voter Participation among Non-South Respondents[b]

Elections		Unskilled	Semiskilled	Skilled
Percent Republican (SRC)				
1948	Truman-Dewey	30	31	42
1952	Stevenson-Eisenhower	50	56	63
1956	Stevenson-Eisenhower	54	50	58
1964	Johnson-Goldwater	26	18	24
1968	Humphrey-Nixon	42	41	46
1972	McGovern-Nixon	48	58	72
Party identification (NORC)				
1955		33	28	35
1956		31	38	45
1968		29	13	24
1972		32	20	24
Voting participation (SRC)				
1964[c]		83	74	76
1968		73	67	72
1972		61	68	74

[a]Excludes independents, don't know, and nonvoters.
[b]All data from 1948, 1952, and 1956 taken from Hamilton (1965), and all remaining data from McNamee (1975).
[c]Data from 1968 survey are in response to questions concerning voting behavior in the 1964 presidential election.

McNamee (1975) replicated Hamilton's analysis for the three following presidential elections: the 1964 Johnson-Goldwater contest, the 1968 Nixon-Humphrey-Wallace contest, and the 1972 Nixon-McGovern election. McNamee made three important changes in his research: he included manual workers in the service sector, he included women in the sample, and he analyzed the effect of income independent of skill. Using a path analytic model, McNamee found that workers with higher incomes were more disposed to vote Republican, and that the relationship between income and skill had an indirect effect on party vote. He also concluded that sociological factors strongly affect party choice.

The Hamilton and McNamee studies together point to several important findings (see Table 5.6). First, voting participation is more constant for the skilled; in three elections, variation in participation was 4 percent for the skilled and 22 percent for the unskilled. Second, consensus among the skill levels varied considerably on presidential candidate preferred and party identification. Some elections were highly consensual (Humphrey-Nixon, 1968), while others were highly non-consensual (McGovern-Nixon, 1972). While party identification did not vary as much as voting, it did vary considerably from one election to another. These fluctuations in voting and party identification held (although in different patterns) even when blacks, foremen, and independent artisans were removed from the sample. Third, the loyalty of the skilled to the Democratic party was more volatile than that of the other manual workers. In the six elections, there was a forty-eight percentage point variation among the skilled in support of Republican candidates compared to twenty-eight for the unskilled. Fourth, in five of six elections, a larger percentage of the skilled than other workers voted Republican. In three elections, over half of the skilled voted Republican; the unskilled voted Republican only once. In short, the skilled as a group were more regular voters than the less skilled, they were more inconstant in their party loyalty, and they learned more toward the Republican party.

A study by Glenn and Alston (1968) examined responses of major occupational groups to 113 questions from twenty-three national surveys to plumb the cultural distance among occupations. As did Hamilton, they concluded that cultural differences between skilled and clerical workers are wider than between any other occupational strata, and that the cleavage between the manual working class and the white-collar middle class reflects political reality better than does a middle mass made up of lower white-collar and skilled manual workers. Two observations from the Glenn-Alston data are more relevant than their central findings. First, consensus on most of the cultural items was low for both the working and middle class, and the range of scores was greater for manual than for nonmanual workers (Glenn and Alston, 1968:372); therefore, the conclusion that working-class culture is more distinctive than middle-class culture seems overdrawn. Second, in terms of critically important political values, the skilled resembled clerical-sales and professional workers more than they did other manual strata (Glenn and Alston, 1968:373).

In two related items (reading and exposure to news, and attention given to current events), the skilled were closer to clerical and sales workers than to other manual workers. Moreover, political values and news exposure scores varied more for manual than for nonmanual workers. Finally, on "attitudes on child rearing and discipline, skilled workers [were] clearly grouped with the middle-class occupations, being as close to professionals as to other manual category with the most similar scores" (Glenn and Alston, 1968:373). The authors underplayed these data by stressing that the skilled resemble other manual workers in authoritarianism, attitudes toward labor unions, optimism about the future state of the world, and drinking attitudes and behavior. Hamilton's conclusion that the skilled may constitute a separate stratum seems to fit the Glenn-Alston data better than does the latter's conclusion on working-class homogeneity. In sum, although data from these studies are not conclusive, they suggest that the skilled are more politically active, more conservative, and more independent than other manual workers. Given the structure of labor politics in the United States, the deviancy of the skilled may indeed inhibit political solidarity in the working class (see Chapter 10).

The Skilled in the Class Structure

Sociologists have polarized the class identification issue by asking whether the skilled belong to the working or the middle class. Framing the question in this way may be just as uninstructive as the embourgeoisement hypothesis. A number of social scientists (e.g., Lipset, 1960:403–17; Kerr et al., 1960) detected certain trends in all advanced industrial societies: workers were becoming affluent, industrial disputes were declining, incomes were drifting toward the mean, and class ideologies were declining. These ideas were labeled "the embourgeoisement hypothesis" by scholars in the Marxist tradition. Social scientists decided to test the hypothesis by comparing the top of the working class (skilled workers) to the bottom of the middle class (clerical workers) on such items as buying a house, moving to the suburb, voting Republican, and identifying with the middle class. They reasoned that if the skilled were more like clerical than unskilled workers, they were becoming middle class; if not, they were still working class. Jehlin (1974) points out that such a research design violates historically important issues associated with embourgeoisement: acquiring capital, acquiring political control, and acquiring business values and status. While her test may be too rigorous, the indicators of conservatism used by many researchers are too crude. Buying a house, moving to a suburb, and occasionally shifting party identification are so common that they are weak political indicators of embourgeoisement.

A more rewarding approach might be to examine how class segments behave toward each other. Perhaps the working-class/middle-class cleavage is not the most important class issue in today's politics. If the skilled fight other workers to maintain their privileges, if the skilled take a more conservative stand on working-class issues, and if they associate primarily with each other, they retard the social solidarity of the working class and thereby influence interclass politics.

Though Hamilton (1964), Mayer and Buckley (1955:84) and Lenski (1955:84) have suggested that the skilled constitute a separate stratum or perhaps a segment of the working class, research on the subject is scanty. The research of Hamilton (1963:67), Goldthorpe and colleagues (1969), DeFronzo (1973), Kornhauser (1965), Glenn and Alston (1968), and others report consistent differences both among the skill levels and between manual- and white-collar workers. Only Mackenzie's (1973) research focused on the separate identity of the skilled. He studied skilled and white-collar workers in Providence, Rhode Island, and found evidence that the skilled were attaining separate status in the stratification system. They not only earned more than other manual and clerical workers, but they had more job security and work satisfaction. They reared their children conservatively, to be obedient, respectful, and honest, yet to have white-collar and university aspirations. The high levels of home ownership and rising consumption among the skilled did not signify a commitment to bourgeois values. Although two-fifths claimed to be independent voters, their allegience to the Democratic party was relatively high; however, party loyalty reflected their ethnic and religious identification more than their political commitment (see Greeley, 1972). Importantly, half of the craft workers believed they were not in the same class as the unskilled (Mackenzie, 1973:135). Like Max Weber, the skilled defined class on the basis of income and life chances. They were also a status group in interactional terms because two-thirds of their leisure-time companions were skilled workers, but they were not class conscious in the Marxist sense of seeing themselves in conflict with other classes. More than any other occupational group, the skilled considered the unskilled/skilled distinction to be important.

Conclusions

The widely-debated issue whether manual workers identify with the working- or middle class hides as much as it illuminates. A more important research task seeks to identify the factors that inhibit the political mobilization of manual workers as a class. Internal class cleavages may be as important as interclass cleavages (Parkin, 1979: 29–44). Class mobilization is inhibited by the tendency of the skilled to define their interests as different from those of other manual workers. Their perception has some objective basis. They earn significantly more money. They are more homogeneous racially and sexually. They constitute a self-conscious status group and they press others to honor their skills. They know that they must struggle to preserve their historic advantages over other manual workers. In this struggle, employers, the less skilled, or both, represent the enemy, depending on the issues.

When the skilled resist the incursions of the unskilled, they may appear conservative, but the label is misleading. Their reservations toward other manual workers are not principled. Whenever the skilled feel they can improve their position by joining other workers, they enthusiastically assume leadership in the struggle against the common enemy (Hanagan, 1977). Here they appear to be radical. In Norway, Cuba, Latin America, and the United States prior to 1940, when organized labor felt oppressed, the skilled led the working-class movement and sometimes embraced a revolutionary ideology of economic equality. Once labor achieved political legitimacy in pluralistic societies or once labor became part of social democratic governments, the skilled again pressed for their traditional advantages. But over the long run and in most countries, the skilled usually seek to maintain a posture of political autonomy and make temporary alliances with other workers and even management to protect their separate interests (see Sable, 1982:127–93). In short, the skilled in the United States are not an aspiring bourgeoisie as Michels claims, nor are they a class in Marxist terms. Sociological terminology is inadequate here, but the skilled appear to be a quasi-social-class segment.

The analysis I have pursued makes the skilled appear as the bête noire of the working class because they inhibit its political solidarity. This impression arises because I have focused on a relatively short time span. If the analysis were to focus, for example, on nonskilled workers in industrial unions (see Chapter 6), they too would appear to be self-serving and indifferent to the problems of the economically disadvantaged in the working class. In short, the

American working class is divided, and more than one stratum inhibits its political solidarity. Importantly, the above analysis has chosen to ignore the repressive actions of business and governmental agencies which also prevent the political mobilization of the working class.

The study of working-class solidarity must consider the internal politics of organized labor at the national level. This topic is pursued in Chapter 9. There I conclude that the American union officials promote a union and a consumer program, not a class program. American labor leadership has been and continues to be recruited from the ranks of skilled labor. The growth of mass industrial unions has not yet produced a genuine class politics.

Note

1. These data are for craft workers exclusive of foremen and for non-farm laborers. The differentials for women are consistently lower than for men, and they rose more slowly from 1940 (1.28) to 1980 (1.60). Women supervisors are included with craft workers. For full-time and year-around workers, the skill differential for 1980 was about 1.35 for men and 1.25 for women.

6

Class Divisions, Unions, and Earnings

Foremen, the self-employed, and skilled workers, as three aristocrats of labor, have resources that increase their earnings advantages over the bulk of the nonskilled. Only a few foremen and self-employed workers are union members, and most of them are concentrated in construction where they sporadically work as employees. Similarly, only a few of the marginally employed are union members because many are partially retired, not committed to or incapable of full-time work. Labor unions do affect the earnings of three major strata of the working class: the skilled, nonskilled workers in core industries, and nonskilled in the periphery, who together make up 85 percent of the class. The skilled, because they arc in shorter supply and more socially cohesive than the nonskilled, command higher wages even without union membership. This chapter examines the impact of unions on the earnings of all strata, but it concentrates more on the nonskilled strata that form the bulk of the working class.

Though union membership is only one factor that influences earnings, Lewis's (1968) detailed comparison of union and nonunion wages in several industries concluded that unions raise wages from 10 to 15 percent. More recent studies examine a wider range of variables and they suggest that the unions' impact is perhaps double Lewis's estimate (Andrisani and Kohen, 1977; Johnson and Youmans, 1971; Kahn, 1977). However, another study suggests a different causal relationship. Schmidt and Strauss (1976) ran two regression equations, the first to determine the effect of unions on earnings and the second to determine the effect of general earnings on union earnings. They found that the effect of general earnings on unions was positive and statistically significant, but the effect of unions on earnings, though positive, was not significant. The authors concluded that unionization does not lead to higher earnings; rather, the conditions that lead to higher earnings also lead to unionization.

Clearly, some union benefits apply to all union members regardless of their skill or social status. Thus, seniority clauses are nearly universal in collective bargaining agreements. Other union gains, such as supplementary unemployment benefits, help some members more than others. Males and whites in core industries may profit more from union membership than do women and blacks in competitive industries. This chapter explores the extent to which unions affect earnings in different strata and the race, sex, and other groups in those strata. First, I review the literature on how union earnings vary by skill and sector, the factors that underlie the formation of the strata, and the literature on race and sex, the main social status cleavages. Second, I systematically compare union and nonunion earnings in the United States today by working-class strata and social status characteristics. Finally, in a multiple-regression framework, I examine the extent to which union membership, stratal category, human capital, labor market participation, and social status variables explain working-class earnings.

Unions, Worker Characteristics, and Earnings

Sociologists and economists emphasize different variables in their explanation of earnings. Sociologists attach significance to the power of organizations to affect earnings while economists stress market effects. Sociologists think that the social status of workers (sex, race, age, marital status, education, and occupation) reflects their social power to affect earnings. But some economists (Becker, 1967) think that some of these variables (age, education, and skill) measure human capital investments that influence workers' productivity and therefore their earnings. While labor economists consider hours and weeks worked simply as indicators of labor market participation, sociologists see them as differences in privileged access to stable jobs. Many economists think that some industries pay high wages because they hire the most productive workers, while sociologists think that unions and high status groups *force* high profit industries to pay high wages. In short, even when sociologists and economists consider the same variables, they interpret their functions differently (Brown, 1977). This chapter examines the earnings of three strata: the skilled, nonskilled core, and nonskilled periphery workers. Since previous research is not organized with these strata in mind, I first review the literature that deals with the variables that make up the strata: skill, sector of employment, and social status.

Economists stress that because the skilled are in short supply, they command higher wages than do the nonskilled in all employment sectors. Although the skilled profit from unionization, they gain less from it than do the nonskilled (Bloch and Kuskin, 1978). In a representative sample of U.S. male household heads, Abowd and Farber (1982:267) found that skilled workers least desired union jobs, while the less skilled very early queued up for them. For both skilled and nonskilled workers, union affiliation became fixed very early in their work careers and it did not change. This suggests the hypothesis that unionized workers, whatever their skill and ascriptive status characteristics (age, sex, race), earn higher incomes in the unionized than in the nonunionized sector.

The fact that unorganized skilled workers earn relatively high and stable wages, while the unorganized nonskilled experience greater fluctuations in demand (Reder, 1955), suggests that skill differences in earnings should be higher among the unorganized where the nonskilled can not resist downward wage pressure (Freeman, 1980). Among the unionized, skilled workers should draw relatively higher wages than do the nonskilled in those situations where the skilled comprise a larger part of the labor force (Weber, 1963). Thus, in craft-dominated unions, where they are the majority, the skilled should draw relatively higher wages than in industrial unions where they are a minority. The wage gap between the skilled and nonskilled should be lower in industrial unions because the more numerous nonskilled can dominate the making of trade union wage policy. Unfortunately, data for craft and industrial unions are not available in my data set, but earnings are available for industries that are known to vary in their proportions of skilled workers. I expect the skill ratio (earnings of skilled divided by those of the nonskilled) to be higher in industries with a higher proportion of skilled employees.

Labor and management differ in their approach to skilled workers. Understandably, unions try to restrict the supply of the skilled in order to maintain their higher wages. On the other side, management seeks to expand the supply of skilled in order to lower the wage bill. Management also prefers to train and upgrade the skills of workers whom they believe show most promise of being productive. Unions think that seniority should be the primary consideration in skill upgrading. Management is more inclined than the union to upgrade the skills of women, blacks, and the young when doing so would lower labor costs (Bonacich, 1976). But white males press unions to reserve the skilled jobs for them (Sexton, 1977).

Ashenfelter (1973) compared the race and sex earnings of unionized and nonunionized workers using data from the census's 1967 Survey of Economic Opportunity. He found that, compared to the nonunion workers, wages of blacks resembled those of whites in industrial unions, while in construction craft unions, wages of blacks were lower. However, he concluded that unions affect the race and sex wage gap in only a minor way.

Antos, Chandler, and Mellow (1980), using a 1976 Current Population Survey of the census, found that the advantage accruing to women by unionization lagged behind that of men, even after sex differences in productivity were taken into account. They concluded that a significant percentage of the male advantage results from their concentration in favored unionized occupations and industries—a reflection of indirect discrimination. For example, skilled women (e.g., dressmakers, cosmetologists) often work alone or in small shops that are not easily unionized. At the same time, women are denied entry into many skilled trades and into industries that use a great deal of skilled labor. When unionized, women are found in the least skilled jobs of the lowest paying industries (Baron and Bielby, 1982).

Taking account of the findings above, I expect earnings of women and blacks to be more ascriptively determined in the unionized than in the nonunionized sector. That is, even though women and blacks may earn relatively more if they work in the unionized sector, union earnings will be more polarized by race and sex than are nonunionized earnings. The human capital (skill, education, and experience) of women and blacks will be rewarded relatively less in the unionized sector.

Compared to industries in the periphery, core industries are more highly unionized, pay higher wages and fringe benefits, offer their workers more steady employment, and provide them with more advancement opportunities (Gordon, 1972; Berger and Piore, 1980:25). Yet many firms in the core sector are not unionized and some firms in the periphery are. If employment sector more powerfully affects earnings than does union membership, workers in the unorganized core should earn more than those in the organized periphery. This situation would reflect the higher profits of core industries (Doeringer and Piore, 1971). Accepting this assumption, I expect workers in the unionized core to receive the highest earnings, followed by those in the nonunionized core, the unionized periphery, and finally the nonunionized periphery.

Earnings of skilled workers, less than others, are affected by union and sector membership. Since earnings of the nonskilled, especially women and blacks, are strongly affected by both union and sector (Small, 1976), I expect their earnings to be more equalized in the unionized core (Duncan and Leigh, 1980). This equalizing tendency should hold for white males as well as women, blacks, and the young (Pfeffer and Ross, 1981). But union and core sector earnings are also affected by the ascriptive traits of workers: sex, race, marital status, head of family, and, possibly, age. Although the literature stresses that women, blacks, and the young are crowded into periphery and unorganized industries (Stevenson, 1978), core and unionized firms do hire employees from discriminated groups. Where do they suffer relatively less discrimination? Since these groups earn more in core and unionized industries, the issue in human capital terms is whether the disprivileged are paid *relatively* more for their skill, education, and work experience in core and unionized industries or in periphery and nonunionized ones. Since few blacks and women hold skilled jobs, the issue is especially pertinent for the nonskilled core and periphery strata.

In the unionized core, pressures develop both for and against discrimination. Because these industries have higher labor costs, management is pressed to use employees efficiently. This may involve training and promoting them rather than hiring from the outside. Unions also urge management to consider seniority in promotions and vacancies. Together, these pressures help build internal labor markets. But anomalies persist. Although many women, blacks, and young workers have more education and higher skill potential than do older white male employees, women and blacks have the least seniority, so they linger in the worst jobs.

Presumably, unorganized firms, more than the organized, pay workers in accordance with their present and potential productivity. In the absence of unions, managers can release their least productive workers with impunity, regardless of their seniority, and can train and promote whomever they think will be most productive, including members of disadvantaged groups. Even in the unionized periphery, managers can follow an individually oriented personnel policy because unions reluctantly recognize that business must remain competitive to survive. Firms in the unorganized core are larger and more profitable than are firms in the periphery, so these core firms can behave more like unionized core firms.

What should be expected in the four comparisons: unorganized periphery, organized periphery, unorganized core, and organized core? Although the evidence is mixed, I expect unorganized periphery industries to respond relatively more to the human capital characteristics of employees, including members of disprivileged groups. This means that higher skilled workers will be rewarded relatively more and the lower skilled, relatively less. Organized periphery industries follow next in responding to the human capital of their employees, followed by the unorganized core, and the organized core. Put differently, the relative inequality of earnings, in human capital terms, should be highest in the unorganized periphery and lowest in the organized core.

Age, seniority, and work experience are highly associated with weeks and hours worked that, in turn, strongly affect earnings. Scholars disagree whether higher pay for older workers represents pay for higher productivity and more experience, or an ascriptive wage for age. Since seniority provisions are almost universal in collective bargaining agreements, the impact of work experience on earnings should be high for union members, and it should widen with age, especially for the less skilled and ascriptively disadvantaged (Andrisani and Kohen, 1977). Johnson and Youmans's (1971) study of the wage effects of age and education concluded that unions most benefit the very young and older workers. Young workers enjoy an immediate advantage from their union status. But employers prefer more educated and older workers, thus forcing other less educated and younger workers into the nonunion sector, further depressing their wages and employment opportunities. Because core firms develop internal labor markets, they also emphasize seniority. In short, I expect the impact of work experience on earnings to be strongest in the unionized core, followed by the unorganized core, the organized periphery, and the unorganized periphery. This trend should be more apparent for nonskilled strata because they profit relatively more than the skilled from unionization.

Finally, whether unions increase or decrease economic inequality in the working class is not firmly established. Holding market conditions constant, unions raise wages first and the unorganized sector follows, thus creating temporary periods of increased wage inequality (Rees, 1967). Kahn (1977), in a re-analysis of a series of studies on the long-run direct and indirect effects of unions on wages, quit rates, and job advancement, concluded that the studies had underestimated the union's effect on wages and quit rates. Higher wages, lower quit rates, and more job advancement in the union sector increased economic inequality in the working class over time.

Kahn (1980) further compared the wages of nonunionized service workers in low and highly unionized metropolitan areas. In a multiple regression analysis that included extent of metropolitan unionization in the equation, he found that white females earned 17 percent less in real wages in relatively more unionized cities, while nonunion nonwhite males earned 27 percent less. On the other hand, nonunion white males earned 53 percent higher real wages in more unionized than in less unionized cities. These results paralleled an earlier comparative study of San Francisco, a highly unionized city, and Los Angeles, a less unionized city (Kahn, 1978). Kahn concluded that a highly unionized environment widens wage differentials between nonunion white males on the one hand and nonunion women and nonwhite men on the other. In effect, union environments depress wages in the lower wage part of the secondary labor force, widening economic inequality in the working class. I cannot test this hypothesis directly in this study, although I can compare the earnings of workers with different stratal and social status characteristics in the organized and nonorganized sectors.

In summary, working-class earnings inequality in both the union and nonunion sectors varies with the stratal position and social status characteristics of workers. The above literature review suggests the following generalizations for testing:

1. Earnings of union workers are higher than those of nonunion workers regardless of their stratal position and ascribed social status characteristics.

2. Earnings inequality is highest in industries dominated by skilled workers regardless of workers' union status, stratal position, and ascribed social status characteristics.

3. Earnings of workers, including those of the least skilled, are highest in the organized core, followed by unorganized core, the organized periphery, and the unorganized periphery.

4. Skilled vs. nonskilled earnings equality is highest in the organized core, followed by the unorganized core, the organized periphery, and the unorganized periphery. This holds regardless of stratal position and ascribed social status characteristics of workers.

5. Earnings in the organized core respond the least to the human capital and ascriptive characteristics of workers, followed by the unorganized core, the organized periphery, and the unorganized periphery.

6. Earnings respond to work experience (seniority) most in the organized core followed by the unorganized core, the organized periphery, and the unorganized periphery.

7. Unions tend to increase economic inequality in the working class.

Data and Methods

The data for this chapter were derived from a computer tape provided by the U.S. Department of Labor (USDOL) that contained the March 1971 national survey of union membership conducted by the U.S. Bureau of the Census. The data were supplemented by a similar survey conducted in May 1981. Both data sets had representative samples of over 50,000 United States households in more than 400 regions. The data were corrected for sampling error. Only manual workers, including service workers who worked for pay in 1970, were selected for this analysis. Foremen and supervisors were excluded. Service workers were distributed into skilled, semiskilled, and unskilled categories according to their occupational complexity scores as in Chapter 2.

The dependent variable in this analysis, annual earnings, includes only profits and wages. Profits of the self-employed were increased by 30 percent to partially correct for underreporting of earnings (U.S. Department of the Treasury, 1979). Earnings were logged to reduce skewness. Working-class strata were represented by five dummy variables for self-employed, skilled, nonskilled core, nonskilled periphery, and marginally employed. The other independent variables (sex, race, marital status, chief earner, education, skill, class of worker, sector, and work experience) were coded the same as in Chapter 2. Hours worked last week were coded in single units and weeks worked: $0 = 1$, $1–13 = 2$, $14–26 = 3$, $27–39 = 4$, $40–47 = 5$, $48–49 = 6$, $50–52 = 7$. Union membership was coded member $= 1$, nonmember $= 0$.

The findings from this analysis should not be compared to those published by the USDOL (1972 and 1981) because the DOL reported data only for full-time, year-around workers, whereas this study includes all workers who reported receiving wages or profits.

Profile of Union and Unorganized Workers

About three-tenths of all manual workers in the United States were union members in 1970 and 1980 (Table 6.1). About two-fifths of the skilled and semiskilled and one-quarter of the unskilled were organized. Transport operatives were more highly organized than other semiskilled workers, and unskilled laborers more than service employees. Overall, union members were more highly skilled than unorganized workers.

The industrial distribution of the organized and unorganized differed markedly. Over five-tenths of all union members and three-tenths of nonunion employees worked in manufacturing. In contrast, only one-tenth of union but three-tenths of nonunion employees worked in the services. Half or more of manual employees in transportation-communication-utilities, durable goods manufacturing, construction, and mining were organized; in nondurable goods manufacturing and public administration, about a third were unionized. In contrast, 20 percent or less of the manual employees were union members in finance, insurance, real estate, wholesale and retail trade, and professional and other services. More simply, 69 percent of manual employees in core industries were union members compared to 36 percent in periphery industries.

In 1970, union members received mean annual earnings that were 64 percent larger than nonunion earnings. This large difference only partially reflects differences in weeks and hours worked. Only six percent more of the union than nonunion members worked the full year, and only eleven percent more of the union members worked over 40 hours a week. Although the organized were older and had slightly more work experience than the unorganized, the differences were too small to account for the earnings disparity. The sex composition of the two groups differed considerably: 15 percent of the union members were women compared to 37 percent of the nonunion labor force. Finally, a larger proportion of the organized were white and married. Except for the increased representation of blacks in unions, all the above differences between organized and unorganized workers remained in 1980 (USDOL, 1980).

In short, union members represent a higher stratum than nonunion workers in levels of skill, social status, and earnings. Although the data indicate that union members receive 64 percent higher earnings than do nonunion workers, this figure underestimates the difference because it does not include fringe benefits. Freeman (1981) pooled three annual surveys conducted by the Bureau of Labor Statistics on Expenditures for Employee Compensation. These surveys covered 10,000 establishments that included all large firms and a sample of smaller ones. He found that, compared to nonunion firms, union firms had significantly higher voluntary fringe benefits, especially in the areas of insurance, pensions, and vacation pay. The union vs. nonunion firm advantage in fringe benefits was greater than the percentage wage advantage. In 1967 prices, union firms paid 70 cents an hour for fringe benefits compared to 29 cents for nonunion firms. Feuille, Hendricks, and Kahn's (1981) study of 505 collective bargaining contracts in manufacturing also revealed a strong and positive correlation between wage level and nonwage benefits. Therefore, the working class is more economically stratified by union membership than our data revealed.

Table 6.1. Social Characteristics of Union and Nonunion Manual Workers in the United States, 1970 (percent)

Characteristics	Union	Nonunion
Hours worked last week (40+)	80.8	69.3
Weeks worked last year (50–52)	70.8	64.7
Skill level:		
skilled	35.2	29.9
semiskilled	46.3	34.5
unskilled	18.5	35.6
Males	85.1	63.2
Married	81.6	66.7
White	87.3	81.3
Age (mean years)	41.0	38.6
Work experience (mean years)	21.7	18.4
Core sector employment	69.1	36.5
Industry:		
Agriculture and mining	1.8	1.6
Construction	12.5	8.1
Manufacturing (durable)	34.7	16.6
Manufacturing (nondurable)	18.4	14.5
Transp., comm., utilities	14.1	6.7
Wholesale and retail trade	7.1	19.2
Finance, insurance, real estate	.5	1.1
Services and public admin.	10.8	33.3
Strata:		
Self-employed	.1	6.2
Skilled	34.1	26.5
Nonskilled core	37.8	18.4
Nonskilled periphery	22.2	36.2
Marginally employed	5.7	13.7
Annual earning (mean $)	$7,802	$4,754
Totals	30.7	69.3

Source: USDOL tape, Report 417 (1972).

Excluding the self- and marginally employed, who together made up 15 percent of all workers, the skilled, nonskilled core, and nonskilled periphery strata were roughly equal in size. As anticipated, the skilled and the nonskilled core strata were a much larger part of the unionized sector, while the nonskilled periphery and marginally employed strata made up a larger part of the unorganized (Table 6.2). In the census data, the self-employed earned the highest incomes, but in the DOL sample the skilled earned the most. This difference probably reflects a larger sampling error in the DOL survey.

Among the unionized, the skilled earned 25 percent more than did the nonskilled core workers; the difference was 15 percent for the nonunionized. Again, for the unionized, nonskilled core workers earned 23 percent more than did nonskilled periphery employees. A 53 percent difference between the two strata appeared in the nonunion sector primarily because unorganized periphery workers earned so much lower wages than did the unionized. The smallest union advantage of 30 percent appeared for the nonskilled core stratum, followed by the skilled and self-employed. Much larger differences appeared for nonskilled periphery workers and the marginally employed. The relative earnings of the strata in the unionized sector remained the same for full-time, year-round workers as for all workers, suggesting that the union effect is constant. Except for the self-employed, for whom the earnings data are not reliable, the absolute dollar differences between parallel union and nonunion strata was about $1,800, a sizable difference. Discounting the marginally employed, the main earnings gap between strata in both the union and nonunion sector was between the nonskilled core and nonskilled periphery strata. One may conclude that though differences in stratal earnings are substantial for both the organized and unorganized, they are especially important for the lowest three strata. This suggests that differences in sector earnings deserve more attention.

Table 6.2. Mean Annual Earnings by Strata for Union and Nonunion Workers, 1970

Strata	Union	Percent	Nonunion	Percent	Union Nonunion
Self-employed	$8,252	—	$ 5,332	6	1.49
Skilled	9,700	34	6,878	26	1.41
Nonskilled core	7,732	38	5,956	18	1.30
Nonskilled periphery	6,305	22	3,896	36	1.62
Marginally employed	3,182	6	1,380	14	2.30
Total	7,802	100	4,750	100	1.64
N	8,497		14,524		

Source: USDOL tape, Report 417 (1972).

Mean annual earnings in the core sector were 72 percent higher than in the periphery, but the advantage varied by union membership, race, and sex (Table 6.3). Union members in core industries earned 30 percent more than did nonunion workers in the core, but earnings in the nonunion core and unionized periphery were virtually identical. Thus, union members in the periphery earned 69 percent more than did nonunion workers in that sector. The largest disparity clearly is between the organized and the unorganized in the periphery.

Table 6.3. Mean Annual Earnings Advantage (1970) of Core Over Periphery Workers for Race, Sex, and Union Member Status[a]

		Union Members			
Total	EA[b]	Whites	EA[b]	Males	EA[b]
$8,414	30%	$8,590	27%	$8,881	13%
$6,481		$6,761		$7,883	
				Females	
				$5,026	28%
				$3,929	
		Nonwhites		Males	
		$6,996	39%	$7,211	23%
		$5,044		$5,850	
				Females	
				$3,929	0%
				$3,937	
		Nonunion			
Total	EA[b]	Whites	EA[b]	Males	EA[b]
$6,339	65%	$6,593	64%	$7,044	33%
$3,835		$4,018		$5,296	
				Females	
				$3,947	51%
				$2,612	
		Nonwhites		Males	
		$4,912	56%	$5,095	23%
		$3,146		$4,134	
				Females	
				$3,666	50%
				$2,428	

Source: USDOL tape, Report 417 (1972).
[a]Core earnings in numerator, periphery in denominator.
[b]Earnings advantage.

Among the unionized, sector advantage in earnings was only 13 percent for white males and zero for nonwhite females. Clearly, white females and nonwhite males gain the most from union affiliation and core sector employment. Among the nonunionized, the earnings advantage of core over periphery workers was 65 percent, more than double that among the unionized. This larger sector disparity for nonunion workers was maintained for white and nonwhite females, but reduced by half for males. Thus, male earnings suffered less than did female earnings from employment in the nonorganized periphery. In short, sector earnings inequality is much larger for nonunionized workers, especially for women.

Earnings advantages of union membership vary considerably by skill, sector, race, and sex. The nonskilled profit especially from unionization. They earned 73 percent more than their unorganized counterparts, compared to the 48 percent advantage for the skilled (see Table 6.4). At both skill levels, the union advantage in the periphery was double that of the core. Within the periphery, the union advantage for whites was greater than for nonwhites. Nonwhite men in the core profited relatively more from unionization than did whites at both skill levels, but nonwhite women showed an inconsistent pattern. Overall, the union effect on the earnings of sex and race groups varied.

Finally, earnings inequality was examined between the skilled and nonskilled. The advantage of the skilled was much higher for nonunion (60%) than for union workers (37%), and the advantage was higher in all industries. In line with the hypothesis, in the unionized sector, the earnings advantage of the skilled was lower in durable and nondurable goods manufacturing where the nonskilled are in the heavy majority. The advantage of the skilled was larger in construction, mining, services, and government where the skilled are more highly represented.[1]

The skill advantage in earnings was considerably higher in the periphery than in the core, especially among the unorganized, pointing to the lower pay for nonskilled labor in the unorganized perphery. Since skilled whites earned more than skilled nonwhites in both sectors whether or not they were unionized, clearly whites were paid more for their skills wherever they were employed. Nonwhite women received almost no reward for their skill in the core compared to white women and men, regardless of union status. But skilled nonwhite males were severely underrewarded only in the unorganized periphery. Inexplicably, skilled nonwhite women were rewarded more than white women in the periphery, regardless of union status. However, the main pattern was an underreward for the skills of nonwhites and women in the core for both union and nonunion workers (Table 6.5).

In summary, union members represent an economically privileged segment of the working class. Earnings equality is higher among the organized primarily because nonskilled workers gain relatively more from unionization than do the skilled. Although the earnings advantage of core over periphery workers is large, it is greatly reduced for union members. In any event, men suffer less than do women by employment in the periphery. Earnings inequality is highest in industries where

Divided We Stand

Table 6.4. Annual Earnings Advantage (1970) of Union over Nonunion Workers by Skill, Sector, Race, and Sex[a]

	EA[b]		EA[b]		EA[b]		EA[b]
Skilled $9,445 $6,408	48%	Core $9,785 $7,881	24%	White $9,864 $8,062	22%	Male $9,924 $8,124	22%
						Female $6,401 $5,106	25%
				Nonwhite $8,315 $6,106	36%	Male $8,450 $6,106	38%
						Female $4,872 $3,907	25%
		Periphery $8,182 $5,152	59%	White $8,380 $5,306	58%	Male $8,860 $6,784	31%
						Female $4,393 $3,076	43%
				Nonwhite $6,286 $4,028	56%	Male $8,415	24%
						Female $4,890 $3,975	23%
Unskilled $6,903 $3,996	73%	Core $7,457 $5,563	34%	White $7,592 $5,585	36%	Male $7,966 $6,096	31%
						Female $4,796 $3,867	24%
				Nonwhite $6,689 $4,612	45%	Male $6,901 $4,778	44%
						Female $4,685 $3,646	28%
		Periphery $6,002 $3,376	78%	White $6,258 $3,502	79%	Male $7,479 $4,568	64%
						Female $3,885 $2,468	57%
				Nonwhite $4,865 $2,985	63%	Male $5,685 $3,939	44%
						Female $3,853 $2,321	66%

Source: USDOL tape, Report 417 (1972).
[a]Union in numerator, nonunion in denominator
[b]Earnings advantage.

the skilled are more numerous than the nonskilled, especially in the nonunion periphery where skilled whites preserve their earnings advantage while nonwhites and nonskilled lose dramatically.

Table 6.5. Earnings Advantage of Skilled over Nonskilled for Sector, Race, and Sex, by Union Status[a]

	EA[b]		EA[b]		EA[b]		EA[b]
					Union Member		
Total	$9,455 37% $6,903	Core	$9,785 31% $7,457	White	$9,864 30% $7,592	Male	$9,924 25% $7,966
						Female	$6,401 33% $4,796
				Nonwhite	$8,315 24% $6,689	Male	$8,450 22% $6,901
						Female	$4,872 4% $4,685
		Periphery	$8,182 36% $6,002	White	$8,380 34% $6,258	Male	$8,860 18% $7,479
						Female	$4,393 13% $3,885
				Nonwhite	$6,268 29% $4,865	Male	$6,615 16% $5,685
						Female	$5,090 32% $3,853
					Nonunionized		
Total	$6,407 60% $3,996	Core	$7,881 42% $5,563	White	$8,062 44% $5,585	Male	$8,129 33% $6,096
						Female	$5,106 32% $3,867
				Nonwhite	$6,006 30% $4,612	Male	$6,106 28% $4,778
						Female	$3,907 7% $3,646
		Periphery	$5,125 52% $3,376	White	$5,306 52% $3,502	Male	$6,784 48% $4,569
						Female	$3,076 25% $2,468
				Nonwhite	$4,082 35% $2,985	Male	$5,114 30% $3,939
						Female	$3,092 33% $2,321

Source: USDOL tape, Report 417 (1972).
[a]Skilled in numerator, nonskilled in denominator.
[b]Earnings advantage.

Regression Analysis of Earnings

While the above findings describe economic inequality associated with union affiliation in the working class, they do not measure how different variables contribute to the inequality. To do this, I ran a series of multiple regression equations for earnings. In the first equation, union membership was included along with variables such as human capital (education, skill, experience), labor market participation (weeks worked, hours worked), and social status or ascriptive characteristics of workers (race, sex, marital status, head of family). Then, separate equations were run for union and nonunion employees. Finally, equations for union and nonunion workers were run separately for sector of employment and sex, the variables that most strongly affect their earnings.

Most of the variables in the regression equations correlated below .50. This suggests that the analysis was not confounded by serious problems in multicollinearity. The correlation of union status and the log of earnings was moderate (.30). As expected, week and hours worked, sex, marital status, head of family, and skill were moderately correlated with earnings. In almost all instances where the correlations were larger than .10, they were larger for nonunion than union members. This suggests that the union population is more homogeneous and/or that unions buffer the impact of market, human capital, and ascriptive status factors on earnings. Among the nonunionized, weeks worked, hours worked, and skill were more highly associated with earnings than among the unionized. The correlations for race and education were similar for both populations. Finally, greater stratal inequality existed in the nonunion sector because the negative correlations among the skilled, nonskilled periphery and marginally employed were larger.

Earnings for Two Stratification Models

Table 6.6 presents regression coefficients for two stratification equations that have the same terms except for skill and sector. In the "skill" model, the two variables were kept separate, while in the "working-class" model, they were combined to form the skilled and the two nonskilled strata.[2] The two models have about equal power because both their variances are close to 60 percent.[3]

Comparing the standardized betas in the two equations and disregarding for a moment the effect of stratal position, weeks and hours worked contributed most to earnings and explained a large part of the total variance. In both models, union status had a

Table 6.6. Regression of Natural Log of 1970 Annual Earnings on Two Stratification Equations

Variables[b]	Skill Stratification			Working-Class Stratification[a]		
	B	S.E.	beta	B	S.E.	beta
Union	.324	.009	.161	.348	.010	.170
Weeks	.258	.003	.394	.181	.004	.272
Hours	.108	.003	.179	.117	.003	.191
Skill	.156	.006	.125			
Education	.034	.002	.091	.036	.002	.100
Experience	.003	$.378^{-3}$	.047	.003	$.378^{-3}$	.041
Sex	.291	.012	.135	.334	.012	.152
Race	.094	.012	.035	.130	.012	.047
Marital status	.218	.010	.099	.233	.011	.104
Head	.223	.012	.108	.213	.012	.101
Sector	.204	.010	.104			
Self-employed	−.133	.063	−.009[c]	.503	.074	.031
Skilled				.725	.022	.334
Nonskilled core				.660	.022	.291
Nonskilled periphery				.466	.021	.219
N	20,317			20,633		
Constant	4.862	.03		5.080	.03	
R^2	.615			.602		

Source: USDOL tape, Report 417 (1972).
[a]Marginally employed, the omitted term for strata.
[b]Significant below the .001 level.
[c]$p = > .05$.

relatively high unstandardized coefficient, raising earnings by about a third when all other effects were controlled.

In the skill model, the contribution of union membership, as reflected by the standardized betas, was relatively high. It was higher than the effects of such human capital assets as skill, education, and experience, higher than employment sector, and higher than such ascriptive factors as sex, family head, marital status, and race. Only weeks and hours worked per week contributed more to earnings than did union membership. In short, union membership affects earnings more than do sector, ascriptive, and human capital variables, but not as much as labor market participation.

Important changes in the explanation of earnings resulted from introducing working-class strata into the equation. Recombining sector, skill, and class (self-employment and employee status) to form the strata made the indirect contribution of these variables more important (Table 6.6). Self-employment now became statistically significant, and the betas for the skilled and nonskilled core

strata became larger than weeks and hours worked. The union beta
was smaller, ranking sixth of thirteen, but it was larger than the
human capital variables of education and experience, and larger
than all of the ascriptive status variables. In short, introducing the
working-class strata into the equation raised their contribution to
earnings and lowered that of union membership. But the contributions of weeks and hours worked remained quite high and those of
human capital and ascriptive variables remained relatively low.
Since the strata represent groups with different amounts of market
power, I conclude that, controlling for other effects, strata and labor
market participation (weeks and hours worked) influence earnings
more than does union membership.

Earnings of Union and Nonunion Workers

Since the effect of union membership on earnings is moderately
high (about 32 percent), the earnings of organized and unorganized
employees may be determined differently. Earlier I speculated that
unions may reduce the impact of human capital and market participation on earnings. To explore this question, I ran separate regression equations for union and nonunion workers and then ran
regressions for both groups by sector and sex.

   Data in Table 6.7 show that the amount of total earnings variance explained was 14 percent lower for union than for nonunion
workers. The standardized betas for weeks and hours worked ranked
higher for nonunion employees, suggesting that they were more
exposed to market vicissitudes. For the unionized, hours worked
were much less important. Sex affected earnings by about the same
amount in both groups: males earned 30 percent more than did
females, controlling for all other factors. As hypothesized, education
was slightly more important for the nonunionized and ascriptive
factors of marital status and head of family, slightly less important.
Surprisingly, work experience ranked low for both the organized
and unorganized and contributed little to earnings. The greater
exposure of the nonunionized to unemployment and underemployment
suggests the importance of examining how sector especially affects
the earnings of the two nonskilled strata.

Sector Earnings and Union Status

Core sector employment and union membership are both associated
with high earnings. Yet, in our sample, almost one-third of union
members worked in the periphery, and their earnings were closer to

Table 6.7. Regression of the Natural Log of Annual Earnings on Characteristics of Union and Nonunion Workers

Variables[a]	Union[b]			Nonunion[b]		
	B	S.E.	beta	B	S.E.	beta
Self-employed	.421	.133	.037[c]	.470	.090	.031
Skilled	.655	.030	.498	.676	.030	.281
Nonskilled core	.525	.030	.407	.673	.030	.247
Nonskilled periphery	.394	.031	.264	.424	.028	.192
Weeks	.123	.005	.245	.209	.006	.315
Hours	.045	.004	.096	.139	.004	.228
Education	.019	.003	.075	.045	.003	.116
Experience	.002	$.474^{-3}$	.051	.003	$.541^{-3}$	.037
Sex	.318	.019	.183	.333	.016	.150
Race	.142	.016	.075	.118	.016	.043
Marital status	.166	.015	.102	.258	.014	.112
Head	.193	.018	.122	.219	.016	.101
N	7,781			12,839		
Constant	.431	.04		4.764	.04	
R^2	.441			.583		

Source: USDOL tape, Report 417 (1972).
[a]Significant below the .001 level.
[b]Marginally employed, the omitted term for strata.
[c]$p = > .05$.

the organized than to the nonorganized core.[4] To examine the relation of unionism to sector earnings, we ran regression equations for each sector by union status of workers (Table 6.8).

Explained variance increased as we moved from the union core to union periphery, nonunion core, and, finally, nonunion periphery. Variance for the nonunion periphery was 21 percent higher than for the union core. This points to the homogenizing influence of the union and the core sector on the determination of earnings. The beta patterns clearly showed that the union, controlling for other factors, was relatively more important in the core than in the periphery. But the unstandardized coefficients showed that, controlling for other factors, unions increased earnings in the periphery by 38 percent compared to 28 percent in the core. Expectedly, weeks worked was the most important determinant of earnings in both sectors, but hours worked per week was much more important in the periphery, pointing perhaps to more part-time work and underemployment in that sector.

Contrary to expectation, skill and education betas, as human capital indicators, ranked higher in the core than in the periphery.

The beta pattern for workers' ascriptive characteristics revealed that being a male and married counted relatively more in determining earnings in the periphery, while being head of the family counted much more in the core. Interpreting the effect of ascriptive characteristics is not intuitively obvious.

Table 6.8. Regression of Natural Log of Earnings on Social and Economic Characteristics of Workers by Union Status and Sector of Employment

	Union				Nonunion			
	Core		Periphery		Core		Periphery	
Variables[a]	B	beta	B	beta	B	beta	B	beta
Weeks	.158	.364	.232	.416	.269	.466	.286	.448
Hours	.028	.067	.059	.115	.078	.148	.47	.248
Experience	.033	.074	.001	.019[b]	.003	.059	.003	.044
Skill	.122	.161	.119	.116	.133	.123	.175	.132
Education	.020	.092	.016	.055[b]	.041	.139	.045	.112
Class	.185	.014[b]	.308	−.024[b]	−.195	−.018[b]	−.151	−.011[b]
Sex	.308	.156	.240	.153	.185	.080	.300	.138
Marital status	.132	.090	.224	.133	.139	.072	.266	.118
Head	.205	.134	.242	.154	.285	.153	.225	.103
Race	.103	.061	.183	.094	.173	.075	.043	.016[b]
Union	—	—	—	—	—	—	—	—
N	5,255		2,453		4,483		8,126	
R²	.361		.471		.515		.574	

Source: USDOL tape, Report 417 (1972).
[a]Significant below .001 level.
[b]Non-significant at .01 level.

Among the organized, number of weeks worked again had the largest betas for both core and periphery workers. Skill, education, and experience, as human capital factors, remained relatively more important in the core. While the beta for sex ranked third in both sectors, all other ascriptive characteristics (family head, marital status, and race), ranked consistently higher in the periphery than in the core.

Among nonunion employees, sector differences persisted but they were not as strong or as consistent as among the organized. The importance of hours worked for earnings was greater for the unorganized in both sectors; the unstandardized coefficients for the unorganized were twice those of the organized, but hours worked were still much more important for unorganized periphery than core workers. The unstandardized coefficient for skill was larger in the core, but that for sex was much larger in the periphery. The coefficient for heading a family was much higher in the core, but the meaning of this is not clear. In short, the analysis for union and sector point to the greater importance of human capital for union and core workers and the greater importance of weeks worked and ascriptive factors for nonunion and periphery workers. Earnings in the organized core appear to be more universalistically determined than elsewhere because the betas for human capital factors rank higher and those for ascriptive factors rank lower.

Yet in terms of absolute contribution to earnings, weeks worked, hours worked, skill, and education contributed relatively more to the earnings of nonunion periphery workers than to the earnings of organized workers in either sector and the nonunion core. The size of other unstandardized coefficients is informative. Weeks and hours worked increased steadily from union core to nonunion periphery. A similar but weaker trend appeared for skill. Married workers earned 13 percent more than the nonmarried in the organized core, but 27 percent more in the unorganized periphery. Sex made the largest contribution to earnings in the unionized core. To conclude, the relative contributions of human capital and ascriptive factors to earnings suggest that the union promotes universalism in the core, but not with respect to sex, while the picture with respect to ascriptive factors is mixed in the periphery.

Sex, Union Status, Earnings

Most researchers report that even after all factors that affect earnings are controlled, women earn less than men. In the stratal regression model of Table 6.6, males earned 33 percent more than females. This effect was about the same size as the union effect. In Table 6.9, regressions were run for union members and nonunion workers for each sex. Controlling for all other variables, union membership raised women's earnings more than it did men's: 44 as opposed to 32 percent. Among the unionized, the betas for the two nonskilled strata and hours worked ranked higher for women than for men, but skill, education, and ascriptive characteristics of race, marital status, and chief earner ranked much more highly for men.

The variance explained for earnings of organized males is 12 percent less than for females; i.e., the variables explain male earnings less than they do female earnings. Women's earnings are explained entirely by their stratal position (sector and skill) and weeks and hours worked. Put differently, the ascriptive variables of family headship, marital status, and race, and the human capital

Table 6.9. Regression of Natural Log of Earnings on Social and Economic Characteristics of Workers for Union Status and Sex[a]

| Variables[c] | Union | | | | Nonunion | | | |
| | Male | | Female | | Male | | Female | |
	B	beta	B	beta	B	beta	B	beta
Self-employed	.379	.030[e]	—[b]	—	.496	.042	.205	.010[e]
Skilled	.621	.544	.646	.275	.674	.343	.616	.213
Nonskilled core	.483	.423	.611	.438	.606	.279	.830	.241
Nonskilled periphery	.363	.247	.406	.322	.381	.186	.455	.213
Weeks	.110	.233	.172	.411	.198	.314	.219	.365
Hours	.040	.092	.072	.150	.111	.196	.180	.292
Education	.022	.096	.005	.019[e]	.004	.137	.046	.110
Experience	.002	.055	.004	.068[e]	.003	.044[d]	.002	.023[e]
Race	.148	.085	.101	.062[e]	.141	.055	.084	.033[e]
Marital status	.152	.096	.095	.073[e]	.198	.094	.346	.160
Head	.242	.128	.055	.039[e]	.302	.135	.281	.113
N	6,608		1,186		7,921		4,918	
R²	.313		.4334		.525		.494	

Source: USDOL tape, Report 417 (1972).
[a]Marginally employed, the omitted term for strata.
[b]No cases for Union-Female.
[c]Significant below .001 level.
[d]Significant at .01 level.
[e]Non-significant at .01 level.

variables of education and experience explain only men's earnings. These effects are sizable. Controlling for other variables, heading a family increases men's earnings 24 percent; marriage and race each contribute 15 percent; and each additional year of education contributes 2 percent. The work experience variable is significant only for males, suggesting that the variables does not capture seniority for women, or that their experience is ignored by employers and unions. Being the family head and married may be honored claims to good jobs for men but not for women. In any event, women appear to be treated much more categorically than men in unionized plants because women's labor force attributes are ignored.

Among nonunion workers, the explained variance of earnings for both sexes is nearly equal, buttressing the earlier observation that unions dampen the impact of forces that affect earnings. Though earnings respond more to women's characteristics in the nonunion than union sector, the lower contribution of human capital to their earnings remains. Weeks and hours worked count heavily but work experience remains unrewarded.

These findings tend to support most of my predictions. The union slightly increases the skill, sector, and experience advantages that men already have and decreases the risk of unemployment in terms of weeks and hours worked. Although unionized males' earnings respond more to human capital and status characteristics than do females' earnings, the large coefficients for the stratal position of men diminish the explanatory power of other variables. Without union protection, both sexes respond more to almost all factors that affect earnings: current labor market participation, human capital, and ascriptive factors. But in both union and nonunion employment, women's earnings depend much more on their current labor market participation, their overwhelming presence in the nonskilled periphery, and less on their work experience, human capital, and ascriptive status characteristics.

Conclusions

The economic advantages of union membership in the working class are so pervasive that the unionized may well be considered a privileged stratum. Union members have higher skills than other workers, are employed in industries that pay higher wages and offer greater fringe benefits, suffer less unemployment, and occupy more favored ascriptive positions in society. Regardless of unionization, the five working-class strata are highly stratified in their earnings. The lower the strata, the deeper and more important the economic disparities. Yet the union provides an economic floor for the two lowest strata which is not available to the unorganized. Consequently, stratal economic cleavages are smaller among organized workers. This greater equality holds both in the core and periphery. Contrary to expectations, earnings in the unorganized core were slightly below those in the organized periphery. Earnings inequality increased as we move from organized core to organized periphery, nonorganized core, and nonorganized periphery. This order held for all skill, race, and sex categories. But the advantage of union over nonunion earnings was greater for all skill levels in the periphery than in the core.

As anticipated, in unionized industries where their percentage was highest, the skilled increased their earnings advantage over the nonskilled. In the reverse situation, where the nonskilled were more numerous, they were able to bring about greater equality in earnings. Yet, the rewards of skill were not equally available to nonwhites, whatever their union status or sector of employment.

In a multiple regression analysis of earnings, I found that union membership contributed more to earnings than did sector, human capital, and ascriptive social status, but not as much as did weeks and hours worked. Earnings attributed to stratal position were generally larger than the effects of union membership, human capital, and ascribed status. Separate regression analyses for union and nonunion members pointed to the much greater contribution of hours and weeks worked to earnings of the nonunionized. Thus, union members were more insulated from unemployment and underemployment.

The variance of earnings explained was consistently higher for nonunion than for union workers, even when the analysis was run separately for sector and sex. This suggests that the union muffles the impact of market forces on earnings. This situation was most impressive in the core sector where male seniority (work experience) had the greatest impact. Cain (1976) thinks that the contribution of work experience to productivity applies only to skilled workers in internal labor markets. For others, seniority may be an unearned increment.

Whether unions disproportionately reward ascriptively favored groups (males and whites) is not altogether clear. To be sure, unionized women and blacks do earn relatively more than their non-unionized counterparts, but the picture varies by sector. Thus, unions do not reward the skills of blacks and women in the core as much as they do whites and males; in the periphery, the situation is the same for both organized and unorganized. Regression analysis shows that human capital is rewarded more in the organized core than in the periphery. Males are rewarded for their favored ascriptive characteristics (being white, married, head of family) in the union sector, but women's ascriptive roles are ignored. Women in unions suffer more than men because women's work experience, education, and marital-family status contribute nothing to their earnings. Earnings in the unorganized sector respond more to all women's labor force characteristics. In all the above comparisons, the contribution of race to earnings was negligible and often absent in both union and nonunion sectors.

Because only a minority of manual workers are union members, unions probably increase economic inequality in the working class. While unions advance the earnings of already privileged workers, other employees are left more exposed to economic vicissitudes. In unorganized industries in the periphery, management rewards married men with higher skills and education at the expense of lower-skilled women workers. Thus, both the union and the social inclinations of management combine to widen economic inequality in the working class, especially for women. How this is managed is the subject of the next chapter.

Notes

1. For example, the advantage of the skilled in manufacturing, who make up about one-quarter of all employees, is about 30 percent. In construction, mining, services, and government, where the skilled are more numerous, the advantage is about 50 percent. Transportation-communications-utilities is an exception to the generalization.

2. The marginally employed are omitted in Table 6.6 to prevent perfect multicollinearity.

3. The variance is slightly lower than that obtained by using the Public Use Sample of the 1970 U.S. Census, 1/1,000 county file, which did not contain union membership information (see Chapter 2).

4. Organized core workers at the skilled and semiskilled levels earned 19 percent more than similar workers in the organized periphery, and the unskilled, 32 percent more. But organized skilled workers in the core earned 24 percent more than unorganized core employees; semiskilled, 31 percent more; unskilled, 50 percent more.

7

On the Technological Subordination
of Women

The previous chapter documented the importance of the union in
economically stratifying the working class, especially at the lower
levels of the skill hierarchy. Regression analysis clearly showed
that, controlling for all variables that affect earnings, except for
union membership and weeks and hours worked, sex explained
more than any other variable. This fact held even when separate
regressions were run by sector, skill level, and union membership.
In short, women workers formed an economic substratum everywhere.

Most explanations of women's inequitable estate focus on their
occupational and industrial segregation, their being crowded into a
few occupations, and their institutionalized sex stratification (see
the references in Huber and Spitze, 1983). Despite these explanations,
social scientists have not systematically considered how management and the unions have used machine technology to keep women
in their work place. Scholars have described women's encounters
with machines in a few specific occupations and industries (Abbott,
1919; Davies, 1974; Garson, 1975; Baxandall, et al., 1976; Rubin,
1976; Glenn and Feldberg, 1977), but social science still lacks a
general picture of the differences in the machine relationships of
women and men in all occupations. Therefore, this chapter pursues
four important areas dealing with the technological subordination of
women employees: (a) the different machine assignments of women
and men, (b) how these assignments affect the degree of women's
and men's control over their work, (c) how technological change
selectively alters men's and women's work, and (d) how technologi-

---

An earlier version of this chapter was co-authored with David B. McMillen.

cal change affects the attitudes of the sexes toward their jobs and machines. Technology is defined simply as the tools, equipment, and machines that workers use, or the tools, equipment, and machines that directly and indirectly affect work behavior.[1]

Though people commonly associate machines with manual jobs in manufacturing, almost all workers have some contact with machines. The executive operates a dictation machine; the engineer, a computer; the office worker, a typewriter; the domestic worker, a vacuum cleaner; the gardener, a lawnmower; and the cashier, an adding machine. Ever since Adam Smith (1776) and Marx (1844) described the stultifying and alienating aspects of industrial work, studies of the impact of machines on workers have overwhelmingly concentrated on men. Although women were among the earliest industrial workers in textile manufacturing (Abbott, 1919), and although most women since then have worked with machines, the popular image of the alienated worker is still the male auto worker chained to the assembly line (Walker and Guest, 1952; Chinoy, 1955; Faunce, 1958; Blauner, 1964; Goldthorpe, 1966, Form, 1976a). Despite the fact that women now constitute half of the civilian labor force, social science still offers no systematic explanation of how women and men's machine relations differ. However, existing theory about technology, coupled with knowledge of women's distribution in the labor force, suggests what to expect in the four areas under investigation.

Four Themes on Technology

The first area deals with the machine assignments of men and women. Ellul (1967) has shown that in all advanced industrial societies, most jobs have some direct and indirect contact with machines. Moreover, machines increasingly dominate work behavior as one descends from the top to the bottom of the skill and authority ladders (Friedmann, 1955:191). Machines were first introduced where work was most routinized and where workers were least able to protect themselves from managerial power (Marglin, 1974). Low job skill, low power, and low prestige generally appear together. Today, though women's occupations apparently are as prestigious as men's (Treiman and Terrell, 1975), all along the prestige hierarchy, women's occupations have less authority than do men's (Kanter, 1977), lower cognition and manipulative skills (McLaughlin, 1978), and lower income (Oppenheimer, 1970; Freeman, 1976). Therefore, one may reasonably expect that, whatever the prestige level of women's occupations and whatever women's concentration in different occupations, women, more than men, will work with machines that demand less skill. When new machines are introduced, women will be disproportionately assigned to work that is the most mechanized and routinized.

The second area deals with work autonomy or control. One of the most persistent social science themes deals with the amount of work autonomy that machines permit their operators to have (Blauner, 1964). Both the functions of machines and their level of automation affect the autonomy of their operators. Machine functions may be classified according to the extent that the machines themselves can be manipulated. Thus, operators can move vehicles and mobile equipment over large areas, workers who use tools and small-scale production machines can manipulate them around objects, operators of large-scale production machines are usually bound to their pre-set cycles, and operators of office, professional (e.g., x-ray machines), and electronic equipment (e.g., computers) must monitor machines to varying degrees (Meissner, 1976).

The automation level of equipment also provides clues to the boundaries of work autonomy.[2] Equipment is typically classified according to three levels of control: manual, mechanical, or numerical-computer-tape-logical (Mueller, et al., 1969). Manually controlled tools and machines typically permit their operators to control work more so than do mechanically powered machines that perform only a single and repeated operation, while machines that perform multiple functions require more active intervention or monitoring by their operators (Noble, 1979), thus introducing more variety in work. Automated equipment controls itself by electronic feedback devices but requires inputs of information and monitoring from operators. Thus, the complexity of equipment bears no necessary relation to the amount of work autonomy permitted operators (Kohn, 1969). The simple hand tool and the complex computer may both permit their operators to exercise a high degree of work autonomy. These observations lead to the expectation that men will dominate jobs that allow the worker the most amount of physical mobility, jobs that permit the worker to move machines and tools, and jobs that require constant and active monitoring of machine operations.

The third area deals with the selective impact of technological change in men's and women's jobs. Contrary to Braverman's (1974) position that deskilling and loss of operator control of work is inherent in capitalist industrial development, Edwards (1979) has shown that technological change and work rationalization can either increase or decrease occupational skills and work control. Moreover, these changes can simultaneously improve and worsen different aspects of the same job (Shepard, 1971:5). The main job characteristics altered by mechanization and automation are the physical environment of work, skills, and social interaction patterns (Meissner, 1969). Although sociologists have studied how technological change alters some job characteristics, they have not developed a general theory of how technology alters *different* dimensions of a *wide range* of occupations. Findings from some case studies suggest the kind of trends one might expect for manual and white-collar jobs.

Studies show that mechanization and automation generally improve the physical environment of most manual and white-collar jobs, but they also increase the demand for work speed and accuracy (Davis and Taylor, 1976). Second, though the evidence is conflicting, it suggests that technological change increases job complexity more than it reduces it (Spenner, 1979; Rumberger, 1981). Third, mechanization and automation are known to reduce social interaction among workers and increase the amount of supervision (Harvard, 1970:26). Based on these findings, some predictions may be made about how jobs of women and men are differentially affected by technological change. First, little or no sex difference should be expected in changes of the physical environment of jobs. Second, since workers with the highest amount of job skill and authority most successfully cope with technological change, positive changes will likely occur in men's jobs more than in women's. Technological change should result in pressure for faster work and increased supervision in women's jobs. Job complexity should increase less for women than for men, and technological change should reduce social interaction in women's jobs more than in men's.

The fourth area deals with the impact of equipment changes on workers' attitudes toward their jobs and machines. Since research shows that technological change has more positive than negative effects on jobs, those who experience change should be more satisfied with their jobs and have more positive feelings toward their machines than those who experience no equipment change. Since technological change is expected to have more positive effect on men's jobs, men should report increased job satisfaction and liking for their machines.

Research shows that new equipment affects specific job characteristics differently. Since men's jobs tend to become more complex in terms of skill than do women's jobs, men should report more satisfaction resulting from this kind of change (see Miller, 1980). Technological change improves the physical environment of most jobs. Insofar as job satisfaction and liking of machine are affected by improved physical environment, both sexes should report the same positive changes. Fortunately, data from a national study permit the testing of all of these predictions.

Data and Methods

In 1967, Eva Mueller and her colleagues at the University of Michigan's Survey Research Center conducted a national study of the impact of technology and technological change on the U.S. labor force. A probability sample of labor force participants in U.S. households (1,800 men, 855 women) were interviewed to ascertain how work is affected by machines and changing technology. Mueller's (1969) study is unique because it examined workers in a nationally representative set of occupations, industries, and technologies. Almost all studies of machine effects on workers' behavior are case studies selected to represent dramatic and/or novel situations. No matter how well these studies are designed, their summarized results do not mirror the national situation. Bielby and Baron (1982) used Mueller's data to examine the technological organization of work, but they did not examine sex differences in detail.

Mueller's respondents were adults who had worked for twenty or more hours a week during the past five years. They were asked to describe: (1) their tools and equipment, (2) changes in them over a five-year period, and (3) their reactions to the changes. Technology was analyzed along two dimensions: types of machinery and level of automation. Types of machines include: tools, small-scale production, vehicles, small-scale office equipment, large-scale production (presses, lathes), specialized professional equipment (x-ray machines), and computer or electronic equipment (see Table 7.1). Level of equipment *automation* refers to whether machines are regulated by hand, by mechanical means, or electronically (see Table 7.2). Mechanically powered machines are classified according to whether they are stationary or mobile and according to their *complexity:* (a) single-system, i.e., whether they have a simple or fixed mechanical control (on-off, fast-slow) and perform only one operation; or (b) multi-system, whether they are complex and can perform several operations. If workers operated more than one machine, they were queried about their most complex and most automated machine.

Technological change was defined as (1) the introduction of mechanical or automation processes that take over part or all of the tasks previously performed by human labor, (2) equipment changes that perform a greater volume or higher quality of work than that done previously, (3) equipment so repaired or serviced that it changes work, and (4) changes in the equipment of one occupation that resulted in work changes in another occupation related to the first.

This re-examination of the Mueller data uses two samples. The full sample is used to describe workers' technological environments and the effect of technology on work organization. A second sample is used to analyze how technology *changes* job characteristics, job satisfaction, and attitudes toward machines and technological change. The respondents are those who experienced technological change.

Exposure to Technology

Mueller's (1969:26) survey revealed that only 17 percent of the U.S. labor force had no direct or indirect contact with machinery on their jobs. Use of machines varied from a low of 64 percent for laborers and service workers to a high of 90 percent for proprietors. Almost one-half of the respondents operated equipment constantly; one-fifth, some of the time; and the remainder did not operate equipment or machinery.

Contrary to popular impressions, data in Table 7.1 show that a greater proportion of women than men (76 and 69 percent) worked with machines, but the sexes were markedly segregated according to the type of machines they operated. Almost three-tenths of the men, but almost none of the women, operated vehicles or mobile equipment such as forklifts or cranes. These machines permit their operators to move about. Relatively more men than women (34 and 21 percent) could manipulate their tools (e.g., chisels, scissors) or move their machines (e.g., hand grinders, floor polishers). The reverse held for stationary and small-scale office machines which were operated by 43 percent of the women and only 13 percent of the men. The sexes were equally represented (17 percent) only as operators of large-scale immovable production machines (e.g., drill presses, stamping machines). Finally, more of the women than men (19 vs. 7 percent) operated specialized machines in professional services such as hospitals and laboratories, and more of the women operated computer and electronic equipment.

Technological sex segregation is further demonstrated by sex differences in the automation level of their machines (Table 7.2). Employees control their work more when they use hand tools or operate machines with manual controls, both single- and multiple-system. Slightly more than half of the men and only one-eighth of the women operated equipment that is manually controlled—equipment at the first three levels of automation in Table 7.2. Especially notable was the virtual male monopoly over multi-system manually controlled machines like forklifts and turret lathes. In

Table 7.1. Type of Machinery Used, by Sex (percent)[a]

Type of Machinery	Males	Females
Transportation vehicles—all types, passenger and freight	14	1
Mobile equipment—construction, farm, freight	14	—
Small-scale office equipment	13	43
Tools, small-scale production, household, institutional equipment	34	21
Production equipment—large-scale, non-mobile	17	17
Professional, specialized equipment	3	9
Computer, electronic equipment	4	10
Miscellaneous equipment	1	—
Totals (N)	100 (1239)	101 (649)
No equipment used (N)	31 (556)	24 (207)

[a]$\chi^2 = 416.26$; p = < .0001

contrast, twice the proportion of women than men (82 vs. 40 percent) operated simple machines with automatic or mechanically built-in controls; for example, machines with a set pace or machines that turn themselves on and off. Finally, in truly automated equipment, men were slightly more highly represented than women.

Table 7.2. Automation Level of Equipment Used, by Sex (percent)[a]

Automation Level	Males	Females
Operator powered and controlled (hand tools)	2	1
Powered single-system, manual control (drills, mowers)	20	10
Powered Multi-system, manual main control (turret-lathe, forklift)	31	2
Fixed mechanical control (automatic drillers, welders)	40	82
Numerical, tape, or computer control (computers)	7	5
Totals (N)	100 (1257)	100 (644)

[a]$\chi^2 = 338.25$; p = < .0001

When examining machine control, it is important to stress that a machine's mechanization or automation and the extent to which it is humanly controlled are not directly related. Thus, most office machines are mechanical (typewriters), while computers are automated (have electronic feedback), but the great majority of both have built in or fixed controls (see Table 7.3).[3] All office machines and more than four-fifths of the computers and large-scale production equipment have fixed controls. Seven-tenths of all women but only one-third of all men operated such machines. Compared to office machines, professional and specialized equipment vary more in the extent that they are manually controlled. Twice as many men than women operated specialized and professional equipment that could be manually controlled. Thus men were selected to operate machines where the predominance of control was human or manual, and women were assigned to machines with fixed controls (Table 7.3).

Table 7.3. Classification of Machines by Operator Use of Fixed-Mechanical or Human-Manual Controls and the Sex Composition of Operators (percent)

	Females			Males		
	Controls			Controls		
Type of Machine	Fixed	Manual	N	Fixed	Manual	N
Small-scale office equipment	100	0	234	100	0	128
Computers, electronic equipment	82	18	53	100	0	40
Production equipment, large-scale	88	12	91	80	20	182
Professional, specialized equipment	78	22	47	57	43	35
Tools, small-scale production	70	30	107	36	64	367
Transportation vehicles	0	100	2	8	91	134
Mobile equipment	0	0	0	6	94	168

The main conclusion to be drawn from tables 7.1–3 is that the sexes are technologically segregated. Disproportionately more men than women operate machines that permit their operators to move about, machines that they can move, machines that perform multiple operations, and machines that can be humanly controlled. If, as most authors contend, powerlessness or work alienation results from operators' inability to control machines (Israel, 1971; Braverman, 1974), then the image of the alienated worker should be that of a woman worker rather than a man.

Technology and Control Over Work

The design, placement, and use of machines provide information on how work is organized: by the machine, as in feeding machines; by sequencing of machines operations, as in assembly lines; or by the operator, as in bulldozing. Moreover, machines also vary in the amount of necessary monitoring or attending they require—from constant to none at all. The extent of monitoring affects the worker's freedom to move about and speak with others (Meissner, 1969; Form, 1976a). Fixed machines necessarily restrict their operators indoors, while vehicles and mobile equipment permit operators to move about either indoors or out of doors. Many scholars (Blauner, 1964; Shepard, 1971; Seeman, 1974:94–100) have noted that these machine characteristics affect workers' feelings of powerlessness or autonomy. If machines permit operators to organize their own work, move about freely, and converse with others, workers typically experience autonomy, job satisfaction, and a liking for their machines (Kohn and Schooler, 1978).

The differential assignment of sexes to different types of machines has resulted in the almost total cloistering of women: 97 percent of the women and 62 percent of the men worked indoors all of the time (see Table 7.4). Moreover, many more of the women than men (61 and 37 percent) reported they could not move from their work stations. Despite this, sex differences were unexpectedly small in the extent that employees operated their equipment constantly and in the opportunity they had to talk while working.

These general trends undoubtedly hide wide variations in the social environments of machines. For example, truck drivers vary widely in their ability to talk while working. In office machine work, where women are most heavily concentrated, 60 percent of the women and 35 percent of the men reported that they were required to operate their machines constantly. Though this situation has only a small impact on their ability to communicate, it undoubtedly affected the quality of communication. For example, a significantly higher proportion of all women than men were required to talk while operating a machine (e.g., cashiers), but twice the proportion of men than women (43 vs. 20 percent) whose jobs required them to talk did not operate machines. Despite sex differences in the quality of social interaction that machines made possible, about four-fifths of both sexes reported that they regarded their machines more as friends rather than foes (see Table 7.4), and only small differences appeared by machine types and their automation level.

Unfortunately, specific data are unavailable on the quality of social interaction on the job, but clues are gained by examining the way that work is controlled in different machine environments. In Table 7.5, operators of different types of machine were classified according to the ways that their work was primarily controlled: either by humans (the operators themselves, the work group, or boss) or impersonally (by the equipment, production line, workflow, or work-ordering devices). The great majority of operators of all types of machines worked in humanly controlled work situations.

Table 7.4. Work Characteristics of Male and Female Workers (percent)

Work Characteristics	Males	Females
Work inside/outside[a]		
Mostly inside	62	97
Half and half	14	2
Mostly outside	24	1
N	(1691)	(842)
Chance to move about[a]		
Moves	45	23
Usually fixed	19	16
Fixed	36	61
N	(743)	(405)
Organization of Work		
By respondent	50	50
By equipment or production line	8	11
By others	42	39
N	(1455)	(776)
Use of equipment		
Constantly	56	60
Some of the time	27	26
Little or never	16	14
N	(1009)	(602)
Chance to talk		
Can't talk	10	12
Sometimes can't	9	9
Can talk	81	78
N	(1487)	(779)
Job enjoy/drudgery		
Enjoy	77	80
Neutral	18	15
Drudgery	5	5
N	(1781)	(841)
Equipment friend/foe		
Friend	77	80
Neutral	17	15
Foe	6	5
N	(1110)	(551)

[a]p of $\chi^2 \leq .05$

Significantly, most work was controlled by the workers themselves; next, by the work group; and least, by the boss.

The greatest amount of individually controlled work was found among operators of office and electronic equipment, and here a somewhat larger proportion of men than women controlled their own work. In two situations (professional and small-scale production), where a larger percentage of women than men controlled their own work, more of the men's work was controlled by the work group, suggesting that more women worked in isolation.

Sex differences among operators of impersonally controlled machines were relatively small, with two notable exceptions: large-scale production machines and electronic equipment. About 45 percent of the women and 19 percent of the men operating large-scale production machines worked on production lines. This means that women, rather than men, tended to be assembly line workers. Electronic equipment operators whose work was impersonally controlled by a work-flow process again were predominately women (see Table 7.5).

To summarize: machine assignments substantially differentiated the work organization of men and women, their patterns of work control, and the quantity and quality of their social interaction.[4]

Effects of Technological Change on Job Characteristics

New equipment typically changes some job characteristics more than others. In some instances, it eliminates jobs and/or creates new ones.[5] Where jobs are preserved, technological change may simultaneously improve some job characteristics and damage others. When workers change jobs, they may confront technology that compares favorably or unfavorably to that in previous jobs. Finally, some job changes result from technological changes in related and interdependent jobs. All such changes are included in the following analysis.

Respondents were asked to report their experiences with equipment changes during the last five years. If they experienced more than one change, they were asked about the change that had the greatest effect. Sixteen percent of all workers reported that equipment changes moderately altered their jobs and 5 percent reported significant changes in their jobs. Slightly more manual than white-collar jobs were changed, and slightly more men than women reported changes in jobs.

Technological change can affect 12 major job characteristics that were grouped into three broad areas. With respect to *physical* characteristics, equipment change can alter the physical environment, the amount of exertion required to do the job, work speed, and job danger. With respect to *skill*, changes may affect skill demands, chance to learn new skills, need to plan work, work interest, and opportunity for advancement. Finally changes may occur in *social*

Table 7.5. Type of Work Control by Type of Machinery and by Sex (percent)

Work Controlled By:	Transportation	Mobile Equipment	Office		Production Small-Scale		Production Large-Scale		Professional Equipment		Electronic Equipment	
	Males	Males	M	F	M	F	M	F	M	F	M	F
Human control	80	84	88	90	83	77	62	46	75	89	88	71
Worker	37	45	74	62	46	54	34	17	38	49	67	46
Group	23	21	10	18	24	11	20	20	37	28	18	22
Boss	20	18	4	10	13	12	8	9	–	12	3	3
Impersonal control	20	17	11	10	16	23	38	55	25	12	12	28
Equipment	1	4	–	–	1	1	7	3	4	–	5	5
Production line	1	4	1	1	4	8	19	45	–	–	2	–
Flow, order	11	7	8	7	8	8	8	–	17	6	3	20
Combination	7	2	2	2	3	6	4	7	4	6	2	3
Total	100	101	99	100	99	100	100	101	100	101	100	99
N	135	101	144	261	348	117	196	105	24	51	40	59

dimensions of the job, such as the chance to converse, the amount of supervision, and the steadiness of employment.

Table 7.6. Methods of Work Control According to Level of Automation, by Sex (percent)

					Level of Automation				
	Manual		Mechanical					Numerical, Computer, Tape	
Work Controlled By:			Fixed Mechanical		Single- System		Multi- System		
	M	F	M	F	M	F	M	F	M	F
Humans (worker, group, boss)	95	63	73	79	82	75	82	31	94	89
Equipment or production	5	25	12	10	9	17	6	46	3	—
Flow, order, mixed	—	12	15	11	9	8	12	23	3	11
Total	100	100	100	100	100	100	100	100	100	100
N	19	8	432	488	197	53	279	13	68	28

Confirming earlier findings, data in Table 7.7 reveal that technological innovation generally improved job characteristics. Workers reported more positive than negative changes in nine of twelve job characteristics and more negative change in work speed and increased supervision. Blue-collar workers experienced more increase than decrease in job danger, work speed, and supervision. In ten of the twelve job areas, more blue- than white-collar workers reported larger negative effects emanating from technological changes. Among blue-collar workers, men were more advantaged than women in most areas, especially in the need to plan work, chance for advancement, job interest, and steadiness of employment.[6] In the white-collar area, relatively more women than men indicated that new equipment decreased the need for supervision and increased their chance to converse, while men showed both more positive and more negative effects in perception of job danger. In short, these data suggest that changes in the white-collar area were few and they affected both sexes in similar degree. Changes in blue-collar work importantly affected career advancement, skill, and job interest, and here innovation clearly favored the men.

Ideally, the effects of technological change should be examined in all major occupational groups. Since the sample was too small to do this, we divided the white-collar sector into a lower clerical stratum and an upper stratum of professionals, managers, and

Table 7.7. Changes in Job Characteristics Attending Technological Change, by Occupational Sector and Sex (percent)

Changes in Job Characteristics	White-collar		Blue-collar	
	Males	Females	Males	Females
Work Environment				
More pleasant	39	47	44	41
Same	50	38	31	37
Less Pleasant	11	16	25	22
Physical Work				
Increased	21	22	39	43
Same	34	33	25	22
Decreased	45	44	36	35
Speed of Work				
Increased	43	44	37	43
Same	41	33	38	35
Decreased	16	23	25	22
Danger of Work[a]				
Increased	23	8	47	37
Same	41	67	24	33
Decreased	36	25	29	31
Skill Required				
Increased	66	67	59	48
Same	26	19	23	27
Decreased	9	14	18	25
Chance to Learn				
Increased	71	76	69	55
Same	28	15	18	27
Decreased	7	8	13	18
Need for Planning[c]				
Increased	69	67	59	37
Same	22	23	28	47
Decreased	9	10	13	16
Chance for Advancement[c]				
Increased	64	59	58	31
Same	26	26	27	53
Decreased	10	16	15	16
Interest in Job[d]				
Increased	73	79	73	57
Same	18	14	12	22
Decreased	9	7	15	20
Chance to Talk[a]				
More often	43	54	39	45
Same	44	22	36	33
Less often	13	24	25	22

Table 7.7. Continued

Changes in Job Characteristics	White-collar		Blue-collar	
	Males	Females	Males	Females
Need for supervision[b]				
Increased	34	36	44	38
Same	39	24	25	34
Decreased	27	40	32	28
Steady Employment[d]				
More steady	38	48	52	34
Same	52	48	34	44
Less steady	10	4	14	23
N	106	72	202	49

[a]p of χ^2 0.01 for white-collar workers   [c]p of χ^2 0.01 for blue-collar workers
[b]p of χ^2 0.08 for white-collar workers   [d]p of χ^2 0.08 for blue-collar workers

proprietors. The blue-collar sector was split into a lower unskilled and service stratum and an upper semiskilled and skilled stratum.

Though the data for this four-fold occupational breakdown are not presented here, they support earlier findings. Among white-collar workers, clerical males reported larger negative effects from technological change in six job areas compared to one such effect for professionals, managers, and proprietors. Among white-collar women, both the professional and clerical strata suffered three negative effects, but in different areas. Among blue-collar workers, skilled and semiskilled males reported larger negative effects in two job areas compared to four for the unskilled. For women, the situation was reversed: higher stratum workers suffered more in six job areas compared to three for the lower stratum. In short, higher stratum males suffered less from new technology than did lower stratum males in both blue- and white-collar jobs, but upper stratum women in all jobs suffered as many negative effects as lower stratum women.

Among all white-collar workers, women suffered more negative effects than did men in four job areas, but men did not suffer more than women in any area. In the higher white-collar occupations, women reported more negative effects in seven areas compared to one for men. Similar results appeared for blue-collar work. In the lower stratum, more women reported negative effects in six job characteristics and men in four; and in the upper stratum, women were more disadvantaged in eight areas, and men in one. In three vital job areas (steadiness of employment, chance for advancement, and job interest), men in all four strata were more disadvantaged than women in just one area, no sex difference appeared in two areas, but women were more disadvantaged in nine instances. The conclusions are clear. Higher occupational status protected men from technological change more than it did women; technological change had more negative effects on women than it did on men in all occupational strata, especially for the vital areas of work interest, steady employment, and opportunity for advancement.

Technological Change, Job Satisfaction, and Machine Evaluation

The final issue is whether technological change affects workers' job satisfaction and attitudes toward machines. Of course, job satisfaction may also be affected by changes that accompany equipment change, e.g., promotions or increases in pay. Data in Table 7.8 clearly reveal that both men and women who reported equipment changes also reported more job satisfaction than those who did not. Even though women suffered more than men from new technology, sex differences in changed levels of job satisfaction were trivial.

Table 7.8. Changes in Job Satisfaction and Machine Evaluation by Equipment Change, by Sex (percent)

	Male		Female	
	Equipment Change			
Change	Yes	No	Yes	No
Change in Job Satisfaction				
More satisfied	67	51	63	49
Equally satisfied	24	39	24	43
Less satisfied	9	10	13	8
Totals	100	100	100	100
N	420	1315	142	615
	$\chi^2 = 36.20$	$p = .000$	$\chi^2 = 17.41$	$p = .002$
Machine Evaluation[a]				
Friend	81	75	83	80
Friend and foe	12	19	12	15
Foe	7	6	5	5
Totals	100	100	100	100
N	781	329	133	418
	$\chi^2 = 6.421$	$p = .040$	$\chi^2 = .875$	$p = .646$

[a]Question not asked of respondents who did not work with machines.

For workers who experienced equipment changes, did changes in job satisfaction vary according to changes in job characteristics? Among male white-collar workers, six of twelve changes in job characteristics were accompanied by statistically significant changes ($p = < .05$) in job satisfaction, all of them positive. But among women, only one such positive change was observed. Among male blue-collar workers, five of the six changes were accompanied by increases in job satisfaction, but only two such changes occurred for women. Thus, at both white-collar and blue-collar levels, men's job characteristics were changed more than women's, and men reported greater increases in job satisfaction (see Table 7.9).

Table 7.9. Coefficients of Contingency (uncorrected) of χ^2s between Changes in Job Satisfaction and Changes in Job Characteristics Produced by Equipment Change, by Occupation and Sex

	Coefficients of Contingency			
	White-Collar		Blue-Collar	
Job Characteristic	Males	Females	Males	Females
Work environment	.224[a]	.094	.081	.086
Physical work	.157	.073	.108	.184
Speed of work	.203	.162	.196[b]	.185
Danger of work	.207[a]	.239	.027	.191
Skill required	.270[b]	.851[a]	.192[b]	.059
Chance to learn	.265[c]	.207	.279[c]	.186
Need for planning	.110	.196	.187	.423[c]
Chance for advancement	.415[c]	.242	.242[c]	.137
Job interest	.360[c]	.374[c]	.304[c]	.358[b]
Chance to talk	.235[b]	.232	.041	.269
Need for supervision	.193	.208	.060	.151
Steady employment	.257[b]	.286[a]	.113	.152

[a]$p = < .10$ [b]$p = < .05$ [c]$p = < .01$

The above analysis does not control for the possibility that changes in equipment were accompanied by changes in pay or promotions, and that such changes, rather than equipment changes, account for increased job satisfaction. Mueller (1969:71) reported that 84 percent of the workers who did not change jobs when new equipment was introduced received no pay change while 16 percent did, but the reason for the pay increase was not specified as being tied to changes in job content. Half of those who transferred to other jobs (twenty-five workers) were promoted, and these received a pay increase. For the job changers (thirty-two cases), decreases in pay were as frequent as increases. Because almost two-thirds of the workers who experienced equipment changes on their jobs reported increased job satisfaction, the direct impact of an accompanying pay raise for a minority could have had only a moderate effect on the whole sample.

Almost three-tenths of the respondents were promoted during the five year interval, and they experienced slightly more equipment change than the non-promoted. Promotion could have positively disposed them towards technological change. In tabulations not presented here, the relation between job satisfaction and equipment change was examined, controlling for promotions. For the non-promoted, the results reported in Table 7.8 remain unchanged; both males and females who encountered new equipment reported more job satisfaction than those who did not. For promoted males and females, no significant differences in increased job satisfaction were found between those who encountered and did not encounter new equipment.

Table 7.9 provides correlations between changes in job satisfaction and changes in job characteristics for workers who reported equipment changes. The size of the sample was too small to also control for promotion; however, I did examine the relationship between promotion and job satisfaction change for white- and blue-collar workers who reported that new equipment changed their jobs. Among white-collar males and blue-collar females, no differences in job satisfaction change appeared between the promoted and not promoted, but more of the promoted blue-collar males reported increased satisfaction. These results suggest that the positive relationship between equipment change and increased job satisfaction tends to hold, and that the confounding effects of promotion and income changes were relatively small.

During the interviews, those who worked with machines were asked whether they regarded their machines as friends, both friend and foe, or as foes. Over three-quarters of both sexes regarded their machines as friends (Table 7.8). Those who encountered new equipment were somewhat more likely to regard their machines as friends, and this tendency was more marked among men than women. For white-collar workers of both sexes, no changes in job characteristics were associated with perceiving machines as friends or foes. Among blue-collar men and women, only one job change was so related.

Finally, Mueller and colleagues (1969) created a technology adjustment scale which was scored as the algebraic sum of positive and negative replies that workers made to eleven questions dealing with technological change.[7] Over seven-tenths of the men and women respondents gave only positive replies, and no sex differences were found by type of equipment or its automation level.

Since several conditions can simultaneously affect workers' attitudes toward their machines, a multiple regression analysis was made of their attitudes toward machines (friend or foe) and their automation adjustment scores, with the following variables in the equations: extent of equipment use, experiencing a machine change, automation level of machine, type of work-control organization, years of work experience, and occupational level.[8]

Variables in the regression equation for machine as friend or foe accounted for less than 2 percent of the total variance (see Table 7.10), and the only statistically significant variables were the amount of time the equipment was used and the type of work control. Expectedly, increased time spent with machines and human (as opposed to impersonal) control of work contributed to evaluating the machine as a friend. In contrast to this pattern, all but one of the independent variables were statistically significant for adjustment to automation, and they accounted for 17 percent of the total variance. Confirming some of the trends reported above, relative youth of the worker, higher occupational status, human work control organization, and experience with machine changes promoted adjustment to automation. Increased education, being male, and constant machine use decreased adjustment. This pattern suggests that the more experienced, higher-educated, male, blue-collar workers who worked constantly with machines felt most threatened by automation.

Multiple regression analyses were run for each sex (data not shown here). Differences in the sample size of the sexes could affect the contributions of the partial regression coefficients in both the general and sex-specific equations (Blau and Duncan, 1967:207–410). In general, the results for the total sample persisted in the sex-specific analyses because no sign changes occurred for any of the independent variables. In the total sample, however, the positive effects of human control of work and time spent operating machines on evaluating machines as friends probably reflect a greater female than male contribution because the two variables were statistically significant only for women in the sex-specific models.

Similar sex differences appeared in the analysis of automation adjustment: constant machine use contributed to greater adjustment only for women, while higher education decreased adjustment only for men. Two other statistically significant variables in the total sample retained significance only for men in the sex-specific models: the positive effects of machine change and the negative effects of

Table 7.10. Partial Regression Coefficients of Machine as Friend or Foe
and Automation Adjustment on Job Worker Characteristics

	Friend/Foe		Automation Adjustment	
Variables	B	beta	B	beta
Time with equipment	.088[a]	.067	−.115[a]	−.073
Education	.006	.059	−.024[b]	−.186
Experience machine change	−.088	−.040	.178[a]	.063
Sex	−.046	−.022	−.488[b]	−.159
Work control organization	−.057[b]	−.077	.116[b]	.100
Machine's automation level	.008	.012	−.037	−.053
Occupational status	−.039	−.047	.353[b]	.299
Work experience	.003	.039	−.025[b]	−.274
Constant	1.919		4.185	
R^2	.016		.173	
N	1510		1141	

[a]Significant at $\geq$ .05
[b]Significant at $\geq$ .01

length of work experience. Thus, the general pattern is supported
by the analysis of the sex differences: technological change is most
threatening to older, well educated men who recently experienced
equipment change.

To conclude, when technology changes jobs, it increases the
job satisfaction of both sexes, more for men than for women, but job
changes generally have little effect on how the sexes regard their
machines. Workers may become dissatisfied with their jobs and/or
dissatisfied with specific aspects of their jobs that are affected by
technological change, but these negative effects do not alter their
positive feelings toward machinery. Automation mostly threatens
older, well educated men, but it is generally accepted by women.

Conclusions

Data from the first national study of technological change generally
support hypotheses that link sex stratification to occupational and
technological stratification. Contrary to popular belief, relatively
more women than men operate machines that perform repetitive
tasks and restrict their physical mobility. Relatively more men
operate machines that require skill and permit work autonomy.
These differences in worker-machine relations parallel differences
in work control patterns. Women's work is more impersonally controlled by their equipment, the assembly line, and workflow devices,
while more of men's work is under the control of the operator or

work group. These findings hold for both blue- and white-collar work.

The data support the hypothesis that technological change generally improves the characteristics of both blue- and white-collar jobs, but more for men's than for women's jobs. Moreover, the changes enlarge men's job skills and improve their advancement opportunities, while changes improve only the physical and inter-actional work environment of women. But for both sexes, equip-ment changes increase job satisfaction. Most increase in satisfaction is reported by men whose jobs are upgraded in skill.

Expectedly, most workers of both sexes revealed positive atti-tudes toward their machines, but the prediction that women would dislike their machines more than men do was not confirmed. Apparently, most employees who work with machines and experi-ence automation accept it as normal and adjust to it, especially if they retain control over work, as generally appears to be the case. Job changes induced by new equipment have almost no effect on men's and women's feelings toward their machines. The paradox is that, even though women are assigned to technologically more restrictive work than men, and even though women suffer more from technological change, their job satisfaction and liking for machines differ little from men's.

Weaver (1979) also found that sex differences in occupational status, education, work experience, motivation to work, quality of work environment, and many other factors did not explain the paradox. He concluded that women are so segregated from men on their jobs that only a small minority (8 percent) perceive any job discrimination. That is, women have little opportunity to observe discrimination and therefore do not feel it. My study suggests that the technological isolation and subordination of women insulate them from situations that would enable them to compare them-selves to men and thus lead them to a greater sense of inequity and grievance.

Alienation theory, from Marx to Marcuse (Seeman, 1971) stresses that technological change reduces workers' autonomy and increases their feelings of powerlessness, work dissatisfaction, and machine hatred. Shepard's (1977) review of the case studies concludes that the evidence is mixed. But Mueller (1969) is the only national study of a representative set of workers that permits testing of these ideas. Her evidence and the present analysis suggest that studies that report largely negative effects of tech-nological change may be selective. Contrary to the thesis of Braver-man (1974) and his supporters—that technological change degrades work and that workers become hostile toward their machines—

Mueller's national study, though based on a short five-year interval, suggests that workers accept technological change as normal and that they like their machines. Workers are not disenchanted by technological change, and women, who are most adversely affected by it, are neither dissatisfied nor hostile toward their machines.

Notes

1. Indirect use refers to machine-dependent work. Thus, workers may be fed supplies by a moving belt, but they may not regulate the belt's movement; workers may repair machines, but not operate them.

2. The technology literature refers to automation in two senses. Automation *level* refers to operational type of control (manual, mechanical, and electronic), while *automation,* as opposed to mechanization, refers only to equipment controlled by preprogrammed knowledge usually fed back electronically—distinguished from machines that have mechanical controls.

3. Strictly speaking, the machines are classified according to whether their operators use mechanical or manual controls.

4. Women also earn significantly lower incomes than do men who operate the same types of machines: large-scale production, multi-system power-controlled, and electronic equipment.

5. The percentage of workers experiencing machine changes (Mueller et al., 1969:55) are professional, 20; managers, 18; proprietors, 14; clerical, 22; craft, 28; operatives, 26; service, 13; laborers, 30; farmers and farm laborers, 20. The spread by industrial categories ranged from 15 percent for health and welfare to 28 for manufacturing.

6. Among those experiencing a significant impact of technology on the job, relatively more males than females reported an increased demand for skill, while relatively more of the females reported a more pleasant work environment.

7. Responses to the friend-foe and automation adjustment scales were correlated +.60.

8. The variables were scored as follows: equipment use (constant = 1, some = 2, little or none = 3), machine change (no = 0, yes = 1), automation level (fixed mechanical control = 1, powered single-system, manual control = 2, numerical and related controls = 3, multi-system, manual controls = 4, operator powered = 5, no machine use = 6), work control organization (impersonal = 1, boss = 2, group = 3, worker = 4, no machine = 5), sex (female = 1, male = 2), work experience (for males, age − years of education − 6 years; for females, 0.6 × [age − education − 6]), education (number of years completed), occupational level (lower blue-collar and service = 1, skilled manual = 2, clerical = 3, other white-collar = 4). For the dependent variables, machine evaluation was scored on a range of 1–5, with machine

as friend = 1, as foe = 5. Automation adjustment score based on responses to 11 questions; positive responses to each machine change was scored as +1 and −1 for each negative response.

8

Economic Justice and Political Ideology

Economic Interests and Economic Ideology

In the first part of this study, I examined the extent to which the American working class is economically differentiated and the extent to which earnings disparities parallel status distinctions. The results pointed to considerable economic and social inequality. These inequalities converged around broad occupational groupings, including foremen, self-employed, craftsmen, nonskilled unionized workers, nonunionized workers, and women. A preliminary inspection of the politics of these groups revealed some systematic differences, but we need a more extensive and systematic analysis of political cleavages within the working class. The purpose of undertaking class analysis, after all, is to ascertain whether economic and status distinctions have political consequences. Marx's distinction of a class for itself, Weber's question about whether classes become status groups and parties, and Giddens's analyses of class structuration all probe the question whether strata become cohesive in the pursuit of political goals. Most theorists, whatever their ideological preferences, agree that struggles that are limited to the economic arena cannot decisively alter class relations unless they also attack political problems and the control of government.

In the following four chapters, I pursue the complexities of political cohesiveness in the American working class. First, on the assumption that a class cannot agree on its political objectives unless it also agrees on its economic situation with respect to other classes, in this chapter I systematically compare the economic ideology of the working class with that of other classes. I also examine whether economic disagreements within the working class are large enough to weaken its posture of political class conflict. In Chapter 9, on the assumption that if union members do not share beliefs about union activities in political affairs, a working-class political program may be unachievable, I examine problems of political consensus among union members. In Chapter 10, I probe working-class voting behavior over an extended period to ascertain the extent of political consensus among the main strata. Finally, in Chapter 11, I compare the economic, status, and political cleavages of the American and French working classes to address the question whether the working class in class-conscious France is structured differently than the U.S. working class, which lacks such class consciousness.

The failure of the American working class to develop a coherent liberal or radical ideology is partially explained by the structure of the United States' two-party system. Even though the Democratic party is more liberal than the Republican, both parties must capture the loyalties of voters who have different class interests. The most anomalous party coalitions have been middle-class southern Democrats who have had to compromise with northern urban liberals, and working-class northern Republican Protestants who have had to accommodate to business groups (Nie, Verba, and Petrocik, 1979:383). The failure of working-class elements (ethnics, Catholics, Jews, native-born workers) to consolidate behind the Democratic party before 1932 impelled Greenstone (1977) to comment that the American working class was not truly enfranchised before the New Deal. Yet, despite the Democratic mobilization of working-class groups, the party still had to appeal to other groups to secure a wide base of support. After the 1960s, the party's appeal to working-class constituencies weakened, with the notable exception of the continuing support of blacks (Nie, et al., 1979:229–34). In prosperous times it may not have been necessary for the Democrats to appeal strongly to working-class groups. Currently, it appears that party slogans and rhetoric are not as clearly class-linked as they were during the Roosevelt-Truman era. In Britain, the situation is quite different. Even though Britain also has a two-party system, the Labour party must, however imperfectly, sustain a working-class rhetoric because it cannot deny its socialist and working-class origins.

In the United States, the working-class appeals of the Democratic party sometimes mix inharmoniously with appeals to other classes. In a non-class, two-party system, party officials strain to retain the loyalty of both working- and middle-class groups. The Republican party has been more successful in retaining the loyalty of upper-middle and business class interests than the Democratic party has been in retaining the loyalty of the working class. Though allegedly in the minority, the Republican party has been remarkably able to attract working-class support in national elections. Greenstone's (1979) contention that the Democratic party became a working-class party in pursuit of broad consumer goals may have been true during the prosperous post–World War II period when the government was able to respond to pressures from a broad spectrum of class groups. This became more difficult during the economically depressed years since 1970.

Scholars in the Perlman (1928) tradition have argued that the American working class is mainly interested in bread and butter issues. On these matters, it may be as class conscious as European working classes. These issues deal with wages, retirement benefits, working conditions, health and safety, union protection, and unemployment. When the Democratic party responds directly to these issues, it obtains working-class support. The rest of the party's liberal agenda has less or sometimes even a negative working-class appeal. Though civil liberties, such as the rights of dissident groups (communists, criminals, pacifists) to free speech are important to liberal elements in the party, they are peripherally important to most workers. The stance that many workers take on civil rights, voting rights, equality of educational opportunity, racial integration of schools, and affirmative action for women and minorities sometimes departs from that taken by middle-class liberals. Workers may even be more comfortable with the stand taken by Republicans on relations with the Soviet Union, the struggle of working classes in Latin America, and other foreign relations concerns. Pollution, environmental protection, regulation of monopolies, and truth in advertising are also of peripheral interest to many workers. However, some scholars contend that on these types of issues, the working class is as liberal or at least not more conservative than the general population (Hamilton, 1972). Although the evidence is mixed (Wilensky, 1976), the point remains that, although civil liberties, civil rights, foreign relations, consumer protection, and government regulation of business are central issues to some groups in the Democratic liberal coalition, the issues may obscure the party's attraction to many workers.

The research question here is whether the working class has a distinctive view of its economic interests when compared to other classes. If it does, then the failure of the working class to become politically mobilized can be partly explained by the Democratic party's inability to respond consistently to working-class economic interests. If a consensual ideology is lacking, then the working class may be nothing more than a category invented by social scientists to serve their research interests. The third possibility is that the working class is split and that only some of its segments develop a consistent economic ideology that can be linked to a political agendum. The nonskilled core stratum should have the most consensual economic ideology because the stratum is highly unionized and most exposed to political guidance by labor's Committee on Political Education (COPE).

Four research questions are in order. First, are the differences in economic ideology between the working and other classes large enough to be considered distinct? Second, if they are, are ideological differences within the working class large enough to undermine unified political action? Third, do working-class differences on beliefs about unjust pay generate differences in economic and political ideology? Fourth, does union membership differentially affect the economic and political ideologies of segments or strata of the working class?

Marxist theory has traditionally neglected the social psychological processes that tie the development of political ideologies to political mobilization (Lockwood, 1981). Ideological development must proceed somewhat as follows. In contrast to the ideology of elites and favored classes that their economic rewards are earned and just (Huber and Form, 1973), central to the development of working-class ideology is the belief that wages and earnings are undeservedly low. Not only must individual workers feel aggrieved about their earnings, they must also believe that other workers like themselves suffer equally (Ollman, 1970). In addition, workers should conclude that people with high earnings do not deserve them. Finally, workers must conclude that both their unjustly low earnings and the unjustly high earnings of others result not from individual luck, ability, merit, or circumstance, but from institutional arrangements designed to perpetuate economic inequities. This pessimistic and cynical outlook must lead to common feelings of individual powerlessness, that nothing can be done to change conditions by individual action. Only collective union and party action can change economic institutions. Although some improvement can be achieved through strikes, ultimately the economic system itself must be changed by seizing control of the government. Conscious political support must be given to parties that are dedicated to changing or reversing institutionalized class inequalities.

Only a few researchers have systematically examined the full range of beliefs that comprise economic ideologies: beliefs about the justice of individual earnings to beliefs about the justice of institutional economic arrangements (see Jones, 1941). Therefore, in examining the economic ideology of the working class, I began by exploring workers' sense of justice about economic areas closest to them (for example, wages), and then I extended the inquiry to beliefs about the justice of incomes of increasingly distant groups, e.g., those of other workers in the same occupation, workers in other occupations, and people in other interest groups and classes. Then I explored workers' beliefs about the equity of governmental measures to redistribute wealth through income taxes, welfare, social security, and other schemes. Finally I examined whether beliefs about the fairness of income distribution and the redistribution of income were related to liberal and conservative political self-labeling.

The data are based on my 1979 survey of almost 700 adults in the state of Illinois. The six broad areas of beliefs dealing with economic justice included the following:

1. *Earnings:* beliefs concerning the fairness of the workers' earnings, earnings of their occupational group, earnings of other occupations that represent the entire occupational structure, and satisfaction with level of income and standard of living.

2. *Basis of equitable pay:* beliefs concerning the extent to which pay should be determined by seniority, physical effort, education, supervisory responsibility, individual productivity, skill, and the company's ability to pay. This section also explores the extent to which workers endorse an ideology of pay equalization, how disputes about the basis of pay ought to be resolved, and what action workers should take when they believe they are being paid less than they deserve.

3. *Equity of other groups' income:* beliefs concerning the fairness of incomes received by four interest groups (corporations, labor union members, small business owners, and farmers), three broad strata (professionals, middle class, and manual workers), and four disprivileged groups (women, blacks, Spanish-speaking, and welfare recipients).

4. *Fairness of income boundaries:* beliefs concerning the just income gap between rich and poor, the income level that makes a household rich, and the just financial limits of personal inheritance.

5. *Fairness of governmental measures to redistribute income:* the fairness of federal taxes on different income levels, the adequacy of welfare payments, and attitudes toward various governmental measures to provide an economic safety net. These items measure degrees of economic liberalism, and they are compared to workers' political identifications as conservatives or liberals.

6. *Trends in societal and personal economic equity:* beliefs

about national trends in economic inequality, equality of opportunity, and economic well-being.

The Sample

This research is based on a subsample of labor force participants (N = 495) of a larger Illinois sample (N = 691) of persons eighteen to sixty-five years old in 1979. Because I needed adequate numbers of high-, middle-, and low-income respondents, I used a two-stage disproportionate sample design. Forty-five Primary Sampling Units (PSUs) were selected for three income levels with probabilities proportionate to size.[1] In high-income areas, the measure of size was the number of households with total household income of $20,000 or more; in low income areas, $3,500 or less; in middle income areas, the measure of size was all households.

A PSU was defined as a community area in Chicago, as a suburb in the Chicago SMSA, or as a county elsewhere in the state. The sampling frame outside the Chicago SMSA was based on telephone directories; respondents were selected by random procedures. In the Chicago SMSA, where random digit dialing (RDD) was used, the frame was based on telephone prefixes. RDD was used in the Chicago SMSA to eliminate the bias of unlisted numbers. Elsewhere, that bias is so small that RDD is not cost effective.

Combining data from three types of PSUs ordinarily requires weighting because of the varying probabilities of selection by income level. Since a comparison of the marginals of weighted and unweighted strata showed only minor and random differences, no weights were used.

Measuring Economic Ideology

Economic ideology was measured with fifty-five items covering six general areas.

1. Fairness of earnings was tapped by three questions:

a. OCCPAY: "Is the pay *most* people get for your type of work much less than they deserve, somewhat less, about the same, somewhat more, or much more than they deserve?" coded 1 = much less to 5 = much more.

b. OWNPAY: "Is your pay much less, somewhat less, about the same, somewhat more, or much more than you deserve?" coded 1 = much less to 5 = much more.

c. JUSTPAY: "Now I am going to tell you the actual average

yearly earnings of people with three dependents in some occupations in this country. In terms of the work they do, would you say that the incomes of these people are much too high, too high, about right, too low, or much too low?" coded 1 = much too high to 5 = much too low.

For the last question, the occupations and their incomes were: top executive of a large corporation, $200,000; corporation lawyer, $470,000; personnel manager in a large company, $35,000; electrician, $21,000; accountant, $18,000; truck driver, $16,000; assembly line auto worker, $15,000; clerk typist, $9,000; telephone operator, $7,300; person employed at minimum wage, $6,000. The earnings were based on U.S. Bureau of the Census (1980) nationwide survey for 1978 adjusted for inflation and data provided by knowledgeable informants of labor market conditions in Illinois. A Pearsonian correlation between the evaluation scores of just income and the occupational earnings was calculated for each worker. A positive correlation signifies that the higher-paid occupations were overpaid and the lower, underpaid.

d. Satisfaction with current standard of living was tapped by response to the question: "How satisfied are you with your standard of living—the things you have—like housing, car, furniture, recreation, and the like?" Very satisfied coded 1; satisfied, 2; dissatisfied, 3; and very dissatisfied, 4.

2. Bases of equitable pay was measured by presenting workers some choices to make in five situations. The questions are:

a. "Which of the following should be the most important in determining how much workers get paid on their job? Their seniority, education, supervisory responsibility, or the physical demands of the job?" Then the others were ranked in terms of their importance.

b. "A company pays workers according to how much their work group produces. Some workers feel they should be paid more because they produce more. Do you strongly agree, agree, disagree, or strongly disagree?"

c. "A foreman is paid less than some skilled workers he supervises because these workers are hard to find. The foreman thinks he should be paid more. Do you strongly agree, . . . ?"

d. "Two people are doing the same kind of work, but the one with more education gets more pay. Do you agree or disagree that the person with more education should get more pay? Do you strongly agree, . . . ?"

e. "Skilled workers get much more pay than assembly line

workers. The assembly line workers say that they should be paid more because their work is hard and tiring. Do you strongly agree, . . . ?"

f. "When workers feel that they get less pay than they deserve, should they not work as hard on the job, go out on strike, do the work poorly or incorrectly, or quit their jobs?" Each choice was presented separately with a choice of yes or no.

3. Fairness of the income received by major interest and class groups in the nation was tapped by this question: "Some people say that some groups in this country get more money than they deserve while others get less. Please tell me whether the following groups get much more money, more, about right, less, or much less money than they deserve," coded 1 = much more money to 5 = much less money.

The groups included corporations, labor unions, small business owners, the middle class, women, blacks, manual workers, professional people, people on welfare, and the Spanish-speaking. Though these groups cannot be scaled, a factor analysis revealed that the responses to three "minority" groups (blacks, women, Spanish-speaking Americans) formed a single factor called MINLESS. Thus, we have evaluations of the justice of the incomes received by eleven groups and women and minorities as a whole.

4. The justice of stratal income boundaries was tapped in response to three questions:

a. RANGE, an indicator of the justifiable income gap between the rich and the poor was constructed by calculating the difference in response to two questions: "What do you think should be the highest yearly income anyone should be able to make for working full-time?" and "What do you think should be the lowest yearly income anyone should make for working full-time?"

b. RICH: "How much money would a person have to earn in a year to be considered rich?"

c. TAX: "How much money do you think people should be able to inherit without paying a tax on it?"

5. Equity beliefs about various forms of income redistribution were tapped with fifteen items compressed into ten variables. To derive a measure of the justness of the federal income tax as a mode of redistribution, respondents were asked:

a. TAXES: "Now, I'm going to read you the average amount of income tax that people with three dependents pay. Please tell me whether you think this tax is much too high, too high, about right, too low, or much too low," coded 1 = much too high to 5 = much too low. Then respondents were presented six incomes, each with an associated tax based on information supplied by a tax accountant. "For $12,000 an average tax of $1,000; $35,000, a tax of $6,500; $18,000, $2,100; $70,000, $20,000; $200,000, $85,000; $9,000, $500." Each respondent's score on TAXES was a Pearsonian correlation between the evaluation and the amount of tax.

In addition, respondents were asked the extent of their agreement to five statements concerning taxes and inheritance, coded 1 = strongly agree to 5 = strongly disagree.

b. "In this country the tax system is more favorable to the poor than to anybody else."

c. "In this country the tax system is more favorable to the rich than to anybody else."

d. "Middle income people suffer the most from taxes in this country."

e. "Basically, the tax system in this country is fair to everybody."

f. "There should be a limit on the amount of money people can inherit."

Respondents' views of government programs that affect income redistribution were obtained in response to four questions which formed a factor we called economic liberalism (ECONLIB). The variables were not recoded and all weights were positive. The response categories were coded 1 = strongly disagree to 4 = strongly agree. The questions making up the factor are:

g. "The government should guarantee a job for everyone who wants one"; "The government should pay the college expenses of students if their parents cannot"; "The government should limit the amount of profits business can make"; "The government should pass a law to guarantee adequate health care for everyone."

Another form of redistribution is to pay everyone more or less equally. Our measure, PAYMARX, was a three item index, constructed from the following questions, coded 1 = strongly agree to 4 = strongly disagree.

h. "It would be more fair if people were paid by how much they need to live decently rather than by the kind of work they do"; "It would be a good thing if all people received the same amount of money no matter what jobs they do"; "Workers should receive additional wages for each additional child they have." The index was constructed by adding responses for the three questions since the items loaded equally on one factor in a factor analysis.

Support for government policy on minimum wages was determined by the following question, coded 1 = much too low to 5 = much too high:

i. "A person working at the minimum wage makes about $6,000. Is this much too high . . . or much too low?"

Liberals and radicals push for greater economic redistribution while conservatives want either no change or changes that increase inequality. Therefore, a simple measure of political self-identification (POLITLEAN) was made from responses to the following question, coded 1 = very conservative to 5 = very liberal.

j. "Would you describe your political views as very conservative, conservative, middle of the road, liberal, or very liberal?"

6. Pessimism or optimism about societal and personal economic equity was tapped with seven questions. Three questions dealt with societal economic equity:

a. "Would you say that the difference in income between the rich and the poor in this country is increasing, about the same, or decreasing?" coded 1 = increasing to 3 = decreasing.
b. "Would you say that equality of opportunity is increasing, staying about the same, or decreasing in this country?" coded 1 = increasing to 3 = decreasing.
c. "Would you say that the poor are treated worse in the United States than in other countries, the same, or better?" coded 1 = worse to 3 = better.

Three questions that emerged as a factor, called BADTIME, tapped personal economic pessimism or optimism. The variables were not recoded and all weights were positive.

d. "Would you say that you are better off, about the same, or worse off financially than you were a year ago?" coded 1 = better off to 3 = worse off.
e. "Do you think that a year from now you will be better off financially, about the same, or worse off?" coded 1 = better off to 3 = worse off.
f. "During the past year, would you say that you have kept ahead of inflation, stayed even, or fallen behind?" coded 1 = kept ahead to 3 = fallen behind.
g. "Taken all together, how would you say things are these

days? Are you very happy, pretty happy, or not too happy?" coded 1
= very happy to 3 = not too happy.

All these measures of economic ideology were statistically
reliable. After randomly assigning each case to one of two groups,
the means of each measure were compared and in no instance was
the difference between the means significant at the 0.05 level.

Do Classes Differ in Their Economic Ideology?

I divided all workers into three classes: professional and administrative, clerical, and manual. Since some economic beliefs of clerical
workers resemble one class rather than another, I indicate which
way the resemblance goes for the different beliefs. It is noteworthy
that, while earnings of clerical workers averaged about $2,000 less
than those of manual workers, family incomes of clerical workers
averaged $2,500 higher than manual workers' family incomes.
Obviously, many clerical workers were part of two-earner families.
Over 80 percent of them were women, and their mean years of work
experience were only two years fewer than employees in the other
two classes. Unless otherwise indicated, I report *only* findings that
are statistically significant by the chi-square test, using the 5 percent level of significance.

The responses of the three classes differed on half of the
fifty-six items, and some differences appeared in all six belief areas
(see Table 8.1). Almost half of the workers in each class thought that
their earnings were less than they deserved. Expectedly, more of
the clerical and manual than the top class felt that their occupations
were paid less than they deserved. The correlations between the
pay of occupations chosen to represent the occupational structure
and judgments about the fairness of their pay (JUSTPAY) were
substantially high, about .60 for all three classes. This suggests that
all occupations were perceived as somewhat unfairly underpaid.
Importantly, the earnings that respondents were asked to judge
were the actual earnings then current for the occupations. In short,
the evidence suggests that half of the respondents in all classes saw
their own pay as unjustly low; the lower the class, the more the
dissatisfaction with occupational pay. This sense of inequity was
counterbalanced by high levels of satisfaction with their standard of
living. Workers in the clerical and manual classes were only slightly
less satisfied than those in the professional-administrative class.

Often members of different groups differ in the way they judge
equitable pay (Brown, 1977). The data showed little class consensus

Table 8.1. Economic Beliefs of Workers in Three Classes (percent)

	Classes		
Beliefs	Prof.-Admin.	Clerical	Manual
Occupational income equity			
OWNPAY—less than deserved	40	47	56
OCCPAY—less than deserved[a]	43	58	60
JUSTPAY—(mean correlations)[b]	.56	.58	.61
Standard of Living—satisfied[a]	83	73	76
Income—satisfied[a]	76	66	58
Pay Equity			
Most important in determining pay			
Seniority[a]	13	16	20
Education	22	27	31
Superv. responsibility[a]	54	30	19
Physical demands[a]	11	27	30
Bases of pay			
Indiv. > group productivity	84	80	82
Education > performance	29	25	24
Foremen paid > skilled	55	60	55
Tiring work > skill[a]	14	33	40
PAYMARX scale[a]	8.3	8.8	8.1
Fairer if paid by need[a]	28	38	51
Same pay for all jobs[a]	3	6	12
Extra pay for each child[a]	21	26	45
When paid less than deserved, workers should . . .			
Not work as hard[a]	6	12	17
Go on strike	38	39	46
Do work poorly[a]	2	2	7
Quit jobs	73	56	54
Income equity of national groups			
More income than they deserve			
Corporations[a]	78	84	93
Labor unions[a]	86	85	75
Small business[a]	3	8	8
Professionals[a]	48	66	65
Middle class	2	5	5
Manual workers	3	8	8
Welfare clients [b]	49	43	38
Women[b]	2	4	7
Blacks	7	10	12
Spanish-speaking	10	13	14
MINLESS ($\overline{X}$)[a]	.17	.00	−.12
Fairness of income boundaries ($\overline{X}$ in 000 $)			
RANGE of justifiable income[a]	501	408	299
Highest justifiable income[a]	513	417	322
Lowest justifiable income	9	9.5	11

Table 8.1. Continued

Beliefs	Classes		
	Prof.-Admin.	Clerical	Manual
RICH	252	289	231
TAX—inherit w/o taxes ($)	1,741	1,824	1,621
Minimum wage—too low	86	88	91
Equity of income redistribution			
Tax system is fair	10	15	17
Tax system favors poor	23	17	20
Tax system favors rich	84	86	89
Taxes worst for middle class	93	92	91
Same taxes for everybody[a]	38	54	64
ECONLIB—scale[a]	.31	−.01	−.17
Government should guarantee job[a]	51	62	69
Government should guarantee health care	70	78	84
Government should pay education for poor	50	67	71
TAXES, Fairness of income tax schedule(r)	−.07	−.09	−.03
Government should limit profits	54	58	57
Conservative political identification	42	38	37
Societal and personal optimism			
Income gap increasing	72	75	79
Equal opportunity increasing[a]	69	62	54
U.S. poor treated better[a]	83	73	66
BADTIME—personal economy scale	−.08	.04	.05
Personally happy[a]	74	74	60
Family annual income ($\bar{X}$ $)	27,661	19,732	17,348
N	174	192	247

[a]p of chi-square ≤ .05, based on original tables.
[b]p = .06 − .10, based on original tables.

on the basis for determining equitable pay. Manual and clerical workers placed greater importance on the physical demands of the job, educational requirements, and seniority than did the professionals and administrators. Understandably, the latter stressed supervisory responsibility more (Table 8.1). In a related question, over eight-tenths of workers in all classes felt that individual productivity should be rewarded more than group productivity, and only one-quarter believed that education of the worker should be considered more important than performance in determining occupational pay. Surprisingly, almost half thought that foremen should not be paid more than skilled workers when the latter are in short supply. Although the majority in all three classes thought that skill should be more highly rewarded than unpleasant and tiring work, the differences were substantial. Forty percent of the manual and only 14 percent of the professionals and administrators thought that physically demanding and boring work justified higher pay than skilled work. Substantial differences also appeared in beliefs about pay equalization, with manual workers pressing for more equalization than the other two classes. But very few workers in any class thought that all jobs should be paid equally, supporting Hochschild's (1981) observation that Americans do not believe in equality of pay. Almost half of the manual workers believed that paying on the basis of the workers' needs is fairer than the present method of paying, but very few in other classes agreed.

Important stratal differences appeared on the question of what workers should do when they perceive themselves underpaid. Although all classes preferred quitting to other alternatives, the top class most preferred this solution. Almost two-fifth of each class approved of striking, but only negligible minorities thought that not working hard or doing work poorly was justified. Yet the two lower classes preferred these solutions more than the top one. In sum, on most items dealing with pay equity, the basis of pay determination, and action to take when justice norms are violated, pervasive class differences appeared, with clerical workers responding more like manual than like professional-administrative workers.

All classes agreed that four groups receive more money than they deserve: corporations, labor union members, professionals, and welfare clients. More of the manual than professional-administrative workers felt that corporations and professionals were over-rewarded, and fewer of the manual workers felt that labor union members and welfare clients were over-rewarded. Importantly, all classes agreed that the majority of employees, that is, manual workers and the middle class, make much less money than they deserve as do the disprivileged groups: women, blacks, and the Spanish-speaking. Though the differences were small, more of the manual than other workers felt that the disprivileged receive higher incomes than they deserve (see MINLESS in Table 8.1).

The three classes differed in their conceptions of justifiable high and low incomes. The top class thought that $500,000 should be the top limit compared to $300,000 for the two lower classes. These figures roughly represent eighteen times the present incomes of families in each class. All classes agreed that about $9,000 was the lowest justifiable annual income, a figure that was about $3,000 above the then annual federal minimum wage, which all classes considered too low. Thus, highest justifiable incomes were fifty to eighty times greater than the lowest justifiable ones. Curiously, all classes thought that an annual income of over $200,000 would make a person rich, a figure much lower than the highest justifiable income (see RICH in Table 8.1). All classes agreed that there should be no limit on the amount of inheritance people could receive without paying taxes on it. Thus, all classes would tolerate inherited incomes that were much higher than incomes they defined as justifiable.

If people believe that the range of incomes is too large, then they should approve of some income redistribution. Taxes constitute the main vehicle to achieve this in the United States. Data in Table 8.1 clearly reveal class consensus regarding the tax system. The great majority agreed that the system is unfair, that taxes hit the middle class (the average worker) hardest, and that the system favors the rich. One-fifth thought that the tax system favors the poor. Respondents were asked to evaluate the fairness of current federal income taxes on incomes ranging from $9,000 (the minimum wage) to $200,000 (being rich). The correlation between tax levels and judgments of their fairness (TAXES) was almost zero for all classes, suggesting that respondents were unable to judge the fairness of graduated income taxes. They preferred a system where everyone would be taxed at the same level.

In responding to questions about what the government should do about economic injustice, more than a majority in all classes agree that the government should limit business profits, guarantee jobs and health care to everyone, and provide free college education for the poor. In short, the majority in all classes agreed that taxes were inequitable and that government should provide an economic safety net. Apparently these views are not viewed as "political" by any class because over three-quarters saw themselves politically as being either middle-of-the-road or conservative (Table 8.1).

Some class differences appeared in response to questions dealing with societal and personal economic optimism. On the societal level, over 70 percent felt that the income gap between rich and poor is increasing, about 60 percent thought that equality of economic opportunity is increasing, and even more thought that the U.S. treated its poor better than most countries treated theirs. In all these beliefs, manual workers were more critical than those in the other two strata. Respondents were not optimistic about their economic well-being during this period of high inflation. Over 40 percent in all three classes reported that they were worse off than a year earlier and that they would be worse off a year hence because their incomes were not keeping up with inflation. Yet over 60 percent of manual workers and 74 percent of those in the other two strata said that they were personally happy, somewhat lower figures than have appeared in earlier national surveys (Campbell, et al., 1976:29).

Overall, the evidence of a sense of economic injustice runs high in this study. Most people believe that the earnings of the middle class, the working class, and minorities are unjustly low. Taxes are unfair, favoring the rich. Support for governmental income redistribution runs fairly high as does pessimism about future economic well-being. However, respondents considered themselves to be moderates and conservatives politically, and their political identifications appeared to be unrelated to their beliefs about economic injustice. Responses to one-half of the items differed by class, and for forty-six of fifty-six items the trends were precisely hierarchical. Thus, the working class appears to be differentiated from other classes in economic ideology, but political polarization between classes is relatively low. The question now is, how heterogeneous is the working class in its views of economic justice?

Do Working-Class Strata Differ in Economic Ideology?

On formal statistical grounds, the working class appeared to be as internally divided as the classes themselves. At the five percent level of statistical significance, the responses of the working-class strata (self-employed, skilled, nonskilled core, and nonskilled periphery) differed in twenty-five of fifty-six beliefs, compared to twenty-eight of fifty-six beliefs for the three major classes. The difference might easily reflect the larger number of working-class strata than classes. The more important question is, to what extent do beliefs of the working-class strata change in a consistent direction as one moves from self-employed to the nonskilled periphery? Employing the most severe test and permitting ties, responses to thirteen of the fifty-six items changed in a single direction and eight other items changed monotonically from skilled to nonskilled periphery. At most, twenty-one of fifty-six items changed systematically by working-class strata compared to forty-six of fifty-six for the classes. Clearly the five working-class strata do not differ in their economically ideology as much as the three classes, yet working-class differentiation is not negligible.

The responses of the foremen deserve special attention. In almost half of the belief items, the foremen were outliers in that they represented either the highest or lowest value. In the other half of the items, the foremen resembled one of the other strata. The foremen's modal position (eighteen of twenty-nine items) was between the self-employed and the skilled. On statistically significant items, the foremen's position typically resembled that of one of the other strata (see Table 8.2).

The foremen's responses were also compared to those of the classes in Table 8.1. In thirteen items, foremen's beliefs resembled those of the professional-administrators rather than those of clerical and manual workers. In the remaining forty-three items, the foremen placed between the top and clerical group in thirteen items, between the clerical and manual in eleven items, and in an outlier position closest to the manual in nineteen items. These data reinforce the conclusion that the foremen's beliefs are closer to those of the working- than those of the middle class.

Not surprisingly, the lower the working-class stratum, the more workers in it felt that their occupational pay was less than they deserved and the more dissatisfied they were with it. Similarly, the lower the stratum, the more the workers felt that job seniority and physical demands were important bases for determining pay, and that supervisory responsibility was less important. Over twice the percentage of the two nonskilled strata than the self-employed and foremen thought that tiring and boring work should be paid more than skilled labor, and that paying workers according to their needs and family responsibilities is more fair. Although equality of pay was endorsed only by a small minority, the lower strata supported that equality more than did the higher strata. In situations where workers perceived that they got paid less than they deserved, again, the lower the stratum, the more respondents endorsed striking, not working hard, and doing work poorly, but the less they thought workers should quit their jobs. This response pattern conforms to Marxist theory of class crystallization that the most deprived most oppose the status quo.

Only in a few instances did the strata disagree on the fairness of incomes received by other groups. The three lowest strata almost unanimously felt that corporations made more money than they deserved. The lower the stratum, the fewer workers thought that labor union members received undeservedly high wages. Fewer workers in the most unionized stratum (nonskilled core) thought that union wages were unjustly high, while more workers in the other strata thought that union wages were too high. Although not statistically significant, the lower the stratum, the more its members concluded that professional and middle-class earnings were unjustly high. Concerning the incomes of the four economically disprivileged groups, only beliefs concerning welfare clients differed by strata. Fewer of the foremen and nonskilled periphery employees than members of other strata thought that welfare clients' incomes were too high. The two highest strata also had more sympathy for economic status of women, blacks, and the Spanish-speaking.

With only occasional exceptions, the lower the stratum, the smaller was the justifiable gap between the highest and lowest incomes. Importantly, all strata agreed that inherited incomes should not be taxed and that the minimum wage was too low (Table 8.2).

Table 8.2. Economic Beliefs of Working-Class Strata (percent)

			Strata		
				Nonskilled	
Beliefs	Foremen	Self-Employed	Skilled	Core	Periphery
Occupational income equity					
OWNPAY—less than deserved[a]	75	36	58	30	16
OCCPAY—less than deserved	47	30	45	46	48
JUSTPAY—(mean correlations)[a]	.59	.54	.66	.60	.59
Standard of living—satisfied	95	81	78	86	77
Income—satisfied	80	75	62	56	62
Pay equity					
Most important in determining pay					
Seniority[a]	0	12	10	32	25
Education	26	26	29	26	28
Superv. responsibility[a]	37	47	29	7	8
Physical demands[a]	37	14	31	35	39
Bases of pay					
Indiv. > group productivity[b]	58	93	81	83	95
Education > performance	21	24	27	24	29
Foreman paid > skilled	68	49	60	46	55
Tiring work > skill[a]	18	18	25	52	53
PAYMARX scale[a]	8.8	9.1	8.3	7.9	7.9
Fairer if paid by need[a]	30	35	51	55	62
Same pay for all jobs[a]	5	2	7	15	13
Extra pay for each child[a]	20	24	35	59	53
When paid less than deserved, workers should . . .					
Not work as hard[a]	0	4	9	21	28
Go on strike[a]	32	30	38	51	56
Do work poorly	5	2	3	9	8
Quit jobs[a]	74	81	57	47	49
Income equity of national groups					
More income than they deserve					
Corporations[a]	76	81	94	93	94
Labor unions[a]	79	87	77	68	83
Small business	5	2	6	7	11
Professionals	65	56	59	71	76
Middle class	0	4	4	2	10

Table 8.2. Continued

			Strata		
				Nonskilled	
		Self-			
Beliefs	Foremen	Employed	Skilled	Core	Periphery
Manual workers	0	8	8	5	20
Welfare clients[a]	13	59	42	54	30
Women	5	2	6	12	6
Blacks	10	8	16	18	10
Spanish-speaking	0	21	16	24	3
MINLESS ($\bar{X}$)	−.07	−.26	−.03	−.26	−.12
Fairness of income boundaries ($\bar{X}$ in 000 $)					
RANGE of justifiable income[b]	378	449	283	264	319
Highest justifiable income[b]	390	582	314	285	328
Lowest justifiable income[b]	12	8	11	12	9
RICH	140	377	231	288	158
TAX—inherit w/o taxes[a]	1,430	1,822	1,698	1,894	1,010
Minimum wage—too low	20	89	92	90	87
Equity of income redistribution					
Tax system is fair[a]	15	29	9	15	18
Tax system favors poor	20	28	18	17	23
Tax system favors rich[b]	100	82	86	96	87
Taxes worst for middle class	95	22	38	33	20
Same taxes for everybody	50	58	63	68	66
TAXES—fairness of income tax					
schedule(r)	−.13	−.18	.02	.01	−.04
ECONLIB scale[a]	.30	.47	−.14	−.29	−.40
Government should guarantee job[a]	53	47	59	70	72
Government should guarantee					
health care[a]	70	76	83	86	97
Government should pay education					
for poor[a]	60	48	64	67	87
Government should limit profits[a]	20	33	51	61	46
Conservative political identification[a]	40	44	49	27	26
Societal and personal optimism					
Income gap increasing[a]	80	64	81	84	68
Equal opportunity increasing[a]	74	74	43	54	56
U.S. poor treated better	100	74	75	64	58
BADTIME—personal economic scale	−.25	−.32	.00	.01	.03
Personally happy	90	70	69	55	51
Family annual income $)	21,250	22,222	16,164	14,917	8,118
N	20	45	99	77	62

Note: Significance chi-square tests omit foremen and are based on the original tables.

[a]$p = \leq .05$

[b]$p = .06 - .10$

Given these patterns, I expected the lower strata to most oppose the tax system and be more favorable toward governmental programs to help the poor and to limit business profits. No consistent trend appeared in responses to the tax questions; however, the expected pattern held up for beliefs about governmental redistribution programs. The lower the stratum, the more workers favored governmental guarantees of jobs, health care, educational subsidies for the poor, and the restriction of business profits. The increasing economic liberalism of the lower strata was matched by their increasing self-identification as political liberals. Finally, in the area of societal optimism, a curvilinear trend appeared: fewer of the self-employed and nonskilled periphery believed that the income gap between rich and poor is increasing, but, the lower the stratum, the smaller the proportion who believed the United States treats its poor better than do other countries. As expected, the lower the stratum, the more economically pessimistic were its members, and the less they reported being personally happy.

Finally, I ran regression equations that included other independent variables besides stratal position that might explain beliefs about economic fairness or justice. The independent variables included being in a working-class strata (the nonmanual were the omitted category), education, income, union membership, years of work experience, sex, race, and marital status. For the dependent variables, I selected some of the more important belief items. In the pay area, I selected JUSTPAY (equity of pay in the occupational structure), the most important basis for determining pay, preferences for individual over group productivity in determining pay, higher pay for tiring rather than skilled work, and action to take when pay is less than that deserved. In the income boundaries area, I chose RANGE (justifiable range of income). In the area dealing with income equity of national groups, I chose as groups union members, manual workers, MINLESS (minorities), and welfare clients; for income redistribution, the fairness of the tax system, TAXES (fairness of federal income tax schedule), ECONLIB (economic liberalism scale), PAYMARX (equality of income scale), and POLITLEAN (liberal-conservative preference); in the personal optimism area, BADTIME (scale of personal economic difficulties).

The variances explained by the independent variables were small. In fact, in six of the twenty beliefs, no variance appeared, and in ten items, it ranged from 6 to 16 percent. In most of the equations, only two or three of the eight independent variables were statistically significant, and they varied by beliefs. The beliefs with the largest variance in declining order were physically hard work should be paid more than skill, PAYMARX, ECONLIB, manual workers receive more pay than they deserve, MINLESS, and individual vs. group productivity for pay. Altogether, the strata were as powerful as other variables in explaining economic beliefs. Although strata, education, and work experience were statistically significant for half of the beliefs, for no single belief were all of the strata statistically significant. Self-employed, skilled, and nonskilled core appeared most frequently. Importantly, the R^2 for ECONLIB and POLITLEAN was 11 and 4 percent respectively. This suggests that economic ideology is better explained than radical-conservative political identification.

To conclude, working-class disagreements about economic justice in society are fewer and smaller than disagreements among the classes, yet systematic differences appeared among the working-class strata for almost two-fifths of the beliefs. In general, the lower the stratum, the more its members saw economic injustice as a societal feature. Regression analysis showed that we cannot explain much of the variance by critically important economic beliefs, but that the strata contribute as strongly (or as weakly) and as systematically as other variables in explaining beliefs.

Do Beliefs about Pay Inequity Generate System Blame?

Scholars have paid insufficient attention to the process of how group beliefs about inequities are generalized to blaming the system and wanting to change it (Della Fave, 1974; Kluegel and Smith, 1981). The idea that beliefs about personal incquities are transformed into system blame (Lane, 1962) is found in both Marxist and group-interest theories. Both theories hold that feelings about economic inequities help generate grievances about the functioning of other institutions, thus providing coherence to ideology and stimulating a desire to change the system. I took the position that when workers feel individual rather than occupational outrage about their pay level, they tend to blame their bosses or their bad luck, but when workers feel that their occupation is inequitably paid, they are more inclined to blame the system. Since beliefs about the inequity of one's own pay and beliefs about inequitable occupational pay correlated about .50 in all strata, workers apparently made some distinction between the fairness of their personal and occupational pay.

The research task then was to ascertain whether a sense of inequitable occupational earnings (OCCPAY) is associated with beliefs about injustice in other areas of economic ideology; e.g., the basis of occupational payment, the extent to which other occupations are over- or underpaid, the extent to which other classes, interest groups, and disprivileged workers are underpaid, the justice of the income gap between rich and poor, fairness in economic redistribution, and faith in economic justice in the nation. High correlations between equitable occupational pay and other measures of economic equity do not establish a causal relationship, but they are a prerequisite.

Data in Table 8.2 show that 30 to 50 percent of workers in each stratum believes that their occupation's pay level is less than it deserves. Using the 10 percent level of statistical significance, data in Table 8.3 show that equity of occupational pay failed to correlate with other beliefs in only thirteen of fifty-six instances. Yet for any individual stratum, only one-quarter of the items on the average were correlated with pay equity, and over half of these were below 0.11. Thus, there is limited evidence that beliefs about occupational pay equity spill over to beliefs about economic injustice in other areas. Importantly, for only two beliefs did all strata exhibit correlations with pay equity.

Evidence of ideological polarization would consist of a monotonic trend of statistically significant correlations of increasing or decreasing size as one moves from the self-employed to the nonskilled periphery strata. Polarization would also be indicated if the signs of the correlations of the top and bottom strata would differ or if the correlations of the higher strata were statistically significant while those of lower strata were not, or vice versa.

With these guideposts to detect trends, at most twenty of the fifty-six items showed some indication of stratal polarization (see Table 8.3). For most of the findings in Table 8.3, I ignored the foremen and considered the self-employed and the nonskilled periphery employees as polar groups. The correlations between beliefs about the fairness of one's own pay (OWNPAY) and that of one's occupational pay (OCCPAY) were moderately high, and they increased slightly for the lower strata. In the following discussion, a positive correlation signifies that workers who have a sense of inequitable occupational pay affirm a given belief; a negative correlation signifies a rejection. On two beliefs about the *basis* of equitable pay, the two nonskilled strata disagreed. While for nonskilled core workers inequitable occupational pay was associated with believing that seniority should count the most in determining pay, nonskilled periphery workers did not agree. Understandably, jobs in the core sector are usually protected by union seniority agreements while those in the periphery are not. For the nonskilled periphery workers, equitable occupational pay was negatively associated with the belief that heavy physical demands of the job should be rewarded more than skill or other job demands. Almost three-fifths of these workers are

Table 8.3. Pearsonian Correlations Between Occupational Earnings Equity (OCCPAY) and Economic Ideology Variables (demical points omitted)

Beliefs		Strata			
	Foremen	Self-Employed	Skilled	Nonskilled Core	Periphery
Income equity					
OWNPAY	58[a]	41[a]	52[a]	59[a]	57[a]
Pay equity					
Most important in pay					
Seniority	—	−01	04	20[b]	−22[b]
Physical demands	17	08	10	01	25[b]
Tiring works > skill	38[b]	−25[b]	14	17	06
Fairer if paid by need	43[a]	—	24[a]	48[a]	−28[a]
If pay undeserved, quit job	—	26[b]	−07	−02	−11
Income equity of national groups					
Corporations	39[b]	00	06	06	25[b]
Labor unions	−29	−24[b]	−02	−17	10
Women	27	29[a]	−20[a]	06	16
Blacks	—	02	07	−13	32[a]
Manual workers	—	−19	−19[a]	−19[b]	−13
Professionals	−17	−12	−11	−05	−24[a]
Welfare charts	36[b]	22[b]	−10	−05	15
MINLESS	−10	01	−29[a]	−14	−34[a]
Equity of Income Boundaries					
RICH	20	19	12	−24	−26[a]
Equity of Income Redistribution					
Tax system favors poor	−24	16	−21[a]	24[a]	−18
Tax system favors rich	—	−11	18[a]	−01	37[a]
Taxes worst for middle class	24	46[a]	19[a]	09	01
Government should guarantee health care	20	09	16[b]	25[a]	28[b]
Government should limit bus. profits	31	13	12	09	22[b]
Societal and personal optimism					
Income gap increasing	13	−06	11	−04	40[a]
BADTIME	−14	−34[a]	02	−21[b]	−19
Personally happy	−38[b]	−33[a]	−08	−16	−28[a]
N	20	45	99	77	62

[a]p = ≤ .05
[b]P = .06 − .10

women who probably resent the fact that men get paid more than women just because men do heavy physical labor. Skilled workers should share this belief, but they did not, probably because the skilled are mostly males. For all strata, except for the self-employed, inequitable occupational pay was associated with the belief that workers should be paid according to their needs, but again the reverse held for the nonskilled periphery employees. I cannot account for this pattern given the fact that the stratum is so poorly paid.

Apparently, beliefs about the fairness of occupational pay affected stratal views about the just pay of different national groups and classes. For the skilled, it was associated with the belief that manual workers, women, and welfare clients receive undeservedly low pay. Among the self-employed, it was associated with the belief that women and blacks are overpaid but that union members are underpaid. Among the skilled and nonskilled core workers, occupational pay inequity was related to seeing manual workers as underpaid. While for nonskilled periphery workers, the most insecure stratum, pay inequity tended to be associated with seeing corporations and blacks as having more money than they deserved, professionals and welfare clients were seen as receiving less than they deserved. In short, the skilled appeared to have the most systematic and non-punitive sense of class consciousness, the self-employed had some resentment toward the disprivileged groups, the nonskilled core workers were concerned only about manual workers, and the nonskilled periphery employees verged on being the most class conscious, having both resentment toward corporations and sympathy for disprivileged minorities and professionals.

In the area of economic redistribution, for workers in the three lowest strata pay inequity was associated with the belief that the government should guarantee adequate health care for everyone. While this should be expected (Huber and Form, 1973), it is surprising that other governmental programs for redistribution were not supported. Stratal responses to the fairness of the federal tax system conformed to theory. In the highest stratum, inequitable occupational pay for the self-employed was associated with the belief that the middle-income people (themselves) suffer the most from high taxes. Among the skilled, unjust pay beliefs were not only related to the belief that the tax system favors the rich, but to the belief that taxes disfavor the middle class and the poor. While for nonskilled core employees pay inequity was related only to the belief that poor are unfairly taxed, for nonskilled periphery workers pay inequity was systematically related to views of the system: the tax system favors the rich, government should limit the profits of business, and government should guarantee adequate health care for all.

Finally, beliefs in the area of personal and societal optimism were consistent with the above pattern. Only for the nonskilled periphery workers was inequitable pay associated with a dismal view of society: the income gap between poor and rich is increasing, and they were personally unhappy with the way things were going in their lives. The self-employed, who were experiencing financial difficulties, also were relatively unhappy.

Unions and Pay Equity[2]

Three hypotheses have been offered to explain how unions affect their members' beliefs about equitable pay. First, by raising their pay relative to the nonunionized, union members increase their sense of just payment (Survey Research Center, 1970). Second, union leaders instill in their members a sense of inequitable pay in order to mobilize them for battles against management (Freeman, 1978; Borjas, 1979). The third hypothesis, generally untested, is that unionization affects members' beliefs differentially. Those who profit most from union membership feel a sense of just pay, while those who profit less increase their sense of unjust pay. For example, the unskilled profit relatively more from unionization than do the skilled (Rosen, 1970). This increases the sense of pay equity for the unskilled while it lowers a sense of equity for the skilled. Similarly, blacks and women (Antos, Chandler, and Mellow, 1980) gain less from unionization than do whites and men. This leads women and blacks to feel a greater sense of pay injustice.

Curtin's (1977) national survey of income equity found that blue-collar union members felt significantly more satisfied with their pay than did nonunionized workers. Hammer (1978) found that the more unions succeeded in raising wages, the more their members felt a sense of pay satisfaction. But other variables intervene in the relationship. Lawler's (1971) extensive literature search showed that, holding income constant, higher levels of education, skill, and job performance lead to lower levels of job satisfaction. These findings generally support the basis thesis of equity theory, that people's sense of equity results from their balancing the ratio of their inputs (work) to outcomes (earnings) against their estimates of the ratios of other reference groups' inputs and outcomes (Adams and Freedman, 1976). The research also shows that employees prefer equity to equality or need as the basis of determining pay (Lane, 1959; Lawler, 1966; Della Fave, 1974; Curtin, 1977; Jasso and Rossi, 1977).

Using my Illinois survey of income equity, I constructed a path diagram with pay satisfaction as the dependent variable, inequitable personal pay (OWNPAY) and earnings as intervening variables, and union membership, education, and supervisory responsibility as independent variables. These five variables explained 22 percent of the variation in pay satisfaction, suggesting that other variables also influence pay satisfaction. Expectedly, the standardized coefficient for OWNPAY (.44) was positively related to pay satisfaction, and it was the only statistically significant path. Since job earnings were not related to pay satisfaction, clearly the sense of pay equity is more important than the level of pay. Importantly, union membership, educational level, and supervisory responsibility did not affect pay satisfaction.

Since union membership, controlling for education, vocational training, weeks worked, skill, sector, age, sex, and race increased workers' earnings by 6 percent, the question now arises: Does the union differentially affect the sense of fair pay of men and women, blacks and whites, and skilled and nonskilled workers? The regression equation for earnings showed that for blue-collar males, union membership increased their earnings by 8 percent, but it had no effect on women's earnings. Using personal pay equity as the dependent variable in the regression equation, union membership was found to have no effect, while earnings had a positive effect and supervisory responsibility, a negative one.

The path model for pay satisfaction was run separately for males and females, blacks and whites, and skilled and nonskilled workers. For both sexes, pay equity was the only statistically significant variable. Job earnings were significantly related to pay satisfaction for males but not for females. Supervisory responsibility had a strong negative impact on pay satisfaction for males and a weak positive one for females. Union membership had no impact for either sex. When pay equity was considered the dependent variable, again union membership had no impact on it for either sex.

A multiple regression analysis of personal pay equity was run for union and nonunion workers separately with skill, education, vocational training, age, sex, race, and marital status as independent variables. The purpose of this analysis was to discover whether the sense of pay equity of different groups is affected by the union environment. For nonunion workers, the sex variable did not reach statistical significance, but for unionized workers the sex variable was strong and statistically significant (standardized beta of .46). Thus, although women clearly gain economically by union membership, their sense of being inequitably paid was exacerbated. The situation for race almost paralleled that of sex. No relation existed between race and equity of pay beliefs among nonunionized workers, but among the unionized, the standardized beta for race was .52, strongly pointing to an increased sense of pay inequity among blacks. Finally, the impact of skill level on pay equity belief did not approach statistical significance. To conclude: of the three groups that display a tendency to be relatively deprived economically in the process of unionization, two of them, women and blacks, felt a greater sense of pay injustice when unionized. Perhaps the union, by proclaiming pay equity as a policy, increases the sense of economic injustice for those groups for whom pay equity can not be realized.

Conclusions

Data in this chapter show that the sense of economic injustice runs deep in American society. Workers believe that earnings are unjustly low, taxes favor the rich, the government needs to do more to redistribute income, and the economic future is bleak. Many systematic differences appear between the working class and other classes that point to a differentiated economic ideology; however, political polarization between the classes is relatively low.

Belief differences about economic justice among the working-class strata are not as common or as deep as between classes, but they are substantial and hierarchically arranged. The lower the strata, the more workers see economic injustice. My attempt to explain these differences was not very successful. Regression analysis showed some stratal effects.

The hypothesis, that beliefs about the justness of low occupational pay generate beliefs about justice in the economic system, received some unsystematic support. Beliefs about inequitable pay among the self-employed generated concern about their future economic status; for the skilled, inequitable pay was related to beliefs that economic inequities exist in society, especially for disprivileged minorities; for nonskilled core workers, inequitable pay beliefs were self-centered and related to punitive ideas about the income of minorities. Beliefs of nonskilled periphery workers approximated those of the Marxist proletariat that sees institutionally organized economic inequity, associates it with the power of the rich, and wants to change society to increase economic equity and personal happiness. Finally, the analysis of labor union effects suggested that its female and black members feel economic injustice more keenly than do its male and white members. Unions appear to have neglected workers in the periphery who are the most receptive to political mobilization, and unions have probably aggravated the sense of economic grievance among their women and black members.

The above picture points to considerable fragmentation in the economic ideology of the working class, but it does not point to persistent and systematic stratification of beliefs. If the working-class strata formed a hierarchy, then beliefs about personal and societal economic injustice would increase from self-employed to the nonskilled periphery strata. Though this pattern clearly occurred more often than by chance, I could not explain why and where it occurred. For each stratum, beliefs about inequitable occupational pay did not increase a sense of injustice in the important belief areas of: justness of pay in the occupational structure, equality of pay scale, equity of federal income tax rates, the tactics to take against the employer when pay is unjust, the equitable range in income between rich and poor, economic liberalism scale, and conservative or liberal political orientation. Perhaps this pattern reflects little variation in beliefs about the equity of occupational pay. The most anomolous finding was that the differences that did appear within and between strata were not associated with liberal or conservative political self-labeling. Either these labels mean something different to workers than they do to politicians, or differences in workers' politics are not linked to issues of economic justice. Possibly workers in all strata resist the systematic organization of both their economic and political beliefs, a problem I take up in the next chapter.

Notes

1. I am grateful to Seymour Sudman of the Survey Research Laboratory of the University of Illinois for designing the sample.
2. I am indebted to Gary L. Miller for research work on this subject.

9

Political Cleavage at the Local Union Level

Source of Political Cleavages

Most students of union politics have analyzed how members vote in national elections and what they want in social welfare legislation (see Ra, 1979). These studies say little about the politics of members in different industries and occupations and even less about the politics of skill, sex, racial, regional, and other groups. Moreover, researchers rarely report on the disagreements between members and their officers on the issues that are most important to the members. Consequently, no one, not even union officers, can provide a reasonably accurate picture of the diverse political views of union members. Without this picture, a strategy for building political solidarity can hardly be realized.

National studies have shown that union members strongly support governmental aid for medical care, old age assistance, unemployment, education, and housing (Campbell, et al., 1964; Pomper, 1975). However, as McClosky (1960) reported more than two decades ago, most workers, irrespective of union or nonunion status party affiliation, or political involvement, approve of these social welfare programs. Evidence that union members endorse liberal legislation on other matters is far from clear. Organizations in the Democratic party coalition call on the unions to support them on such issues as civil liberties, civil rights, foreign relations, and pollution. These issues often have low salience for both unionized and nonunionized workers. When they are salient, union members may differ from their officers and not heed their advice. The questions raised in this chapter are, What issues are important to different segments of the rank and file? and What positions do they take on them?

The issues that appeal most to workers deal with problems they encounter daily in the plant and community (Bok and Dunlop, 1970). In the plant, the issues are level of wages, occupational wage differentials, fringe benefits, overtime pay, dues to the international union, health and safety, occupational training for women and minorities, and contributions to local political campaigns. Important community issues include level of real estate taxes, tax support for public housing, busing to achieve racially balanced schools, racial integration of neighborhoods, and the size of the welfare load. Not all of these issues divide voters along party lines, but they may divide workers from different occupational, ethnic, racial, and political backgrounds, and they may divide rank and file union members from their local and national officers. No one has systematically analyzed union members' disagreements on the issues that interest them most, how members differ from their officers on certain issues, and how these divisions affect the political mobilization of the working class. Although the data are limited, this chapter focuses on studies that deal with union politics at the local level. This approach is necessary for two reasons. First, most of the literature on union politics comes in the form of observations, interpretations, and judgmental commentaries about union officers. The assumption is that the officers know how their members think. Second, union officers formally speak for the membership, but they rarely report disagreements. Therefore, neither commentators nor union officers can explain why members vacillate in supporting the unions' public stands.

I examined the research literature from 1960 to 1980 to identify empirical studies of local union politics. "Recent Publications" titles of the *Industrial and Labor Relations Review* were examined as well as titles in the *Social Science and Humanities Index* for 1974-80. Of the 101 titles that seemed appropriate, only 35 turned out to have some empirical basis. Of these, only 16 were serious enough to merit intensive study. Most articles were commentaries by partisan observers (Catchpole, 1968; Sexton and Sexton, 1971). Articles in socialist journals, notably *Dissent* on problems of black workers (Brooks, 1970; Sexton, 1971) or of union democracy (Kornblum, 1971), were discussions that offered insight into political organizations rather than political issues (Polaskoff, 1959; Gamm, 1979; Cook, 1963). Historical studies of labor's struggles (Foster, 1975; Nash, 1977) gave little insight into current issues. Finally, studies of labor's stand on racial integration (Marshall, 1963, 1967) and the Vietnam War (Wright, 1972) did not examine internal disagreements.

The studies I selected for intensive examination were based on surveys of union members. The United Automobile Workers (UAW) figured in six studies and the International Typographical Union (ITU) in one, while other unions were represented in multi-union samples. Altogether, these unions comprise an unrepresentative group of politically active and liberal unions, yet the majority of unions and union members in the AFL–CIO today belong to ex-AFL craft unions that tend to be more politically conservative than are the ex-CIO unions (Wilson, 1979).

A theory that explains political disagreements should guide the analysis of local political studies. Unfortunately, a refined theory is not yet available, but the bases used to stratify the working class should provide clues to their political disagreements (see Chapter 2). For example, very few of the self-employed and foremen are unionized, but those who are should be slightly more conservative than the skilled employees whom they most resemble in social origin, social status, and earnings. The skilled, in turn, are more conservative than are the less skilled workers. The skilled are less affected by their employment sector and union membership because they have greater individual bargaining power (see Chapter 6). The skilled are primarily concerned with protecting their economic and status advantages, and thus they should be more conservative than the nonskilled. Since the skilled are most threatened by affirmative action programs, they oppose sex and racial equality more than do members of other strata. Because the skilled hold a disproportionately large share of local union offices, their resistance to affirmative action programs should be especially evident at the local level.

Nonskilled core workers, especially those in the original CIO unions, should represent the basic kernel of liberal support for union goals. As relatively unskilled but relatively well paid workers who have profited the most from union membership, they depend on their officers for political guidance. Therefore, whatever their race, ethnicity, sex, education, or seniority, they should support the union's egalitarian goals in the plant. Although they consistently support the Democratic party, their involvement in community politics is probably low, but they may resist the racial integration of schools and neighborhoods in order to retain their advantages over racial minorities.

Women, blacks, and Hispanics constitute a large segment of organized nonskilled periphery workers. They probably hold the most liberal political beliefs in the working class (see Chapter 8) even though they may not be aware of the union's official positions. Although less privileged by unionization than are other workers, nonskilled periphery employees sense that their interests are served by any group that supports liberal legislation, but this stratum is perhaps the least informed about politics. Like the marginally employed, they are apathetic about plant, community, and national political issues because they feel powerless to do much about them (Huber and Form, 1973; Schlozman and Verba, 1979: 315).

The Kornhauser and Colleagues (1956) Pivotal Study

This early study of 828 Detroit UAW members is reviewed here not only because it is one of the most elaborate studies of local unions, but also because it has been used as a model for other studies. UAW members were asked about their voting behavior, political involvement, trust of labor, authoritarianism, social alienation, and labor's political orientation. Their responses were analyzed for age, sex, race, ethnicity, occupation, religion, income, socioeconomic status, social-class identification, family income, home ownership, father's occupation, father's political identification, birthplace, years of residence in Detroit, and seniority. The study's main findings now seem commonplace. Union members support the union's political positions, but they are not very active politically. Blacks, ethnics, and young workers of lower socioeconomic status vote Democratic and support the union's political recommendations more than do other union members.

The study had some important shortcomings. Despite the detailed analysis, the authors presented no explanation for political disagreements, and their own biases affected the interpretation of the data. Moreover, the findings were obscured by the method of analyzing the data. Each dependent political variable was separately analyzed by workers' social characteristics. This piecemeal approach resulted in some anomalous findings. For example, both workers with a strong prolabor and a nonlabor orientation were better educated, more highly skilled, and more highly paid than the average worker. Without multivariate analysis, the relative contributions of the variables remained unknown. The independent variables were not intercorrelated, and some socioeconomic status variables were constructed by assigning scores to individuals which were derived from aggregate residential data. Finally, since the characteristics of the total UAW membership were not known, the representativeness of the sample remained unknown.

Ignoring these shortcomings, does the Kornhauser study help illuminate working class politics? The members' political beliefs and behavior must be evaluated against the goals of the UAW officers. The three objectives of the UAW leadership were clear: members should support the Democratic party and Stevenson for president against Eisenhower and the Republicans, trust the union's political recommendations, and be active in politics to increase labor's political influence. In the interviews, members were asked about the union's three objectives. From their responses, four indices of their political orientations were constructed: prolabor and politically involved, prolabor and apolitical, nonlabor (i.e., not prolabor) and politically involved, and nonlabor (not prolabor) and apolitical. These orientations provide cues to the political differentiation of the working class.

My theory states that support for the union's position should decrease as the worker's socioeconomic status rises. Skilled native-born workers should be the least prolabor or the most opposed to the union's position, and the most politically active. Nonskilled second generation ethnic males who are well educated (those resembling core workers), should be the most prolabor and politically active. Nonskilled, poorly educated men and especially women (those resembling the nonskilled periphery stratum) should be prolabor but politically apathetic.

The data (Kornhauser et al., 1956:217–44) partially support the theory. Surprisingly, in one of the nation's most militant and liberal unions, only 55 percent of the respondents were prolabor and 45 percent were nonlabor (i.e., not prolabor) in their political orientations. Workers with *nonlabor political* orientations formed the highest status group. More than others, they were skilled or clerical, male, white, Protestant, urban, and native-born. Also more than others, they were homeowners, had higher family incomes, and were fathers who identified themselves as Republicans.

The *prolabor politicals* represented a middle status group, less skilled than the nonlabor politicals and derived from families with lower than average incomes. They were predominately male, young, highly educated, and had fathers who were semiskilled workers who identified themselves as Democrats. The prolabor politicals resembled workers in the nonskilled core stratum. The *prolabor apoliticals* formed the lowest status group. Although more favorable to the union's political stance than were the other types, they were the lowest paid, the least skilled, and had the lowest tenure. This group had the highest representation of women, Catholics, and recent arrivals to Detroit from small towns, the South, and eastern Europe. In their social characteristics they most resembled nonskilled-periphery workers (see Table 2.1).

Finally, *nonlabor apoliticals* differed little from nonlabor politicals, but the latter were less skilled, less educated, less urban, and less

Protestant in background. The nonlabor apoliticals represented a somewhat higher status group than the prolabor apoliticals, being more skilled, male, white, Protestant, and older. They had higher incomes, higher rates of home ownership, and more seniority. In summary, UAW members were stratified from high to low into nonlabor politicals, prolabor politicals, nonlabor apoliticals, and prolabor apoliticals, with the two nonlabor types resembling each other more than the two prolabor groups.

Other UAW Studies

How do these findings stand up in light of subsequent UAW studies? In 1956, Sheppard and Masters (1959) interviewed 156 Detroit UAW workers, using many of the questions from the 1956 Kornhauser and colleagues' survey. Although statistics were not reported, the findings partially confirmed those of the earlier study. The politically active were young men with higher incomes and education, resembling the prolabor apoliticals. But apparently all members endorsed and trusted the political decisions and recommendations of their officers. The authors present a picture of a politically cohesive union with no cleavages between officers and members. The small sample and the absence of statistical analysis raise questions about the reliability of some of the findings.

The most intensive analysis of the political culture of a UAW local is Blume's 1967 Toledo study. He interviewed 314 members and reported his findings in three publications (Blume, 1970, 1973a, and 1973b). Blume's research has four advantages over earlier UAW studies. First, workers were asked to respond to a range of political issues that extended beyond those taken by UAW leaders. Second, the union had taken a stand on an open housing referendum about to be voted upon. Workers were asked to evaluate the union's stand and present their own views. Third, Blume analyzed the relationship between members' beliefs about the extent of democracy in their local and members' support of its political stands. Fourth, the results were subjected to statistical tests. In short, this study examined consensus between union members and officers on a range of issues that dealt with the union's behavior on the factory floor, its success in operating democratically, and its position on issues thought to be important for welding a politically cohesive working class. A major shortcoming of the research was its failure to analyze political differences among the members.

Though many studies claim that members go along with the union's endorsement of political candidates, Blume's (1970) research showed that only a small minority of 15 percent knew of the endorsements. When members were asked whether they would follow the endorsements, over one-half indicated that they would not, less than one-quarter said they would most of the time, and one-quarter would do so occasionally. As in the Kornhauser (1956) study, one-half of the members did not trust the union's recommendations. Similarly, in Toledo's lowest stratum, the prolabor politicals (those over fifty years old, the poorly educated blacks, and long-term union members) were most likely to follow the local's recommendations.

Not surprisingly, almost all members agreed with union officers' positions on local plant issues involving higher wages, better working conditions, better health and pension benefits, and guaranteed annual wages (only 59 percent). Except for minimum wages, where almost 70 percent approved of the union's stand, barely a majority backed the union's position on repeal of the Taft-Hartley Act, crime control, water pollution, open housing, and federal aid to education. In short, in areas of economic self-interest, consensus was high; where self-interest was not obvious, as in legislation important to labor's liberal coalition partners, barely half of the members went along.

In 1967, the city of Toledo conducted an open housing referendum. The UAW openly and strongly urged its members to support the measure (Blume, 1973a). Though a bare majority in the UAW local agreed that blacks needed better housing and that the union should participate in the open housing campaign, three-fifths were not aware of the union's position on the referendum and a majority did not know that union officials were actively engaged in the fight. More important, one-half opposed the union's open housing recommendation, less than one-quarter supported it, and the rest were undecided. Those in opposition were high school graduates of middle socioeconomic status who had little interest in politics—the nonlabor apoliticals in the Kornhauser (1956) study. But contrary to that study, referendum supporters were politically oriented, older retirees, with little education and low income. Except for being politically oriented, these members resembled the prolabor apoliticals in the Kornhauser study. Unexpectedly, home ownership did not influence a member's position on the open housing issue. In short, the study showed that membership consensus on the racial equality issue was not high, and that only a minority approved and acted in line with their officers' recommendation. The supporters appeared to be a low socioeconomic stratum of union members, and the opponents, a somewhat higher stratum.

Blume's (1973b) third article examined the relationship between members' beliefs about democracy in the union and other political variables. Members' perceptions that the union was democratic were related to their interest in and identification with the union, but not to their political awareness. Those who believed that the members control the union tended to support the union's position on all political issues and endorsements. Expectedly, member satisfaction with the steward was not related to any political variable.

Three conclusions may be drawn from this study. First, members' positions on factory issues are not related to their politics, and members do not see the steward as representing the union's political position. These findings point to the absence of a labor mentality among the workers. Second, the degree of democracy in the union that members perceive is not related to their awareness of the union's political stands. This suggests that members feel that officers can take political stands without member approval. Third and most important, even though members acknowledge the union's right to be involved in politics, many vote against the union's recommendations. This suggests that members consider union politics to be the business or property of their officers, and that they, as members, are not bound by official political recommendations. In short, although the union's political stand is legitimate, the stand has no binding authority on the members. All three conclusions point to missing ingredients needed to build united political unionism (Ollman, 1970).

Another UAW study suggests that members with above-average social status most oppose the politics of their officers. Blaine and Zeller (1965) examined the background of UAW members who appealed to the union's Public Review Board between 1957 and 1965 to reverse decisions made by their officers. In the follow-up questionnaire sent to appealers and a random sample of nonappealers, the authors found that the appealers resembled the independently minded skilled workers' faction in industrial unions described by Weber (1963) and the nonlabor politicals described by Kornhauser and colleagues (1965). Compared to the average UAW member, appealers were more highly skilled, had higher incomes, were older, and more of them lived in the city. The appealers were also more active in community organizations, more politically independent, and more involved in party politics than were nonappealers. Significantly, about two-thirds of the appealers claimed to be leaders of minority factions in their locals. In short, appealers resembled union activists and leaders described in other studies (Lipset, et al., 1956; Seidman, et al., 1958), but appealers differed on the greater stress they placed on the rights of minorities. The mobilization of this high status minority as an opposition faction in the UAW reached its peak at the 1974 national convention, where skilled workers won the right to veto contract clauses that might affect them adversely (*Wall Street Journal,* 1975). This victory signaled a movement among skilled workers in other industrial unions to improve their position at the expense of younger, less skilled workers (Harris, 1983).

Does such a minority see itself in opposition to officers on union issues, as socially superior to the membership, and as politically removed from it? That is, does a link exist between political opposition inside the union, independent social status claims, and political opposition outside the union? A few studies in both craft and industrial unions suggest such linkages. Kornhauser (1956:229, 249) reported that 33 percent of the nonlabor politicals identified with the middle class compared to 18 percent of the prolabor politicals, and that 61 percent of the nonlabor politicals and only 6 percent of the prolabor politicals voted for Eisenhower. This class-party split also appeared in a New York City local dominated by craft workers. Not surprisingly, Levine (1963) found that older, highly skilled Protestant workers who identified with the middle class also identified with the Republican party. Significantly, high participation in union activities did not change the political identification of this group; that is, union participation had no spillover effect on political socialization, on identifying with and voting for the Democratic party. In short, the political cleavage between high-status, skilled, and somewhat conservative union members and their local union officers is counterbalanced by the support given the officers by a small minority of prolabor activists and by prolabor apoliticals who constitute the bulk of membership (Kornhauser, et al., 1956).

Finally, Sidney Peck (1963) conducted group discussions with 184 rank and file stewards from sixteen industrial unions in Milwaukee. The majority of these stewards were relatively young, (under forty) native-born workers of German Catholic background. They had high school educations and were doing unskilled and semiskilled work. Though Peck unfortunately heeded Eby's (1950) advice not to engage in statistical analysis, his account clearly shows that the stewards were activists with a strong prolabor orientation.

Two major conclusions emerged from Peck's discussions with these activists. First, they did not see any incompatibility between job-conscious unionism and class-conscious political action. They saw the Democratic party as the workingman's party and were firmly committed to it and to union political action (Peck, 1963:341). Second, " . . . among rank-and-file union leaders there exists genuine confidence in higher officials of the labor movement. . . . Sharp political differences between rank-and-file grievers and top union leaders simply do not exist" (p. 344). "Because he (the steward) functions as a spokesman in this small realm of industrial conflict, he receives the praise and adulation of labor officials and labor educators. The class bond, which unites the rank-and-file leader to the departmental workers on a personal intimate level in the shop, is notably weakened by these status concerns. While top officials are rarely subjected to intense criticism, union stewards denounce the rank-and-file as apathetic, ungrateful, uncooperative, indifferent" (p. 345). This study shows that where local political activists are politically united with higher union officers, both are politically estranged from the bulk of the membership.

Issue Cleavages and Consensus

Although the studies to be reviewed contain no information on the politics of union subgroups, they do permit a comparison of the political views of the members and their officers. The question here is, to what extent do officers get member support for liberal causes — causes that help deprived segments of the working class, especially blacks, minorities, the poor, and women? To create a class-conscious membership, officers must convince members that a relationship exists between their economic issues in the plant and legislative goals to help unorganized workers — especially those in the lower third of the income distribution. In addition, members should be aware of the issues that their officers support and follow official recommendations. The six studies that deal with rank and file and officer relations vary in sample size, unions represented, and geographic region. They are 1.) Blume (1973a), 314 interviews with UAW members in Toledo, Ohio; 2.) Bartlett (1966), 553 interviews with "local-wide" or "shop-floor" leaders from 343 locals of nine national unions; 3.) Barkin (1967), 1,700 interviews with members of twelve international unions; 4.) Dix and Flory (1970), 213 questionnaires from members of the West Virginia Federation of Labor; 5.) Cook (1975), 478 questionnaires from union members in Monogalia-Preston County, West Virginia; 6.) Tapper and Neal (1977), 201 questionnaires from West Virginia AFL-CIO members.

　　These studies represent a sample of liberal industrial unions. Comparing the results of these studies is difficult because researchers probed member attitudes on political issues that were popular at the moment. However, the issues can be classified into four broad areas: (1) economic issues of wages, working conditions, pensions, and guaranteed annual wage; (2) legislation dealing with social security, regulation of unions, racial equality, and other issues; (3) relations between political parties and unions; and (4) consumer issues such as pollution, compulsory auto insurance, and national resources.

Since no difficulty is encountered in determining the official union position on any issue, to what extent does the membership endorse the positions of its officers? I arbitrarily defined consensus as 60 percent or more of the members supporting their officers' positions. Officers can hardly claim to represent members if only a bare majority support them.

Many studies have shown high consensus between officers and members on traditional bargaining goals. Blume (1973a) found that nine-tenths of the members endorsed traditional collective bargaining goals of higher wages, better working conditions, and improved fringe benefits (pensions). Yet, a guaranteed annual wage, a non-traditional bargaining goal, was supported by only 57 percent of the UAW membership, just shy of the 60 percent required for consensus. Apparently, even the union's economic goals must remain traditionally narrow to obtain broad membership support.

In the five studies of Table 9.1, three union goals (raising the minimum wage, expanding workmen's compensation, and permitting public employees to bargain collectively) received substantial membership support (over 70 percent). Yet even here, members of individual unions deviated from the general pattern. Bartlett (1966) reported that a majority of the Wisconsin sample of the American Federation of Teachers (AFT) opposed increasing the minimum wage. Less than half of the workers in International Ladies Garment Workers Union (ILGWU) approved of spending union dues to influence minimum wage legislation, even though ILGWU wages were below the proposed minimum. Although leaders of the labor movement have consistently opposed right-to-work laws, a substantial number of AFT delegates, Communication Workers of America (CWA) members, and the ILGWU members from right-to-work states opposed the repeal of right-to-work laws. Finally, in none of the three studies that surveyed members on the repeal of Taft-Hartley Act regulating union membership did as many as 60 percent of the members approve (Blume, 1973a; Barkin 1967; Dix and Flory, 1970). In short, while most members support the union on legislation bearing on narrow economic issues, some individual unions stand in opposition and block consensus.

The remaining issues deal with legislation to help all workers, regardless of their union or other social status characteristics. The issues include expanding federal support for medical aid, legislation to equalize educational opportunity (school busing, federal aid to education), open housing, income supplements to poor families, and gun control. With few exceptions, member support for these goals failed to reach a 60 percent consensus. On the issues of open housing, gun control, and welfare aid to the poor, the majority opposed the legislation.

Table 9.1. Six Local Union Studies of Member Opinions on Political Issues (percent supporting)

			Studies[a]			
Issues	1	2	3	4	5	6
Legislation						
Raise minimum wage	—	49–93	71	87	—	83
Expand Workmen's Compensation	—	—	76	89	—	86
Public employee bargaining	—	—	—	—	79	68
Repeal Taft-Hartley Act	43	—	54	57	—	—
Expand medicare to all retirees	61	32–90	74	—	—	—
Federal Aid to education	—	51	67	—	—	—
Federal crime control	53	—	—	37[b]	—	41[b]
Open housing laws	21–39	—	43	41	—	50
School busing	—	—	—	—	—	48
Government owned transportation	—	—	—	—	—	51
Welfare reform needed	—	—	—	—	—	71
Union-Party Relations						
Unions should endorse Democrats	8[c]	—	55	42–54	74	—
Union dues for political action	48–68	39–79	—	—	59	33–48
Aware of union backed candidates	15	—	—	—	73	—
Democratic party identification	—	—	58	—	—	60
Consumer Protection						
More pollution laws	51	—	90	—	—	—
Compulsory auto insurances	—	—	—	97	—	91
Tax on exploitation of natural resources	—	—	—	90	—	91
Prohibit strip mining (no)	—	—	—	—	—	59

[a](1) Blume (1973a); (2) Bartlett (1966); (3) Barkan (1967); (4) Dix and Flory (1970); (5) Cook (1975); (6) Tapper and Neal (1972).
[b]Gun control
[c]Only Democrats

Bartlett's (1966) study of local union leaders suggests that evidence of their political liberalism must be taken with a grain of salt. Although nine-tenths of the leaders favored Medicare or extending free hospital and medical benefits to retirees, only 54 percent wanted these benefits to go to all retirees automatically and 32 percent believed that benefits should go only to retirees who proved financial need. Bartlett concluded that the union's position that Medicare is a retiree's right did not receive widespread approval of local union leaders, let alone approval of the membership.

A basic plank of the AFL–CIO's Committee on Political Education (COPE) is that unions have the right to endorse candidates for public office (Greenstone, 1969), yet in three of four studies that examined members' views on the subject (see Table 9.1), less than 60 percent agreed. Evidence that members vote for union-backed candidates fluctuates, but in the four studies that investigated the issue, member defection for some union-backed candidates was about 40 percent. While the great majority of members are aware that the union endorses candidates, Blume's (1973a) UAW Toledo study showed that only 15 percent were able to name such candidates. Blume (p. 143) questioned Barkin's (1967) assertion, based on a national survey of the AFL–CIO members, that members accept political direction from the union. When less than 60 percent of the members vote in national elections, when less than 60 percent identify themselves as Democrats, and when only 33 percent approve of spending union dues for political action, one can hardly conclude that members follow the political direction of their officers.[1]

Finally, substantial consensus exists between members and their officers on consumer legislation that deals with pollution, compulsory auto insurance, taxation on the extraction of mineral resources, and so on. Although only two studies (Dix and Flory, 1970; Tapper and Neal, 1977) report on these issues, further studies are unlikely to report different findings. Greenstone (1969) asserted that these consumer issues constitute the bases of a new class politics in the United States, but evidence is lacking that supporters of specific consumer interests unite to support legislation to help organized labor, the poor, and other disprivileged groups. Solidarity on consumer issues does not necessarily build class-oriented political discipline among interest groups.

Conclusions

A review of local political studies exposes substantial cleavages among union members on a range of community and national political issues. Opposition to the union's political stand is highest among the skilled, who are the most active politically. Strongest agreement for the union's political positions exists among the low-status members who resemble the nonskilled periphery stratum in their social characteristics and their political apathy. Members who most resemble nonskilled core workers fall in between the two groups in their support of unions' goals and in their degree of political involvement.

The rank and file and union officers agree on economic bargaining objectives, social security, and some consumer protection legislation. Consensus is uneven but relatively high for government legislation that bears directly on the economic well-being of the membership: minimum wages, workers' disability compensation, health protection, and union rights. Consensus is lacking for legislation to improve the economic, social, and civic life of the most dispossessed segments of the working class. Finally, member consensus is unstable regarding union-party relations. Substantial support does not exist for unions to consistently back Democrats for office, for members to vote for union-backed candidates, and for the union to spend dues money to support party candidates. When officials single out "good" or "bad" candidates for public office, members do not know who they are. Even when the rank and file support the candidates and political objectives of their officers, it is not clear that they do so because of the union's stated stands.

These conclusions are based mostly on studies of locals in relatively liberal industrial unions. A more representative selection of locals would likely show more and deeper political fragmentation of the rank and file and deeper cleavages between union members and officers. Union members comprise a relatively privileged minority of the working class. Perhaps the cleavages that are found among union members are even more apparent in the working class as a whole. I pursue this subject in the next chapter.

Note

1. *Dissent* (1981:10) reported: "Meanwhile blue-collar voters nationally divided almost evenly between Carter and Reagan and less than half of all union-household voters backed Carter, a sharp decline from 62 percent in 1976, according to the polls."

10

National Voting Behavior and Politics

Changes in Working-Class Politics

Scholars and political activists have long noted that, in contrast to most industrial societies, the United States does not have a strong socialist or labor party. Although individual scholars have emphasized different reasons for this exception, they have agreed on the central causes. Lipset's (1977) overview of this issue stressed that such diverse writers as Marx and Engels (1936), Sombart (1906), Mowry, (1968), and Harrington (1972) have agreed on the main causes: the absence of a feudal tradition, ethnic diversity, religious conflicts, nonideological unionism, individualism, low class consciousness, the promise of upward mobility, and business repression.

These historical conditions have changed and, with them, the political landscape. Four crises have undermined traditionally stated grounds for American exception: two world wars, the Great Depression, and the tumult of the late 1960s. The reduction of immigration after World War I had the effect of creating an English-speaking, second generation industrial proletariat in the United States. The Great Depression not only dampened the ideology of upward mobility, it also spawned CIO industrial unions that challenged the traditional AFL policy of non-party alignment. After World War II, the CIO abandoned the policy of political neutrality and launched political action committees. Thus, the emergence of an English-speaking proletariat, its sufferings during the Great Depression, and its organization into politically active unions dampened ethnic, religious, and other worker rivalries. The merging of the AFL and CIO and their political committees in 1955 into the Committee on Political Education (COPE) permanently committed labor to the Democratic party, even though non-party alignment remained a whispered policy.

Finally, the civil rights movement, the Vietnam war, and other events in the 1960s further consolidated the political alignments of blacks, middle-class liberals, and intellectuals in the welfare state coalition of the Democratic party. As the largest, most active, and biggest financial contributor to the party, American labor appeared to have achieved what European labor had earlier attained: a party committed to advancing the well-being of the working class. Because most European social democratic parties moved toward a centrist political position as they assumed governmental control, some observers concluded that differences between these parties and the American Democratic party were more nominal than real (Greenstone, 1969; Wilson, 1977; Lipset, 1977).

Despite this history, no strong socialist wing has emerged in the Democratic party, nor have American socialist parties grown substantially. American labor leadership has been vociferously anti-socialist and anticommunist, a position it shares with most workers. The Democratic party, composed of diverse and often competing interests, has not achieved the class solidarity of European social democratic parties. Despite COPE's increasing wealth, strength, and experience, it has not been able to deliver consistent labor support for Democratic presidential candidates. The Republican victories of Eisenhower, Nixon, and Reagan signified that organized labor is not cohesive and that Labor cannot convince nonunionized workers to support the party come what may. This is not surprising given labor's inability to unionize them. In short, Labor has failed to become the political centrifuge of the American working class. Its shrinking influence is demonstrated in legislative defeats in the areas closest to its interests: namely, rescinding restrictive union legislation. Yet labor's newspapers reveal that labor's leaders remain committed to the liberal agenda: supporting ERA, financial aid to cities, civil rights, school integration, affirmative action, ecological preservation, and transfer payments to the poor and deprived segments of the working class. When labor pursues these goals along with liberals, environmentalists, women's organizations, civil rights groups, and others, the coalition is often politically effective; when labor pursues its own trade union objectives, the coalition breaks up and labor is often isolated and impotent.

So the dilemma remains. Despite labor's historically improved political position, its national leaders cannot exert sufficient influence on constituent unions and their members, let alone on the unorganized, to consistently support the Democratic party and liberal causes (see Chapter 9). Why can't the national leadership convince its members that their welfare is furthered by consistent support for the liberal coalition in the Democratic party? Unfortunately, social scientists do not know much about political communication in the house of labor. Although this subject should be of central concern to social scientists, research on the topic has declined since the 1950s. All of the reasons for this decline are not known, but it is clear that union officials, perhaps sensitive to the charge that they disregard the views of members, have not permitted scholars to study their internal politics. In addition, declining union membership and the declining power of labor may have chilled scholarly interest in labor politics.

In the last systematic assessment of labor's electoral politics, Scoble (1963:154) speculated that while the upward mobility of labor leaders has made them more liberal and ideologically committed, it has also estranged them from the views of the rank and file. Parenthetically, Michels (1959) observed just the opposite tendency in Europe. The increased political involvement and power of its labor leaders has made them more conservative (see also Edelman, 1969). As suggested, in the United States, events since the Great Depression have created an increasingly politicized labor leadership, but union members and unorganized workers have remained somewhat detached from the leadership and divided. Roberts (1976) observed that many scholars want unions and the working class to be cohesive and therefore think they really are, thus ignoring the sources of political cleavages.

How can the working class remain divided now that more of it is native born and now that organized labor is more politically organized than ever before? Possibly, although today's working-class cleavages are not as strongly based on ethnic, religious, and other traditional identities, new cleavages have appeared that may have equally fateful political consequences. In earlier chapters I have emphasized that today's class divisions reflect changes in the economy, changes in the composition of the labor force, and new splits between unionized and nonunionized workers. These trends bear a brief review.

Changes in the U.S. economy have split the labor market into a more affluent oligopolistic core and less affluent competitive periphery. This crude dichotomy points to class divisions that may have political effects. Thus, 70 percent of workers in core industries are unionized compared to 36 percent in the periphery. Workers in the two sectors have become socially and demographically stratified. In the core, workers are predominately white males, while in the periphery they are predominately women, Hispanics, blacks, and other minorities. Skilled workers, although slightly more numerous in the periphery than in the core, are predominately white males who earn considerably more than do the nonskilled in either sector, whether or not they are unionized.

After the CIO appeared, labor leaders increasingly saw themselves as representing the social welfare interests of both organized and unorganized workers, but tensions within and between both groups persisted. Hostility between the skilled and nonskilled did not disappear with the merger of the AFL and CIO (Weber, 1963). Even within industrial unions, the skilled struggled to maintain wage differentials between themselves and the less skilled. Responding to the pressures of the nonskilled majority after World War II, union officers permitted differentials to decline until 1960 when skilled workers began to rebel and threaten to disaffiliate (*Wall Street Journal*, 1975). Since then, although differentials stabilized or even reversed somewhat (Schoeplein, 1977), skilled workers still distrust their leaders. In the erstwhile AFL unions, craft workers still jealously guard their wage differentials and try to preserve their jobs for white males.

The very success of organized labor in raising wages has increased economic inequality in the working class. Kahn's important studies (1977, 1978, 1980) showed that labor's economic success tends to depress earnings of the unorganized in cities where labor is strongest, a fact that does not escape the unorganized (Blumberg, 1980). Moreover, opinion polls show that the public now regards labor as a gigantic, self-interested pressure group, much like big business which enriches itself while the public suffers from inflation and unemployment (Lipset and Schneider, 1983). Labor's demand for higher wages and more protective legislation is viewed as self-serving and unwarranted. In sum, new forces have forged new working-class cleavages: the rise of the dual labor market, the socio-demographic stratification of workers along sectoral lines, economic tensions between the skilled and nonskilled in unions, and widening economic inequality between the organized and unorganized.

Yet, solid evidence that these structural changes have widened political cleavages in the working class is not yet available. Therefore, this chapter focuses on the electoral politics of working-class strata over the past two decades. The data are derived from the biennial surveys (1966–78) of the Survey Research Center (SRC) of the University of Michigan and the General Social Surveys (GSS) of presidential elections (1968–80) by the National Opinion Research Corporation. Unlike the studies of local union politics in Chapter 9, these national surveys permit a direct analysis of the political behavior of working-class strata.

Unfortunately, these surveys were not designed to answer political questions of perennial interest to the working class. Even when they were asked, they were rarely repeated and, when repeated, the question wording was changed, making the data noncomparable. I could not use single surveys because the number of foremen, self-employed, and skilled workers in the samples was too small to permit making reliable generalizations. Therefore I combined similar questions that appeared in several surveys. This procedure assumes that workers do not substantially change their views or behavior from one election to another. Later, I examine this assumption as a research question. However, Schlotzman and Verba (1979:135) found that 85 percent of all voters maintained their party preferences in three surveys that covered a four-year span. The figure was even higher for those who strongly identified with a party. The corresponding figure for social-class identification was 75 percent. These figures may be even higher for blue-collar workers.

The questions that surveys repeat most often deal with party preference, party vote, voting participation, and class identification. When the Survey Research Center (SRC) and the General Social Survey (GSS) asked the same questions with the same wording and when the distribution of the responses did not differ as measured by the chi-square test (.05), I combined the surveys in order to have more reliable data. When the wording of the questions and the response patterns differed, I present the results of the two surveys separately. Cases that were dropped because the respondent's stratum could not be ascertained or because questions were not answered considerably reduced the number of usable cases in some instances.

The Politics of Working-Class Strata: Expected Findings

Hamilton (1972) and others have shown that skill and income only slightly affect workers' politics. I reexamined this question, using the five strata of the working class: foremen, self-employed, skilled, nonskilled core, and nonskilled periphery. The five strata roughly correspond to a continuum of earnings from high to low. I expected the higher strata to be more conservative than the lower strata in their politics. The higher the stratum, the less its members should identify with the Democratic party and vote Democratic. I also expected workers in higher strata to change party preference and party vote more often than workers in lower strata. The higher strata should also be more involved politically as reflected by their rate of voter participation and intention to vote in forthcoming elections. Assuming that social-class identification and politics would be related, I expected the higher strata to have higher social-class identifications and be less sympathetic to issues important to the bulk of the working class which makes up the two nonskilled strata. Finally, I expected labor union members to take a more liberal stance than unorganized workers on all questions.

Ideally, political analysis should go beyond demonstrating disagreements. It should demonstrate that disagreements have important political consequences. I hypothesized that the politics of the three highest strata (foremen, self-employed, and skilled) of the working class would deviate sufficiently from the politics of the bulk of the working class (the two nonskilled strata) to make it difficult for labor leaders to guarantee the blue-collar vote to the Democratic party. Even if the bulk of the working class were reliably in the Democratic camp, the uncertain politics of the three upper strata, constituting two-fifths of the total, could upset the balance enough to permit the Republicans to win. The three upper strata could also exercise an indirect effect that I cannot now measure. In the political communication that occurs in the workplace, the three upper strata may convince a sufficient number in the two lower strata to change their votes or to not vote, thus weakening the voting strength of the Democratic party. Although this process is difficult to demonstrate, some evidence suggests that it does occur (Berelson, Lazarsfeld, and McPhee, 1954:93–105).

Foremen probably are the most conservative segment of the working class, the most politically involved, and the least identified with the class. Since socialization influences political dispositions more than any other single factor (Pomper, 1975:29), foremen, because of their working-class background (see Chapter 3), should have political views that resemble those of the working class more than the middle class. Yet the higher education, earnings, social status, and closer association of foremen with management probably influence them to deviate somewhat from the politics of the bulk of the working class, i.e., the nonskilled workers (Dunkerly, 1975). This deviation manifests itself in the foremen seeing themselves as independents rather than as Democrats.

I expected the self-employed and the skilled to have similar politics because they resemble each other in many ways, most importantly in being skilled. Hamilton (1975) found that the petty bourgeoisie had political profiles similar to those of other workers, and that property ownership had no bearing on their attitudes. The question bears re-examination. Both the self-employed and the skilled should be more conservative than the two nonskilled strata for several reasons. First, more of the self-employed and skilled are or have been members of craft unions which are more conservative than industrial unions. Second, since the self-employed and the skilled have higher social status and earnings than the nonskilled, these higher strata do not see themselves as ordinary workers (Bakunin, 1971; Mackenzie, 1973). Third, the two higher strata want to preserve their skill and autonomy and thus do not trust other workers who threaten their monopoly (Sable, 1982:92). This distrust leads the higher groups to vote their own interests and to identify with the upper working class rather than with the nonskilled segment of the working class.

Although nonskilled core and periphery workers in manufacturing and service industries constitute the bulk of the working class, the two strata differ markedly in their earnings, unionization, sex, race, and job complexity. Because core, more than periphery workers, belong to industrial unions that are strongly committed to the Democratic party, and because these unions operate effective political machines (Wilson, 1979), the core workers should be better informed about political issues and vote more regularly in elections than would periphery workers. But no stratal difference should be expected in party and working-class identification. Possibly no difference will appear in voter turnout for several reasons. First, COPE strives to get out the vote in working-class districts whether the residents are union members or not. Second, since 31 percent of nonskilled core workers are not in unions, they receive no political indoctrination in the work place. Third, families tend to be politically homogeneous even though some of their members work in the core and others in the periphery. Finally, the periphery contains more blacks than the core. Their voting turnout has increased in recent years, raising the sector's average turnout.

If the marginally employed stratum were comprised solely of committed workers who were unemployed for more than half a year, they should exhibit the highest identification with the Democratic party, the most radical political beliefs, and the lowest voter turnout (see Schlozman and Verba, 1979:300). However, the stratum also contains part-time workers (women and semiretired) who have varying degrees of skill and young people who work part-time or during certain seasons of the year. Such a heterogeneous group will probably resemble the full range of the working class in its political beliefs and behavior.

In the following section, I first analyze the extent of voter participation by strata and the extent to which the strata identify with and vote for the Democratic party. Second, I examine the social-class identification of the strata and the extent that class and party identification are related. Third, I attempt to determine stratal stability or volatility in social-class and party identification as a clue to the social solidarity of the working class. In all of these analyses, the behavior of union members is examined. In regression analyses, I attempt to weigh the importance of stratal placement as one of a number of variables that affect voter participation, party voting, and social-class identification.

Voter Participation

A sense of civic duty impels most people to say that they intend to vote, but the percentage who actually vote is smaller. In the SRC presidential surveys of 1968–76, about 90 percent of respondents from all strata indicated that they intended to vote, but about 60 percent later revealed that they did vote. Even this figure is high because some people who did not vote report that they did. In Table 10.1, about 80 percent of the foremen and 70 percent of the self-employed and skilled said they voted for president, in contrast to 60 percent for the nonskilled strata. Although the gubernatorial turnout in each state was lower than the presidential, the stratal difference persisted: about 60 percent of the top three strata voted compared to less than 50 percent for the bottom three—again a 10 percent difference.

Table 10.1. Voting Participation in Presidential and Gubernatorial Elections

| Strata | Presidential | | Gubernatorial[c] | |
	Percent[b]	N	Percent	N
Nonmanual[a]	80	5,846		
Foremen	81	378	59	151
Self-employed	71	691	56	200
Skilled	68	2,685	60	817
Nonskilled core	61	3,105	49	756
Nonskilled periphery	59	3,230	45	1,168
Marginally employed	53	1,610	46	480

[a]For GSS only.
[b]Combined GSS and SRC elections 1976–80.
[c]SRC 1966–78.

Apparently, union affiliation increases the workers' intention to vote as well as the voter turnout, especially for the skilled and nonskilled core strata. Confirming Ra's (1978) intensive SRC study of the union's influence on voting, my data showed that union membership raised the level of intention to vote, but it varied by strata: a 10 percent rise for the skilled and nonskilled core strata and only a slight rise for the nonskilled periphery workers. Combining the GSS samples for 1972 and 1976, I found that 77 percent of the unionized skilled voted compared to 58 percent of the unorganized. Though the difference was smaller for the nonskilled strata, it remained a substantial 10 percent.

Intention to vote was regressed on a number of variables that affect voting: education, age, race, income, home ownership, religion, rural-urban residence, union membership, sex, and working-class strata, with the non-manual workers as the omitted variable to prevent perfect multicollinearity.[1] Although the percent of the total variance accounted for was small (.065), all of the coefficients were statistically significant except union membership, sex, and being self-employed or in the skilled strata. Education, age, and home ownership had the highest positive standardized betas, while all those for the strata were negative. Thus, compared to nonmanual workers, and controlling for all variables affecting intention to vote, the lower the stratum, the larger the negative standardized beta, i.e., the lower the intention to vote. This is exactly what our theory predicted.

Party Identification and Vote

More than half of the workers in all strata of the working class except the foremen identified themselves as Democrats, and the differences among the strata were small (see Table 10.2). But, compared to the nonskilled strata, the skilled and self-employed in all elections had smaller percentages of people who identified themselves as Democrats. In both the SRC and GSS surveys, a smaller percentage of the self-employed and skilled than the nonskilled indicated they were strong Democrats, and a larger percentage identified themselves as Independent Democrats or Near-Democrats.

When a seven-point party identification scale (from Strong Democrat to Strong Republican) was regressed on the standard set of variables, .153 of the variance was explained; all the coefficients were statistically significant except age and strata (self-employed, nonskilled periphery, and marginally employed) were significant only at the 10 percent level (see Table 10.3).[2] The relative influence of strata, as expressed by the ranking of the standardized betas, was less than race, religion, union membership, region, education, sex, class identification, or income. Being black, Catholic, a union

Table 10.2. Democratic Party Identification and Vote of Strata

Strata	Identification[b]		Vote[c]	
	Percent	N	Percent	N
Nonmanual[a]	51	5,714	39	5,630
Foremen	47	347	40	305
Self-employed	55	572	49	488
Skilled	62	2,245	51	1,800
Nonskilled core	64	3,631	58	1,845
Nonskilled periphery	62	2,805	58	1,101
Marginally-employed	60	2,281	57	839

[a]For GSS presidential elections only, 1968–80.
[b]Biennial elections: GSS, 1972–82; SRC, 1966–78.
[c]Presidential elections: GSS, 1968–80; SRC, 1964–74.

member, and a southerner, controlling for all other variables, strongly reduced Republican party identification. Higher education and income, and being male, increased Republican identification.

In the presidential elections, a smaller percentage of workers in all strata voted for the Democratic party than identified with it. Less than 60 percent of the nonskilled strata voted Democratic, 50 percent of the self-employed and skilled, and 40 percent of the foremen. In six biennial elections, the SRC asked voters for their usual party vote. Significantly, a larger percent in all strata split their vote between parties than voted Democratic (Table 10.4). Almost half of the nonskilled strata and more than half of the three highest strata split their vote. Put differently, two-fifths of the nonskilled strata and less than a third of the three highest strata usually voted Democratic.

When the Democratic vote was regressed on the standard indicators (Table 10.3), a somewhat different pattern appeared than that for party identification. As reflected by the standardized betas, age now strongly influenced Democratic vote, education became much stronger, and region and strata (except for the nonskilled periphery) became significant only at the 10 percent level. Thus, for Democratic voters, when all other factors are controlled, stratal position was of small consequence, but age, education, union membership, religion, and home ownership remained important (see Table 10.3). When Republican party vote was regressed on the indicators, the only significant betas from high to low were religion (Protestant), race (white), union membership (no), age (younger), region (non-South), income (high), and skilled stratum (negative).

The impact of union membership on the Democratic vote was

Table 10.3. Regression of Democratic Vote and Party Identification on Stratal and Socioeconomic Variables

Variables[a]	Democratic Vote			Party Identification		
	B	S.E.	Beta	B	S.E.	Beta
Foremen	−.063[b]	.043	−.019	.419	.155	.031
Self-employed	.003[b]	.038	.001	−.134[b]	.134	−.012
Skilled	.024[b]	.022	.016	−.244	.080	−.040
Nonskilled core	−.034[b]	.023	−.022	−.182	.082	−.029
Nonskilled periphery	−.040	.020	−.031	−.088[b]	.070	−.017
Marginally employed	.060	.026	−.032	−.094[b]	.093	−.012
Race	−.154	.020	−.108	1.300	.070	.225
Education	.019	.002	.125	.034	.099	.056
Income	−.001[b]	.001	−.018	.010	.003	.053
Union member	.142	.016	.117	−.582	.060	−.117
Home owner	.049	.015	.047	.115	−.052	.027
Class ID	−.010[b]	.007	−.024	.102	.023	.057
Region	.014[b]	.013	.014	−.505	−.049	−.123
Religion	−.085	.136	−.084	.769	.049	.186
Rural-urban	.030	.142	.028	−.140	.051	−.033
Age	.003	.000	.131	.002[b]	.002	.014
Sex	−.013[b]	.013	.014	.208	.048	.053
Constant	.117	.047		1.243	.168	
R² =	.049	N = 5,937		R² = .153	N = 6,820	

[a]Significant at the .05 level.
[b]Significant at the .10 level.
Source: SRC Biennial Surveys, 1966–78.

Table 10.4. Usual Party Vote for Strata in Six Elections (percent)

Strata	Always Democratic	Split	Always Republican
Foremen	14	70	16
Self-employed	32	50	18
Skilled	33	56	11
Nonskilled core	40	49	11
Nonskilled periphery	42	47	11
Marginally employed	40	49	11

Source: SRC Biennial Election Surveys, 1966–78.

impressive: the higher the stratum, the greater was the difference between union and nonunion workers in the Democratic vote. Thus, for the presidential elections between 1964 and 1976, SRC data revealed that about 60 percent of the nonunion nonskilled workers in the periphery voted Democratic and 68 percent of the unionized, an 8 percent increase. But for the skilled, the corresponding percentages were 46 and 67, a 21 percent increase for union members. Similar increases were reported for unionized self-employed and foremen. I tried to determine whether membership in industrial unions influenced Democratic voting more than craft union membership. While the SRC data were far from ideal (the N was only 344), they did support my expectations: a higher percent of skilled and nonskilled periphery workers in industrial unions voted Democratic, but no difference appeared for nonskilled core workers because very few belonged to craft unions.

Class Identification

Sociologists are more committed to the importance of social-class identification than workers are. Sociologists have faith that class identification should say something, directly or indirectly, about class consciousness, and class consciousness should reveal something about class conflict and class politics. The connections between class identification, class consciousness, and politics are rather tenuous among American workers because class consciousness is the least important variable in the string. It has low saliency. Thus, Schlozman and Verba (1979:114–17) found that only 8 percent of blue-collar workers reported that they belonged to the working class, and 50 percent reported "middle class" when asked for their class identification in an open-ended question. In contrast, 65 percent of the French and 33 percent of the British blue-collar workers identified with the working class in response to the question. In response to a forced-choice question, where the alternatives were working class and middle class, United States blue-collar workers chose working- to middle class 2:1, compared to 1:2 for professionals and executives.

In an attempt to measure class consciousness, Schlozman and Verba (1979:121–26) asked whether executives or factory workers are paid too much, whether the interests of workers and management are fundamentally the same or in opposition, and whether America would be better off if workers stuck together or if they worked as individuals to get ahead. Expectedly, blue-collar workers were more class conscious on all three questions than were lower white-collar workers, executives, and professionals. About a third of blue-collar workers thought executives were paid too much and that management and workers were in opposition, and two-thirds said workers should stick together. But more important for this discussion, the associations among the class-consciousness items, as expressed by gamma, were very low (below .15). Unfortunately, the authors did not investigate differences among blue-collar workers, but they did find that union members were more class conscious than were other workers. This loose connection between class identification and class consciousness suggests a muted salience of class identification for the internal politics of the working class.

In an effort to tease the most out of class identification questions, both the SRC and GSS forced respondents to select one of two classes at the bottom and upper parts of the class system. The SRC asked respondents to choose between average-working and upper-working class and average-middle and upper-middle class. GSS asked respondents to choose between lower and working class and middle and upper class. A comparison of the two surveys shows that the SRC classification resulted in 6–10 percent more of the manual workers belonging to the two bottom social classes (see Table 10.5). In both surveys, the clear majority in all strata, including the foremen, identified with the lower and/or working classes (see Table 10.5). In general, though the differences were not large, the lower the stratum, the more its members identified with the working classes. The response distributions of average-working and upper-working classes in the SRC surveys is instructive. While 39 percent of foremen identified with the average working class, 68 percent of the nonskilled periphery workers did so, a difference of 29 percent. The difference between the self-employed and skilled vs. the nonskilled periphery was 10 percent. Clearly, a larger proportion of the three highest strata than the three lowest strata identified with the upper-working, middle, and upper-middle classes. A similar but not so striking pattern appeared in the GSS surveys.

Table 10.5. Class Identification of Strata (percent)

Strata	Average-Working[a]	Upper-Working[a]	Middle and Upper-Middle[a]	Lower and Working[b]	Middle and Upper[b]
Nonmanual	—	—	—	37	63
Foremen	39	23	38	56	44
Self-employed	59	12	29	64	36
Skilled	56	15	29	65	35
Nonskilled core	68	11	22	72	28
Nonskilled periphery	68	8	25	66	34
Marginally employed	59	8	34	68	32

[a]SRC Biennial Surveys, 1966–78. Total N, 4,020.
[b]GSS Presidential Surveys, 1968–80. Total N without nonmanual, 5,665.

Union membership has the distinct effect of increasing the lower- and working-class identification of strata; the lower the stratum, the greater the apparent effect. Thus, in the GSS presidential surveys of 1968–80, 68 percent of unionized skilled and 81 percent of the nonskilled periphery workers identified with the lower and working class, while no difference appeared among the nonunionized strata. Conversely, almost 33 percent of the unionized skilled and 19 percent of the nonskilled periphery workers identified with the middle classes, and no differences appeared among the nonunionized strata.[3] Unfortunately, SRC data were thin with respect to membership in craft and industrial unions. Only for the nonskilled periphery stratum did differences appear: 63 percent of craft union members identified with the working class compared to 74 percent in industrial unions.

Regressing social-class identification on the socioeconomic indicators and working-class strata showed that the variables accounted for a moderate amount (almost 28 percent) of the total variance. Expectedly, the standardized betas for education and income were the most important factors associated with higher social-class identification. Being in a particular working-class stratum was almost as strong in depressing such identification, more so than region, house ownership, and community of residence.

The question remains whether social-class identification has any political significance. One way to probe this is to compare the Democratic vote of strata with and without social-class identification controlled. Working-class identification raised the percent of Democratic vote in all strata. For presidential elections, about 50 percent of the self-employed and skilled voted Democratic, while over 70 percent of working-class identifiers did so, a 20 percent increase. Almost 60 percent of the two nonskilled strata voted Democratic compared to 71 percent of those who identified with the working class, an 11 percent increase. Though the same trends appeared for the congressional elections, they were not as pronounced.

Trend Analysis

The proportion of blue-collar workers voting Democratic in presidential elections varied 28 percent, from 71 percent in 1964 to 43 percent in 1972. The variation for white-collar workers was smaller, 21 percent (Blumberg, 1980:226). Any party has an advantage if it has a substantial core of regular supporters. To what extent do the working-class strata vary in their support for the Democratic party in their voter turnout? Even though the sample size of the three upper strata is too small in individual elections to permit drawing firm conclusions, contrary to expectation the largest strata, the nonskilled core and periphery, varied somewhat more than the three upper strata in the percent indicating that their normal vote was Democratic (Table 10.6). When I examined variation from one election to another in the percentage who thought of themselves as Independent-Republicans, Independents, and Independent-Democrats, again it was larger for the two nonskilled strata than for the upper three. In short, the bulk of working class voters in the two largest strata are more unreliable Democrats and Independents than are workers in the other strata. The three upper strata appear to vote a more consistent independent position. Apparently, when the voting pattern of the larger nonskilled strata conforms to that of the three upper strata, then the Democratic party loses the majority of blue-collar support. This situation is exacerbated by the consistent differences in stratal voter turnout. In the four GSS surveys of presidential elections from 1968 to 1980, the three highest strata in all elections had a higher voter turnout than the three lowest strata. The difference between highest and lowest turnout for the strata averaged close to 20 percent (Table 10.6).

Table 10.6. Voter Turnout in Four Presidential Elections (percent)

	Elections					
Strata	1968	1972	1976	1980	Total	N
Nonmanual	79	82	78	78	80	7,343
Foremen	77	77	85	70	79	232
Self-employed	78	67	70	72	72	443
Skilled	69	68	63	65	66	1,709
Nonskilled core	65	61	56	53	59	2,282
Nonskilled periphery	59	59	54	55	57	1,786
Marginally employed	68	58	57	62	60	915
Range	19	18	31	18	23	

Source: GSS Presidential Surveys, 1968–80.

Conclusions

The hypothesis that the stratification of the working class dissipates its political strength received some support. Voting participation varied according to stratal position: the higher the stratum, the higher the percent who voted. Similarly, the intention to vote varied by strata, and union membership increased it, especially at the higher levels. Regression analysis showed that stratal position had a weak but independent effect. Although identification with the Democratic party typified the working class, persistent stratal differences appeared in the strength of that identification. Moreover, vote-splitting by party was the norm for all strata, and the higher strata split their votes more than did the lower strata. Regression analysis showed only a weak independent stratal effect. Working-class identification was general among all strata, but higher strata identified more with the upper-working and middle classes, and this trend held in regression analysis. Union membership increased working-class identification strongly. Finally, participation in voting varied widely from one election to another, and it varied more in the lower strata. So did variation in normal Democratic voting and party identification.

The implications of these findings are clear. More variation exists in working-class political behavior than previous research has reported. While class divisions are not deep, they are persistent and important. In elections where the turnout matters, the task of COPE is to sustain the political interest of its natural allies, the large unorganized and nonskilled strata. Unions appear to be remarkably successful in increasing the political awareness, class awareness, and Democratic voting of their own members (Ra, 1978). Increasing the number of union members and increasing the voter turnout of the nonskilled strata would undoubtedly tip some elections. As things now stand, foremen, self-employed, and the skilled are numerous enough, active enough, stable enough, and independent enough in their politics to reduce significantly the percentage of the manual vote that the Democratic party needs to win elections.

This analysis has shown that American workers have a low spontaneous sense of class identification and class consciousness. Perhaps its occupational, sector, race, skill, income, and other divisions suppress class feelings and this, in turn, hinders the efforts of labor leaders to mobilize the class consistently to support the Democratic party and liberal legislation. If so, perhaps nothing can be done to increase the class's political effectiveness. The French working class allegedly has the requisite class consciousness and political awareness. Are these a response to its historical and present structural homogeneity? The next chapter, by comparing the French and the United States working classes, examines the issue of the relationship of class stratification to political mobilization.

Notes

1. The coding of the variables in all regression analyses is as follows: strata are dummy variables with being in a particular stratum equaling 1 and other = 0; race: white = 1, other = 0; education in single years; income in hundreds of dollars; home ownership = 1, other = 0; union membership = 1, other = 0; class identification, 1–4 for working, upper-working, middle, and upper-middle; region, non-South = 1, South = 0; religion: Protestant = 1, other = 0; residence: urban = 1, other = 0; age, in years; sex: male = 1, female = 0; Democratic party vote = 1, other = 0; party identification: strong Democratic to strong Republican 1–7.

2. In a regression analysis of intention to vote, where class identification, region, and skill level were added to the equation and strata were removed, coefficients were not statistically significant except for age, race, education, home ownership, religion, and income in declining order. Thus, strata are more powerful indicators of intention to vote than are skill level and class identification, which were not significant.

3. For the nonunionized, 63 percent identified with the lower and working class and 36 percent with the middle and upper. This difference between unionized and nonunionized was statistically significant.

11

Class and Political Division in France and the United States

At its inception, the working class consisted of small local groups of workers who confronted individual employers. Although workers differed in their skills and in other ways, their small numbers and common work experiences enabled them to cooperate in disputes with employers. Indeed, early strikes were conducted by spontaneously formed organizations whose purpose was to resolve particular grievances. These organizations rarely survived as unions after the grievances were "resolved." The formation of a labor movement involved, in Weber's (1945) terms, creating a permanent organization that tied local work groups to other similar groups in the community and society. A class-oriented labor movement required both that national unions confront employers in the market place and that labor parties be created to confront employers in the political arena. This historical shift from local communal economic action to societal economic and political action required extending consensus from local and relatively homogeneous groups to larger and more heterogeneous ones.

In 1902 Simmel (1950:95) pinpointed the problem that arises during the organizational growth of labor. Unconditional solidarity decreases in a group as the size of its membership increases because growth brings more heterogeneous individuals into the organization. In his terms, worker coalitions whose purpose is to improve labor conditions know well that they decrease in cohesion as they increase in size. Moreover, Olson (1965) points out that as cohesion decreases in an organization, individual members are less likely to contribute to the organization because they profit even without participating. In smaller organizations especially, some members receive enough rewards from leadership that they willingly run the organization for the free-riders who refuse to contribute. In larger and more heterogeneous organizations, leaders find it harder to define optimal common interests as members decreasingly perceive how they benefit by making an organizational contribution. Organizational problems are exacerbated by the exponentially rising costs of coordinating an ever larger and more heterogeneous membership.

These considerations suggest that the consensus required for class labor movements may be easiest to achieve at early stages of industrialization when the economic structure is less differentiated, when workers are more homogeneous in their skills and social characteristics, and when more of them are experiencing the pains of being uprooted from traditional structures. Building on Trotsky's (1932) theory of the Russian revolution, Leggett (1968) noted that European working classes rarely mobilized gradually as they were exposed to common industrial experiences, common lifestyles, and responsible unionism. Rather, unions quickly forged links to labor or socialist parties. Engels (1893), Sombart (1906), and many others, in trying to explain the notable exception of American unions to forge these early links, agreed that labor leaders confronted unusually great difficulties trying to unite workers who were split by ethnic, religious, regional, and other divisions (Lipset, 1977). They pointed to the French working class as the polar opposite. French workers were socially homogeneous and early exhibited the consensus required to build a class-oriented movement.

Obviously, factors other than social homogeneity facilitate consensus-building in a class, yet any explanation must consider this important factor. Most observers today believe that American workers are still too divided to form a class-oriented coalition (see Chapter 9 especially), and that French workers are still homogeneous enough to maintain the vigor of class parties. Yet conditions that homogenize or divide working classes may change over time. Technological changes may homogenize (Braverman, 1974) or differentiate skills (Mueller, et al., 1969); changes in immigration policies may increase or decrease ethnic tensions (Yellowitz, 1977); changing markets may concentrate or disperse workers geographically (Gottdiener, 1983); unions and parties may grow or shrink in size (Sturmthal, 1983); and unemployment may have different regional effects. By increasing or decreasing class homogeneity, such changes simplify or complicate problems that working-class leaders face in mobilizing workers politically.

The purpose of this chapter is to compare the social and economic divisions of the French and U.S. working classes in order to assess their possible effects on political consensus. The greater the structural divisions (skill, sector, ethnic, sex, union) within a class, the higher should be the level of economic inequality; the higher its level, the higher the level of political disagreement. First, I present a historical description of the structural divisions of the two working classes and how these divisions affected their politics. Second, I compare current structural class divisions and their possible effect on class economic inequality. Third, after tracing the major economic and political changes in the two classes after World War II, I examine whether their internal divisions are now manifested in different patterns of political consensus. Finally, I discuss why both the French and U.S. working classes remain politically fragmented.

Historical Explanations of Class Consensus

The French disagree as much as the Americans on whom to include in the working class. For example, Mothé (1972) argues that the French unskilled workers in giant manufacturing firms are the core of the working class, while Mallet (1969) argues that the core are the technicians who run the advanced automated industries. Following Weber (1946), class is defined as those occupations that are the common fate of workers and their parents. Many United States studies show that the most important mobility barrier within and between generations for males at least is that between manual and white-collar occupations (e.g., Blau and Duncan, 1967). In his study of social mobility of workers in Paris and Los Angeles, Seeman (1977) found that the manual/white-collar distinction was the most discriminating criterion for both groups. Defining the working class as being comprised of manual workers suffices for the present analysis because including white-collar workers would only further magnify working-class divisions. A preliminary examination of French census data revealed that the five strata I used to divide the American working class also divided French workers by such characteristics as earnings, property, human capital, and unemployment (INSÉÉ, 1974; Documentation française, 1976b; CFDT, 1977).

Most observers agree that the French have traditionally engaged in class politics while the Americans have practiced interest-group politics. Different historical experiences help explain the contrasting patterns. Obviously, in its inception, the French working class was more homogeneous than the American in language, ethnicity, religion, and traditions. In addition, France experienced a pattern of industrialization whose sociodemographic consequences minimized cleavages especially between the skilled and unskilled workers (Sellier, 1973). France industrialized more slowly than the United States, and more of French early industrialization occurred in small communities (Landes, 1966:18). Since artisan industries declined slowly, factory owners could readily recruit skilled labor from the towns; however, unskilled labor was in short supply because the price of agricultural labor, the normal source of factory labor, remained high owing to an unusually low rural birth rate. The demographic transition was completed in rural France by 1830, a singular departure from the normal trend for the transition to appear first in urban areas (United Nations, 1973). After 1850 especially, employers turned to women and foreigners for unskilled labor (Gani, 1972), but the scarcity persisted. This institutionalized the low wage spread between skilled and unskilled labor (Sellier, 1973).

French artisans' unusual tolerance for low earnings differentials was partly motivated by their desire to remain price competitive with factories that produced high quality goods (Hanagan, 1977). From the very beginning, the low wage spread had the added effect of inhibiting craft unions and encouraging industrial-type unions. Local industrialists in the small communities stubbornly resisted collective bargaining, so unions turned increasingly to political action to obtain economic improvements (Lorwin, 1954). Labor unions also formed alliances with political parties of the left, Catholic groups, and independent intellectuals. Although the labor movement remained split by secular/Catholic and other ideological divisions, it clung to the common class legacy of the Revolution of 1789. Reducing economic inequality in the nation and in the working class became a traditional goal that is espoused even today by the communist-led Conféderation Général du Travail (CGT), the Conféderation Française Democratique du Travail (CFDT), and French intellectuals.

In contrast, the working-class movement in the United States was hindered by a changing and heterogeneous class structure and by political disagreements. As long as land was available in the West and even after the closing of the frontier, rural birth rates and geographic mobility remained high. A constant stream of foreigners kept changing the ethnic composition of both rural and urban labor (Griffen, 1969). Unlike France, industrialization after the Civil War proceeded rapidly, especially in the large cities of the East and Midwest. Immigrants increasingly supplied factories with unskilled labor, and natives were trained for skilled jobs. In the absence of a large reservoir of small town artisans, skilled workers were scarce and wage differentials remained relatively high (Ozanne, 1962).

Several class-oriented working-class movements arose in the United States, but they were all subdued prior to World War I (Perlman and Taft, 1966). Even in these labor movements, the skilled were suspicious of the unskilled and opposed the immigration of even British workers. They also tried to keep down the number of apprentices (Yellowitz, 1977). In the "industrial unions" of the Knights of Labor, over half of the locals were comprised solely of skilled workers, and only a few locals had an equal balance of skills (Conell and Voss, 1982). Bennett and Earle (1980) point out that after the Civil War, wage differentials were lowest in small towns of the Midwest, and there the Socialist party had its greatest strength and appeal. In the larger industrial cities of the East, the skilled became organized and pressed for larger wage differentials, thus splitting the working class. The urban Socialist party collapsed between 1912 and 1916, coterminous with the success of AFL craft unions and the rapproachement of the unions and the Democratic party under Wilson. The authors assert that the data support the thesis that wage equalization is more important than union organization for promoting working-class consciousness and political action.

By 1900 the pattern of union organization had stabilized. The AFL unions were organized along craft lines that avoided entanglements with unskilled workers, political parties, and foreign ideologies (Perlman, 1928). Even when the unskilled were finally organized into CIO unions during the Great Depression, they were led by craft workers who carefully guarded traditional wage differentials (Bok and Dunlop, 1971:115). For a time, it appeared that the CIO unions would embrace a class-oriented socialist program, but after World War II, communist and radical leaders were driven from office. Union officials not only disavowed labor and socialist parties, but they showed little concern for wage equalization. Indeed, they competed with each other to get the highest wages for their members. The merging of the AFL and CIO unions further muted class and egalitarian tendencies in the CIO.

In the twentieth century, both France and the United States underwent major economic and social changes that altered the composition of their working classes and their politics. Massive changes took place in the French economy after both world wars. The proportion of workers in agriculture declined rapidly, large-scale urban industries burgeoned, and the per capita gross national product soared to equal that of the German Federal Republic in the 1960s (U.S. Bureau of the Census, 1972b).[1] A labor shortage after World War II produced a rapid and steady influx of unskilled foreign workers whose presence stimulated the upward mobility of

French labor. The Algerian crisis of 1969 resulted in a new constitution and new alignments among unions, parties, and government. Finally, the events of May 1968 signaled worker dissatisfaction with their unions, parties, and government. New alignments were called for.

The United States also experienced vast changes in the twentieth century. Large-scale industry grew even more dominant, and industrial change altered the occupational composition of the working class. The decline of immigration in the 1920s had the effect of producing an industrial working class that was predominately urban and native-born. World War II accelerated the uprooting of black and white workers from the rural South to take unskilled jobs in northern industries. Industrial unions, which gained a foothold during the Great Depression, consolidated their gains during and after World War II. Traditional party allegiances of ethnic minorities, blacks, and even native-born workers changed as the Democratic party became the broker of an increasingly complex coalition. In the 1960s, as in France, the complacency of union leaders and management was shaken by many spontaneous worker revolts and protests; in the 1970s, the labor-Democratic party alliance began to become unglued.

Industrial and Occupational Structures

France's economic structure in the late 1970s resembled that of the United States in 1960 (Table 11.1). Today, agricultural employment is relatively larger in France than in the United States (11 vs. 4 percent) and so is employment in the productive sector of manufacturing, construction, and utilities (36 vs. 30 percent). Although both countries qualify as "postindustrial," the United States has a larger service sector (65 vs. 52 percent). White-collar employees comprise almost half of both labor forces, but the United States has relatively more professional and clerical workers; France has more proprietors and administrators. The United States supports a conspicuously larger percentage of sales clerks. In the manual working class, more of the French are skilled. Overall, France's occupational structure reflects a slower decline in farming, artisan trades, small business, and skilled labor. Finally, more of the French than American workers are employed in the core sector: 56 vs. 42 percent. This reflects the larger French concentrations in construction, government, and durable goods manufacturing. Within manufacturing, about six-tenths of the French and half of American workers are employed in durable goods industries.

Table 11.1. Characteristics of Economic Structures (percent)

	France	U.S.
Industrial Sectors[a]		
Primary	12	5
Agriculture	11	4
Mining	1	1
Secondary	36	30
Manufacturing	26	23
Construction	9	6
Electric, gas, utilities	1	1
Tertiary—services	52	65
Government	21	18
Other services	31	47
Total	100	100
Occupational Composition[b]	(1975)	(1974)
Professional and Technical	8	14
Proprietors, managers, officials	20	11
Office clerks	14	17
Sales clerks	3	6
Craft, skilled	16	13
Operatives, semiskilled	15	18
Laborers, unskilled	7	4
Private household	2	2
Other services	6	10
Farmers	9	4
Total	100	99
Core—Periphery Employment[c]	(1972)	(1971)
Core	56	42
Periphery	44	58
Manufacturing in core	60	57

[a]International Labour Office (1976).
[b]Liaisons Sociales (1978); U.S. Bureau of the Census (1974, Series P-23, No. 54).
[c]Calculated from INSÉÉ (1975), M-43, 44; U.S. Bureau of the Census (1972b: 227).

Skill Hierarchies

Manual workers may be divided into three strata: the aristocrats of labor who include the self-employed, artisans, skilled employees, and foremen; the traditional proletariat, made up of machine tenders, truck drivers, and other semiskilled workers; and the bottom layer of unskilled laborers, domestics, and service workers. Even though the top stratum has declined slightly in France during the last twenty years, primarily because artisans are being forced out of business (Liaisons Sociales, 1978), the French working class has a much larger labor aristocracy than does the American: 41 vs. 28 percent (Table 11.2). Both the proletariat of semiskilled machine tenders and the bottom layer of unskilled and service workers are larger in the United States. Thus, contrary to popular impression, the United States is more heavily proletarian than is France.

Table 11.2. Occupational Trends Among Manual Workers (percent)

Occupations	France[a]		U.S.[b]	
	1954	1975	1950	1975
Aristocrats of labor	46	41	28	28
Artisans	9	5+	4	4
Supervisors	3	5	3	4
Craft and skilled	34	31	21	20
Traditional Proletariat	28	30	40	33
Apprentices	3	1	1	1
Operatives and semiskilled	25	29	39	32
Bottom Layer	26	29	33	39
Laborers and unskilled	14	17	13	10
Household workers	7	5	5	3
Service workers	6	7	15	26
Totals	100	100	100	100

[a]Liaisons Sociales (1978). Supervisors' figure (1954) is for 1960.
[b]U.S. Bureau of the Census (1976a). Artisans are underestimated.

Sex and Ethnic Stratification

Women's labor force participation in France declined from 36 percent in 1900 to 29 percent in 1970, while the rate in the United States doubled from 21 to 43 percent (Liaisons Sociales, 1975b; U.S. Bureau of the Census, 1975:D49–62). The French drop partly reflected declining employment in the artisan trades and agriculture where women had earlier participated heavily. Expectedly, in both nations today, women are overrepresented among the unskilled and underrepresented among the skilled (Table 11.3). They comprise one-half of all unskilled labor in both countries. Women are evenly represented in the semiskilled proletariat of both countries. Although a smaller percentage of American than French women are skilled, more of the French are concentrated in the low-paying, nondurable goods industries: e.g., food, apparel, textiles, leather, and tobacco (INSÉÉ Table 15a; U.S. Department of Labor, 1975:111–12). Altogether, the data suggest that the declining labor force participation of women in France was accompanied by a downward shift into low-skilled jobs of low-paying industries, and that women's employment in the United States expanded into semi-skilled and unskilled service jobs.

Table 11.3. Percentages of Workers in Occupational Strata by Sex, 1970

Occupational Levels	France[a]			United States[b]		
	Men	Women	Total	Men	Women	Total
Craft — skilled	91	9	100	97	3	100
Operatives — semiskilled	75	25	100	69	31	100
Unskilled — laborers[c]	48	52	100	51	49	100
Total	74	26	100	70	30	100
Craft — skilled	48	14	39	37	3	27
Operatives — semiskilled	35	33	35	37	38	37
Unskilled — laborers[c]	17	53	26	26	59	35
Total	100	100	100	100	100	99

[a]INSÉÉ (1974: Table 16.1).
[b]U.S. Bureau of the Census (1972b: 230).
[c]Includes manual service workers.

France is no longer an ethnically homogeneous society. In 1974, 8.5 percent of its work force was foreign-born compared to 5.2 percent for the U.S. Reynaud (1975) reports that the French foreign-born (FFB), by taking over the worst jobs, decreased industrial relations tensions and increased the income and social mobility of French workers. In contrast, the U.S. foreign-born are more highly represented in white-collar employment (44 vs. 31 percent). They earn average incomes and experience below average unemployment (National Commission, 1978:105–115). In the U.S., blacks and Hispanic-origin workers (B–H) rather than foreign-born occupy a labor market position comparable to the FFB. In 1970, the B–H comprised 13.5 percent of the labor force compared to 8.5 percent for the FFB in 1974.[2] More of the FFB than B–H were concentrated in manual labor: 95 vs. 71 percent (Liaisons Sociales, 1975a; U.S. Bureau of the Census, 1978b).[3]

To what extent are the minorities in the two countries industrially segregated? Exact comparisons are difficult because French statistics only cover enterprises employing more than ten workers in twenty manufacturing industries, mining, and construction (INSÉÉ, 1975:Table 18b); U.S. data have no such restrictions. Since about 90 percent of the FFB in these industries are male, I compared them to male B–H manual workers in the same industries.[4] About half of the B–H compared to two-thirds of the FFB work in construction or metal manufacturing, but the same proportions work in nondurable goods industries. About two-thirds in both countries are employed in the high-wage core sector. Like the B–H, the FFB are occupationally heterogeneous, ranging from highly skilled Italians, Spanish, and Yugoslavians to unskilled Portuguese, Maghrébins (North Africans), and Senegalese. Although estimates of their skills vary, more of the FFB than B–H appear to be skilled, but when the skills of the minorities are compared to all workers (Table 11.4), the B–H are more representative than the FFB. Even when the service workers are excluded from the working class, the FFB are more industrially and occupationally segregated than are the B–H.

Table 11.4. Skills of Ethnic and All Workers (percent)

Occupational Level	France[a]		United States	
	Foreign	Total	B–H[b]	Total
Craft and skilled	24	42	18	28
Operatives and semiskilled	39	29	39	36
Laborers and unskilled	37	29	43	36
Total	100	100	100	100

[a]Estimated from Granier and Marciano (1975); Liaisons Sociales (1975).
[b]Blacks and Hispanic origin. Source, U.S. Bureau of the Census (1972c).

To summarize: the French and United States economies are sufficiently alike to permit fruitful comparison. Both are postindustrial, but France has a relatively larger agricultural and manufacturing sector. In nonagricultural employment, more of the French work in the higher-paying core sector. A larger percentage of French are skilled but more French women work in low-wage manufacturing plants. The FFB are more occupationally and industrially segregated than both the U.S. foreign born and B–H. Overall, the French working class is structurally more heterogeneous than is the U.S. working class, which is more heavily proletarian. But does greater heterogeneity in France result in more economic inequality? Before attacking this question, certain problems of data comparability must be clarified.

Data Comparability and "Real Wages" in France

The accuracy of wage data is an ideological issue in France. The Left argues that government reports overestimate earnings because many employers pay below the legal minimum wage and many low earnings are not reported. Conservatives argue that published data underestimate incomes because transfer payments and other hidden labor costs are not included. Everyone agrees that payroll studies could determine the "real wages," but few such studies are conducted. Managers hesitate to release payroll data for fear that union officials, especially the CFDT, would press managers to reduce income differentials while others would demand higher wages. Also, union officials would press managers to pay all workers doing the same job the same wages, but managers insist on their constitutional right to pay individuals according to their job performance.

It is difficult to obtain precisely comparable earnings statistics for the two countries. Despite shortcomings, the U.S. census reports reasonably accurate and comprehensive data (Bielby and Hauser, 1977). INSÉÉ (Institute national de la statistique et des études economiques), the governmental agency responsible for gathering data, depends on employer reports (déclarations annuelles de salaires) of payments made to individual workers. However, the self-employed, government employees, domestics, persons working in family-owned enterprises, and illegal aliens do not report to INSÉÉ (Documentation Française, 1976a).[5] These omissions constitute about one-third of the labor force. My problems were to assess the shortcomings of the INSÉÉ data and to locate other data.

In the U.S., collective bargaining agreements specify the wage rates that workers actually receive, but French agreements specify industry minimums, not the rates paid by specific enterprises.[6] Local agreements are more accurate. Although French law prescribes that all local, bargained agreements must be filed at the local labor agency (Conseil de prud' hommes), I found many dossiers that were inaccurate, unkempt, and out of date. Union wage surveys were also unreliable because they were based on pay slips turned in largely by union sympathizers. While minimum wage laws cover all workers, some employers allegedly circumvented the law by including bonuses and special payments as part of the minimum. Magaud (1974) concludes that official income statistics are unreliable and that only data from personnel files can be trusted.

The major tasks were to evaluate the adequacy of the INSÉÉ data and to get wage data for government workers. In Lyon, I conducted three wage surveys in different sectors: government, glass and plastics, and chemicals. After a wide search I also found estimates of the incomes of self-employed manual workers or artisans (Zarca, 1977).

Wages in Government and the Private Sector

To obtain earnings of government workers, I approached the Lyon metropolitan government. Except for regional cost-of-living adjustments, all national and local governmental employees in France (21 percent of the labor force) in the same job classification are paid identical rates as fixed by the Ministry of Interior. These published rates did not reflect actual earnings in Lyon. No workers occupied the lowest grades of unskilled labor because the rates were too low. Also, bonus and seniority payments were large enough to create overlapping pay grades.

I discovered, though, that actual earnings, exclusive of social benefits,[7] include only the basic salary, bonuses, and seniority benefits. I obtained the bonus rates (for dangerous and unpleasant work) for all labor grades and seniority benefits by grade level. Table 11.5 shows that the difference between the highest and lowest starting rate for manual workers was 31 percent and almost unrelated to skill. The lowest skilled grade paid only 6 percent more than the common labor grade. Most skilled employees did not start at the bottom grade, and wage rates for the maximum seniority of fifteen years were slightly higher than rates in the private sector. These government rates consistently reflected skill level; the bottom grade of skill paid 30 percent more than common labor. Since skilled workers not only moved to higher grades more quickly than unskilled workers, and since skilled workers had more seniority (Documentation Française, 1976b:H-39), I concluded that the skill/unskilled ratio in the public sector approximated the private sector's average of 1.5 (see below).

Wage Equalization in the Private Sector

Two national drives were launched in response to the tumultuous events of May 1968. The first was to persuade all French employers to pay manual workers on a monthly basis (Bunel, 1973). This movement was more or less successful. Second, labor inaugurated a drive to reduce the income spread between management and labor, within management, and within labor. This drive was less successful and is still continuing. I conducted two wage studies in Lyon to provide insights into both the "real wage" and wage equalization issues.

Table 11.5. Monthly Wages (Francs) for Manual Workers in France's Public Sector, 1976

Occupational Grades	Starting Wage				End of Career			
	Grades		Value	Ratios X	Grades		Value	Ratios X
	Base	Adjusted	Francs	2218[a]	Base	Adjusted	Francs	2288[a]
Watchmen	175	187	2,143 (75 bonus)	1.00	190	194	2,213 (75 bonus)	1.00
Common laborer	175	187	2,143 (75 bonus)	1.00	190	194	2,213 (75 bonus)	1.00
Laborer (specialized)	175	187	2,143 (75 bonus)	1.00	253	238	2,213 (75 bonus)	1.00
Cleaning women	175	187	2,143 (75 bonus)	1.00	190	194	2,213 (75 bonus)	1.00
Assistant for skilled	175	187	2,143 (75 bonus)	1.00	282	258	2,213 (75 bonus)	1.00
Street cleaner	203	203	2,297 (70 bonus)	1.07	282	258	2,845 (70 bonus)	1.27
Garbage collector	203	203	2,347	1.06	282	258	2,289 (120 bonus)	1.32
Skilled 1st grade	217	213	2,347	1.06	309	278	2,975	1.30
Skilled 2nd grade	267	248	2,675	1.21	336	298	3,189	1.39
Truck Driver 4th grade	217	213	2,746 (160 bonus)	1.31	309	278	3,135	1.37
Sewer worker	217	213	2,487 (160 bonus)	1.19	309	278	3,135	1.37
Skilled 3rd grade	245	233	2,526	1.14	365	320	3,432	1.50
Work Supervisor	245	233	2,526	1.14	365	320	3,423	1.50
Foreman	254	233	2,526	1.14	365	320	3,423	1.50

[a]Base salary of watchman, plus bonus.

I selected one industry that reputedly paid average wages (plastics and glass) and another (chemicals) that paid above-average rates. Management of the glass firm gave me salary data that covered a three year period for workers in its twelve plants scattered throughout France. During this interval, jobs had been reevaluated, and the unions had pressed a reluctant management to equalize manual workers' wages. Data in Table 11.6 show that the union succeeded in eliminating the lowest wage stratum, but so few workers were affected that the victory was largely symbolic. Moreover, by readjusting the pay rates of several jobs, management succeeded in maintaining the original 1.5 skill/unskilled differential. Later I examined the personnel files of one of the plants chosen at random and found that the wage differential, as reported by management, corresponded to the industry average.

Table 11.6. Distribution of Monthly Wages (Francs) in a Glass and Plastics Industry, 1977

Occupational Level	Occupational Grades	Minimums (francs)	Guaranteed Minimum (francs)	Median Grades	Median Guaranteed (francs)	Ratios
Unskilled-2	110	1,470	—	125	2,058	1.00
Unskilled-3	125	1,838	2,058	129	2,141	1.04
Semiskilled-1	135	1,984	2,203	139	2,291	1.07
Semiskilled-2	145	2,137	2,347	150	2,464	1.15
Semiskilled-3	155	2,279	2,491	161	2,640	1.23
Skilled-1	165	2,426	2,635	167	2,686	1.26
Skilled-2	180	2,646	2,851	184	2,965	1.38
Skilled-3	190	2,794	2,995	194	3,115	1.45
High skilled-1	200	2,941	3,139	204	3,296	1.54
High skilled-2	215	3,161	3,555	217	3,422	1.59

In the chemical industry I examined wage rates at three points over a twelve-year period. During this interval, management and the unions fought rancorously to reclassify all job rates, and the unions pressed to reduce wage and salary disparities. While they succeeded in raising the rates of the lowest paid workers, this was possible because automation had eliminated almost all of their jobs. But automation also introduced new and higher-paying occupations. The process of eliminating some occupations, introducing new ones, upgrading job titles, shifting some occupations to supervision, and increasing seniority benefits elongated rather than compressed the plant's wage profile. As Table 11.7 shows, pay differentials between the skilled and unskilled remained close to the national average throughout the period.

Table 11.7. Chemical Industry: Distribution of Employees and Wages by Wage Levels for Three Periods

Wage Levels Grades	1965		1969		1977	
	Percent of Labor Force	Wage Ratios	Percent of Labor Force	Wage Ratios	Percent of Labor Force	Wage Ratios
115	36	1.00	10	1.00	2	1.00
125	27	1.12	17	1.09	10	1.19
135	18	1.17	16	1.12	18	1.21
145	17	1.27	14	1.17	12	1.32
160	2	1.35	25	1.27	26	1.40
170			17	1.33	1	1.43
175					23	1.50
185					7	1.56[a]
Totals	100		99		99	(1.72)[b]
No. of cases	(340)		(408)		(353)	

[a]For the base 125, the ratio is 1.30.
[b]The lowest ratio for supervisors without seniority bonus.

Finally, I found that some Lyon industries were paying wages below the legal minimum (*Point du jour*, 1977), while others were paying above the levels reported to the government. Interviews with illegal aliens and domestic workers revealed that some of them received wages lower than the minimum level. Interviews with artisans showed that some paid their workers rates above those reported to the government.

I concluded that for the mass of employees in the private sector, earnings reported by most employers to INSÉÉ are probably as accurate as U.S. workers' reports to the census. Moreover, French manual employees in government earn rates close to the national average in the private sector. Overall, INSÉÉ statistics slightly over-estimate earnings of unskilled and semiskilled workers in small enterprises and clearly underestimate the earnings of artisans and their employees. Finally, the union drive to reduce wage inequality has probably failed. U.S. census earnings statistics for manual workers are probably as accurate and certainly more comprehensive than the French. In comparisons of earnings by skill level, the French data probably underestimate the range slightly more than do the U.S. data.

Patterns of Earnings Inequality

From the U.S. perspective, French wage schemes are very hierarchical and status-bound. Most governmental and business documents
divide manual workers into at least two grades of unskilled labor,
two or three grades of semiskilled, three to five grades of skilled,
three grades of immediate supervision, and several grades of
technicians. Since these grade levels (*barêmes*) are typically linked
to educational and other credentials, most workers with higher
grades consider them a coveted property right. Labor union agreements resemble civil service rosters: wages of the lowest grade of
unskilled labor are pegged at 100 and the rates for all other skills are
indexed to it—up to 200 or higher. In most industries the indices
have resisted change for decades (Daubigny, 1969), but recently
they have become controversial. Many union officers want to reduce
the range of the indices, but skilled workers and managers want to
maintain traditional differentials. Some employers assign the FFB to
the lowest wage grade irrespective of their skills or jobs on the
pretext that they lack training. Even the least skilled French workers
are usually assigned grades above the FFB (Linhart, 1978).

Contrary to earlier periods (Brown, 1977:73), earnings inequality in the French working class exceeds that of the U.S. (Table 11.8).
Artisans of both nations earn slightly more than do skilled employees,
but the French artisans probably do relatively better. Zarca (1977:107),
France's leading expert on artisans, holds that official statistics
underestimate their earnings, and that artisans earn significantly
more than do skilled employees. France taxes artisan earnings at
higher rates than employee earnings because officials estimate that
artisans underreport their earnings by about 30 percent. Artisans
have attacked the government's "discriminatory" taxes and have
demanded remedial measures, but labor officials oppose giving
artisans "special privileges" (*Figaro*, 1977). American artisans also
underreport their earnings by at least 30 percent (see Chapter 4).
French artisans derive almost all of their income from self-employment,
whereas U.S. artisans derive a third of theirs from wages.[8] Clearly,
artisans earn the highest working-class incomes in both countries,
but the French do relatively better.

French skilled employees earn about half again as much as the
unskilled and this advantage is about one-fifth higher than the U.S.
ratio. Moreover, virtually all French skilled workers were paid on a
monthly basis at the time of this study, a privilege that was being
extended to unskilled laborers in small firms (Bunel, 1973). French
semiskilled operatives earn 20 percent more than do laborers com-

pared to 14 percent more in the U.S. The French differentials should be even higher because INSÉÉ omits the earnings of poorly paid domestics and many service workers, while most such earnings are reported in the U.S. census.

The conclusion is clear: compared to those in western European and English-speaking countries, French earnings are the most unequal—within the working class, between and within the white-collar and business classes, and among all classes. While American ideology does not stress equality, the U.S. has one of the most equal earnings distribution in the West (CERC, 1971; CFDT, 1977, Documentation Française, 1976).

Table 11.8. Annual Mean Earnings Ratios for Manual Workers in France (1972) and the United States (1969)

Occupational Level	France[a]			U.S.[b]		
	Men	Women	Total	Men	Women	Total
Artisans	—	—	1.57[c]	—	—	1.52[d]
Supervisors and foremen	2.36	2.50	2.46	1.52	1.21	1.47
Craft and skilled	1.47	1.37	1.52	1.35	1.17	1.34
Operatives and semiskilled	1.23	1.17	1.20	1.16	1.10	1.14
Laborers and unskilled	1.00	1.00	1.00	1.00	1.00	1.00

[a]Groupe d'Étude (1976b: H-11). Secteur privé et semi-public.
[b]U.S. Bureau of the Census (1973c: Table 57).
[c]Zarca (1977: 107)
[d]U.S. Bureau of the Census (1970) Public Use Sample, 1/1,000 County File.

Sector Earnings Inequality

A larger percentage of the French than U.S. working class is employed in the core sector of the economy (Table 11.1). The mean earnings of manual workers in twenty identical industries, mining, and construction were ranked for both countries and mean ranks were computed for core and periphery industries. Although core industries ranked slightly lower in France, the Spearman rank correlation (rho) between all U.S. and French industries was quite high: +.86 (Table 11.9). Sector earnings differentials were substantial in both countries. The unweighted mean earnings in French core industries were 15 percent higher than in periphery industries; in American, 10 percent higher. In both countries, mean earnings in the highest paying core industry were twice those of the lowest paying industry in the periphery. In both countries, petroleum workers received the highest pay and apparel workers, the lowest. Skilled workers in petroleum earned almost three times as much as the unskilled in apparel. The ability of French skilled workers to resist sector effects on their earnings is demonstrated by the same skill differential in both core and periphery industries. In the U.S., the differential was higher in the periphery probably because unskilled workers received relatively lower pay (see Chapter 2).

Table 11.9. Core-Periphery Differentials for Earnings of Manual Workers in Industry

	France[a]	U.S.[c]
Mean rank for average earnings		
Core industries	9.5	7.5
Periphery industries	16.8	16.7
Ratio between average earnings of		
highest and lowest paying industries	2.12[b]	2.25[d]
Unweighted mean earnings differentials—		
skilled/unskilled		
Core industries	1.80	1.53
Periphery industries	1.79	1.68

[a]For twenty-four major industry groups including mining and construction, excluding services.
[b]Calculated from Groupe d'Étude (1976b: H-11).
[c]Calculated from U.S. Bureau of the Census (1972c: Tables 1 and 4).
[d]Calculated from U.S. Bureau of the Census (1972b: 709).

Regional Income Inequality

A strong labor movement resists regional inequalities in wages. How do the two nations compare in this regard? The French Ministry of Labor conducted a study of wage differentials in seventeen major industries covering Paris and the provinces for 1956–72 (Documentation Française, 1976:H-30). The skilled/unskilled wage ratios climbed slowly in Paris from 1956 to 1968 (1.68 to 1.71), the fateful year of the Paris riots. Within two years, the ratios dropped 31 percent, signifying a dramatic improvement in the relative economic position of the unskilled. This partly reflected the government's policy to raise minimum wages faster than the rate of inflation. Two years later (1972), however, the ratio climbed 31 percent to reestablish the traditional differential. In eight of seventeen industries, the differential hit an all-time high. In contrast to the above patterns, from 1956 to 1968 the wage ratio increased more rapidly in the provinces than in Paris (11 vs. 3 percent), but by 1970 the rate in the provinces dropped only five percent (vs. 31

percent in Paris) and increased only 1 percent by 1972 (vs. 31 in Paris).

I can only speculate why wage differentials gyrated so wildly in Paris and so undramatically in the provinces. Since Paris is the ideological centerfuge of France and since labor unions are stronger in Paris than in the provinces, one would expect the drive for equality to be better realized in Paris. Yet, since 1850, income inequality in all Parisian industries has been higher than in the provinces (Hannaman, 1979). In 1956, the Parisian differential was 21 percent higher than in the provinces, falling to 13 percent in 1970 and rising to 20 percent in 1972. Before the May 1968 riots, wage inequality rose faster in the nondurable goods industries in both Paris and the provinces, but after the riots, the differential in Paris recovered more slowly in the highly unionized core industries.

Although market forces partially explain differences between Paris and the provinces, political and social factors also play a part. In response to the riots, both the government and unions tried to raise the lowest wages. While the semiskilled/unskilled wage ratio fell faster than the skilled/unskilled ratio (Documentation Française, 1976a:55), Parisian skilled workers quickly regained their traditional wage advantage both where unions were weak and where they were strong. Parisian union officials responded quickly to the ideological demand to equalize wages and then as quickly responded to skilled workers' demands to adhere to traditional wage differentials. Apparently union leaders had neither the power nor inclination to engage in a sustained campaign to raise the relative wage level of Parisian laborers, foreign workers, women, and other low paid workers. If *egalité* could not be approached in Paris where union and political leaders had greatest influence, it had even less chance in the provinces. Provincial reactions to the events of May were muted. Wage differentials changed more slowly, perhaps in response more to market than political pressures.

The U.S. pattern of regional skill differentials stands in stark contrast to France's. Even though U.S. industrial relations were turbulent during the late sixties, wage differentials changed little. Schoeplein's (1977:320) important study of wage differentials in 1952–73 revealed a pattern of national stability and regional convergence. The power of U.S. unions to enforce national agreements undoubtedly contributed to the trend.

Sex Income Inequality

In both France and the U.S., women earn less than men at all skill levels; the higher the level, the more unequal the earnings. Although sex inequalities are massive in both countries, Table 11.10 shows that they are about 15 percent greater in the U.S. The more favorable position of French women is somewhat misleading because the earnings of many poorly paid workers, a large proportion of whom are women, are not reported to INSÉÉ. These include domestics, household workers, artisans (hairdressers, etc.), waitresses in small establishments, and others who together comprise at least 15 percent of all working women.

Because of the traditional shortage of unskilled industrial labor, more French than U.S. women hold stable jobs in manufacturing. A stable job is defined as the worker being in the same occupation for five years. About 30 percent of French and 19 percent of U.S. working-class women work in manufacturing, as Table 11.11 shows, which pays higher wages than the service sector where more U.S. women work (60 vs. 30 percent). Moreover, French women exhibit greater job stability than U.S. women at all skill levels. French and U.S. men have identical job stability (INSÉÉ, 1974:D-32; U.S. Bureau of the Census, 1970:Table 320).

Table 11.10. Ratio of Women's to Men's Mean Annual Earnings for Full-Time Workers

Occupation	France[a]	U.S.[b]
Supervisors	.83	.46
Skilled and craft workers	.73	.57
Operatives and Semiskilled	.75	.61
Laborers and Unskilled	.79	.60
Service workers except domestics	.80	.56
Totals[c]	.69	.56

[a]Documentation Française (1976b: H-11), for 1972.
[b]U.S. Bureau of the Census (1972d).
[c]For total labor force.

Laws in both countries decree equal pay for the same work, yet Charraud (1974) has shown that sex earnings inequality in the same occupations increased in France after World War II, as it did in the U.S. over a twenty year interval (U.S. Department of Labor, 1975:129). Although both governments launched vocational training programs for women, movement into skilled work has been slow and most women continue to be trained for traditional female jobs (Liaisons Sociales, 1975b; U.S. Department of Labor, 1975:233).

Other indicators of inequality show that French working-class women are worse off than their U.S. counterparts. After World War II,

Table 11.11. Proportion of Women Manual Workers in
Selected Industries (percent)

Industries	France[a]	U.S.[b]
Mining	5	4
Construction	1	1
Machinery	11	11
Electrical goods	41	44
Chemical	26	23
Transportation	4	5
Primary ferrous	9	3
Wood and furniture	19	28
Stone, ceramics	13	16
Food	33	24
Textiles	55	48
Apparel	85	84
Paper	30	14
Printing	28	21
Total manufacturing	30	19

[a]Documentation Française (1926b: Table B-4).
[b]U.S. Bureau of the Census (1972e: Table 4).

the U.S. female unemployment rate grew relative to men's, but this occurred as women expanded their labor force participation. In 1974, U.S. women's unemployment was 40 percent higher than men's, while in France it was over 80 percent higher. Silver (1977) has shown that in the French class structure, the male advantage in education is greatest in the working class; in the U.S., working-class women and men attain the same level of education. For years, CGT union leaders have ignored women's protests and have opposed birth control because they believed using it would reduce the size of the working class. While U.S. unions have held no official position on birth control, they have opposed sex equality in the marketplace. The AFL–CIO opposed the Equal Rights Amendment for many years. Despite American labor's traditional conservatism toward women's issues, the U.S. women's movement is stronger than the French, and this may ultimately benefit U.S. working-class women more (Stoddard, 1978).

Ethnic Earnings Differentials

Data on FFB earnings are scant and unreliable. INSÉÉ is the best data source, but it excludes many agricultural workers, domestics, self-employed, illegal aliens, family workers, and others. Using INSÉÉ data, Vlassenko and Volkoff (1975) reported that an earnings gap of 17.4 percent between the French foreign-born (FFB) and French manual workers largely reflected differences in occupational placement rather than discrimination.[9] Controlling for occupation, FFB earnings were within 5 percent of those of the French. Since the FFB were younger and had less seniority than natives (2.5 vs. 5 years), the true gap was even smaller. But the FFB worked more hours and were more heavily concentrated in the larger, higher-paying industries, which tended to raise their earnings. Overall, these factors probably offset each other.

Granier and Marciano (1975) studied a sample of 1,772 FFB who registered with local prefects.[10] Although the representativeness of the sample was undetermined, the study corroborated Vlassenko and Volkoff's findings of a 17 percent difference in FFB and French earnings. In the Granier and Marciano study, FFB earnings equaled those of unskilled and semiskilled French workers, but French skilled workers earned five percent more than did the FFB skilled.

When the relative earnings position of the FFB and the B–H are compared, the FFB do better (Table 11.12). U.S. skilled workers earned 28 percent more than the comparable B–H group; the semiskilled, 20 percent more; and the unskilled earned identical wages.[11] However, skill differentials *within* the ethnic populations were similar in both countries and they conformed to their respective national patterns.

Table 11.12. Earnings Differentials for Male Ethnic Groups and Total Labor

Occupations	France[a]		U.S.[b]	
	FFB	Total	B–H	Total
Nonmanual	1.31	1.69	—	1.85
Skilled	1.42	1.50	1.44	1.47
Semiskilled	1.22	1.23	1.27	1.34
Unskilled	1.00	1.00	1.00	1.00
Total	1.20	1.41	1.37	1.48

[a]Granier and Marciano (1975:Table 1), Monthly Earnings.
[b]U.S. Bureau of the Census (1972e). The total for B–H are for ages twenty-five to sixty-four.

Although one might conclude from these statistics that earnings differentials between ethnics and natives are trivial in France compared to those in the U.S., official French statistics are not representative. The massive protests of the FFB over their economic discrimination would appear unlikely if they involved an earnings gap of only 5 percent. To be sure, the differential at the unskilled level is small because the FFB comprise a major segment of the unskilled labor force (e.g., over 40 percent in construction). French semiskilled and skilled workers typically earn higher incomes than do the FFB, hold preferred jobs, have more seniority, suffer less unemployment, and get more training (Linhart, 1978).

Though Granier and Marciano (1975) did not reveal how their sample was gathered, it contained only *employed men.* Butaud (1973), who did the field work, reported that one in eight Maghrébins in Paris was unemployed at the time of interviewing. His sample omitted FFB unemployed, unregistered aliens (who accept lower wage jobs), workers in small cities and rural areas (where wage rates are lower), and wives (who often do not register as workers). Finally, the study compared FFB male earnings to the earnings of all workers, one-third of whom were women who typically receive lower earnings than do men. The effect of all these deficiencies probably overestimated the earnings of the FFB by 20 percent.

I decided to compare the earnings of the FFB with all workers employed in the same industries studied by Granier and Marciano (1975), who feel that this approach has limited utility. Nevertheless, the comparisons do reveal the position of the FFB in those industries. For the U.S. comparison, except for domestic service, I included only the males in those industries because almost all of the FFB are males. The results in Table 11.13 show that the earnings inequality between the FFB and all workers is higher than the corresponding U.S. figure for all industries except construction and "other production." I suspected that the two French exceptions were underestimations. My computations for 1972 INSÉÉ (1975) data for these industries produced higher differentials: 1.19 for construction and 1.18 for other production. Even these ratios should be higher because, unlike U.S. data, the French data excluded managers and professionals who earn the highest incomes. It is hard to avoid the conclusion that earnings inequality between the FFB and all workers is higher in France than between the B–H and all U.S. workers.

The findings reported above support the hypothesis that greater structural cleavages in the working class are reflected in greater earnings disparities. Skill earnings differentials in France are the largest in the industrialized world. Larger and more persistent earnings gaps exist between workers in different regions of the country. Sex income inequality is smaller than in the U.S., but educational

Table 11.13. Earnings Ratios by Industry

	France[a] All Workers	U.S.[b] All Workers
Sector	FFB	B-H
Construction	1.10	1.55
Mining	1.46	1.41
Metal working	1.62	1.37
Other production	1.10	1.39
Domestic Services	1.46	1.45
Other sectors	2.14	1.37
All sectors	1.59	1.36

[a]Granier and Marciano (1975b: 149).
[b]U.S. Bureau of the Census (1972). Except for domestic services, figures for blacks and Hispanic-origin workers are based on male earnings. "Other production" is interpreted as nondurable manufacturing.

inequality and female unemployment are higher in France. Economic inequality between ethnic groups and natives is also larger in France.

Class Changes and Political Consensus

The final research question is whether social and economic disparities in the French working-class, greater than in the U.S., reflect greater political disagreements. If the French working class exhibits more political consensus than the American, class homogeneity cannot explain it. Yet before one can reject the hypothesis that links class homogeneity with political consensus, other factors must be considered. Perhaps French working-class heterogeneity is too recent to produce political cleavages. Obviously, comparative historical studies of changes in class structure and class politics are needed. Even though this chapter cannot summarize the existing material on the subject, I do want to point to some obvious changes in class composition and the degree of political consensus in the two countries. The following description suggests but does not prove them.

Changes in U.S. Class Composition and Political Consensus

The U.S. working class appears to be becoming more homogeneous. The proportion of foreign-born manual workers has declined steadily from 26 percent in 1920 to 3 percent today, and the second generation has declined from 21 to 8 percent (U.S. Bureau of the

Census, 1970c). Current ethnic changes result largely from the rural-urban migration of blacks and Hispanic-origin workers. Educational equality is increasing: men's rate of high school completion now equals women's; educational inequality between the races is declining; educational differentials among skill levels are trivial (U.S. Department of Labor, 1974:64). Occupational homogenization is increasing as the percentage of artisans, domestic servants, and unskilled labor declines, and as the percentage of skilled workers stabilizes and that of semiskilled and service workers continues to increase (Wolfbein, 1969:56). Finally, occupational and educational homogenization have produced a long-term secular trend toward wage compression (Ober, 1948; Schoeplein, 1977).

While it is difficult to demonstrate causal links between class homogenization and party allegiance, certain trends are clear. After the Great Depression, the U.S. working class increasingly shifted its allegiance to the Democratic party. Blacks and Hispanic-origin workers, as recent entrants into the urban working class, identified even more strongly with the Democratic party. Party loyalty tends to be intergenerational, and both working-class men and women displayed similar party allegiances and political behavior (Pomper, 1975:28, 88).

Hamilton's (1972) exhaustive study concluded that economic differences among non-Southern workers within the working class only slightly affect party preference. However, using more direct measures and a more representative sample, I found greater differences. In addition, I found other differences. Unskilled and semiskilled workers are more apathetic than the skilled, vote less regularly, but vote Democratic more consistently. Self-employed, foremen, and skilled workers are more active and independent politically. Party identification is also slightly affected by union membership, community size, religion, region, and ethnic background (see Chapter 10).

Although their political involvement is low, manual workers are more liberal than are white-collar employees. Union members do not like their officers to become too involved in politics and too influential in Congress (see Chapter 9). Union officers, especially in the industrial unions, are more liberal and more politically active than their members or officers of craft unions. In the bland, two-party U.S. political culture, union officers back legislation of direct interest to their members: union protection, minimum wages, social security, unemployment and consumer protection. Officers hesitate to move too far from their members in such areas as foreign affairs, taxation, and welfare aid. Overall, the historical political tide of the working class has been toward the Democratic party, and the wavering historical drift of the party, aided by union pressure, is to become more programmatically liberal and distinct from the Republican party (Pomper, 1975:183).

Changes in French Class Composition and Political Consensus

After 1850, the French labor force became more heterogeneous. At that time immigrants (mostly Belgians and Italians) formed 1 percent of the population, but today immigrants (over two-fifths of whom are North Africans) form an under-class of almost a tenth of the population. Unlike earlier immigrants, few Maghrébins become French citizens. Educational inequality is increasing because vocational tracking persists in French schools, and untrained immigrants swell the ranks of the less skilled. Sex educational inequality only recently shows signs of abating, but vocational training is still highly segregated by sex (Liaisons Sociales, 1975c). Normally, when the demand for artisans and skilled labor declines, wage compression follows, but the reverse has happened in France. Parodi (1962) and Sellier (1973:97) report that wage differentials declined sharply from 1865 to 1906, but today they are 20 percent higher than at the turn of the century. Increasing economic inequality has clearly accompanied increasing social heterogeneity.

The political ascendancy of the French working class has always been hampered by splintered unions and splintered leftist parties. In the face of economic depression and rising fascism, unions and parties buried their differences in the 1930s to form a popular front socialist government, but it was quickly sabotaged by business and financial interests. Left coalitions emerged again after the Liberation, the Algerian crisis in 1960, and the events of May 1968, but they did not endure. Hoffman (1974:134) suggests that the structural changes that modernized French industry after World War II may have split working-class loyalties: workers with secure jobs in the government sector and in large-scale industry wavered in their support of the Left. In 1982, the strong resurgence of the Socialist party, with the support of a weakened Communist party, enabled the Left to assume power. Whether the Left will remain united is uncertain. Therefore, an analysis of current political divisions is appropriate.

Class divisions seem to be deepening between immigrants and native born, between skilled and unskilled, men and women, workers and union officials, and workers and political parties. Traditionally, unskilled labor in construction, metals manufacturing, and the services were French. Today, the unskilled are increasingly immigrants who are excluded from national politics and discouraged from holding union office (Minces, 1973:154). Antagonism between the French and immigrants is high: 70 percent of the French believe that there are too many North Africans in the country (Tapinos, 1975).

Artisans, once bonded to the working class by family and political ties, flirted with rightist Poujadism after World War II (Hoffman, 1963:60–74) and cast their lot with small business after the 1960s (Michelat and Simon, 1975). Skilled workers have successfully resisted union efforts to decrease wage differentials. Their strikes typically involve protecting their traditional prerogatives, while strikes of semiskilled workers increasingly involve political issues (Maupeau-Abbud, 1974).

Despite their class consciousness, only 30 percent of French workers belong to the two leading unions that support the Communist and Socialist parties. Neither the expansion of large-scale industry after World War II nor the growth of manual occupations increased union membership much above the U.S. level at that time. Public opinion surveys show that the French working class is split over supporting the politics of their union leaders. Durand's (1971:117ff) national study of 1,080 union *militants* in manufacturing, those who presumably endorse class conflict, found that they held moderate views. The majority thought that class inequalities were diminishing, that their economic future looked bright, and that workers, in their wages demands, should take into account their employer's economic condition. On these questions, the skilled were more conservative than the less skilled.

In a study of 1,116 nonimmigrant manual workers in the most highly unionized manufacturing sector, Adam and colleagues (1970) found that only 38 percent belonged to a union and that almost all of them had experienced upward occupational mobility. Over half thought that unions were too preoccupied with politics and insufficiently involved with workers' grievances; 60 percent disagreed that unions had to engage in politics, and 60 percent disagreed that unions should be tied to a single party, preferring instead a loose entente with several parties. In responding to the events of May 1968, a majority in all three major unions expressed dissatisfaction with the behavior of their unions, and over 70 percent of those who had opinions opposed students entering the factories to discuss problems (Adam, et al., 1970: 55, 169, 223). Finally, in a national survey of 2,000 respondents (CERC, 1973:1950), workers were asked who had most influence in raising their salaries: 40 percent named their boss, 33 the union, and 22 the state. Though skilled workers were the most split into pro- and anti-union positions, on most of the above questions they expressed the most conservative views.

The intense interest that French workers show in politics may be mythical. In the Adam and colleagues' study (1970), 65 percent of manufacturing employees expressed little or no interest in politics. About 40 percent favored parties of the left, 30 percent favored parties of the center or right, and 30 percent did not respond. Converse and Dupeaux (1962), who had earlier noted this high nonresponse rate, interpreted it as signifying a lack of political knowledge and involvement, especially among the poorly educated, the young, and housewives. Far from having strong family party traditions, half of the electorate expressed weak party attachments; only 29 percent could characterize their fathers' political preferences—compared to 91 percent for U.S. workers. In DeGaulle's last referendum of 27 April 1969, 30 percent of the skilled workers and half of the unskilled admitted they did not vote (Adam, et al., 1970:191).

French working-class men and women disagree more on politics than do their U.S. counterparts. Michelat and Simon (1975) analyzed the voting intentions of 10,159 citizens included in ten national surveys. Both men and women household heads at all occupational levels and men and nonemployed women differed strongly. A larger proportion of women than men did not answer political questions, but the women who did were significantly more attracted to the center and Gaullist parties and much more distrustful of Communist and noncommunist left parties. Women's party preferences varied little either by their own occupations or those of their husbands.

Mossuz-Lauvau and Sineau (1976) confirmed these findings in a study of 470 men and women, ages sixteen to thirty-four, in two sections of Paris. Among those with working-class backgrounds, 50 percent of the women and 26 percent of the men indicated no interest in politics. Women were also less radical than men but not at higher socioeconomic levels. Mothers with working-class jobs had daughters who were less attracted than men to leftist parties, but sex differences disappeared at higher SES levels. Religious involvements did not affect women's party preferences unless they were not employed. To conclude: the data support the hypothesis that sex inequality in education, sex differences in socialization, and lower female labor force participation, by inducing political indifference and conservatism among women, have increased working-class cleavages.

Several studies point to political disagreements paralleling the skill hierarchy. Hamilton's (1967:22ff) national survey noted that more skilled than unskilled workers thought that a French accommo-

dation with the U.S.S.R. was possible and that a revolution was not
needed to achieve social progress. Even though skilled workers
rejected middle-class identification, they remained more moderate
even when important variables were controlled: job satisfaction,
unemployment experiences, changes in standard of living, and prospects for promotion.

The political surveys of Adam and colleagues (1970) showed
that the skilled were more radical than the unskilled in political
self-identification and party sympathies, but the skilled were also
more attracted to non-communist left and center parties. Michelat
and Simon's (1975) ten combined surveys revealed that unskilled
workers were slightly more pro-communist and Gaullist than the
skilled; the latter were more favorable to the non-communist left;
and men in service occupations were more attracted to non-communist
parties. Among working women, few differences appeared by skill
level. They were less attracted than men to the Communist party
and more favorable to Gaullism. Non-working women's party preferences were the least developed, least favorable to the Communist
party, and unrelated to their husbands' occupations.

A multivariate analysis led Michelat and Simon (1975) to conclude that increasing age and socioeconomic status depressed identification with the Communist party and increased it with the
non-communist left. Increasing age and education pushed the skilled
toward the non-communist left and higher education similarly affected
young skilled workers. High income inflated voting intention, especially among the skilled, an effect that benefited all parties but the
Communist.

In a national survey, CERC (1973) asked 2,000 citizens how they
felt about their own economic well-being and that of other major
occupational groups. Skill differences were small but consistent.
More of the skilled felt that their standard of living had improved
over the last ten years, that their income level was fair, and that
wage increases should not disproportionately favor workers in low
income occupations. Finally, all surveys showed that supervisors
were the least attracted to the Communist party and more inclined
toward the non-communist left and Gaullism. Artisans similarly
rejected the Communist party and supported the Gaullist party
more strongly than did other workers.

Comparing French and U.S. working-class politics is complicated by three structural differences: France has a multi-party
system while the U.S. has a two party system; France's parties cover
a wider ideological span; and France's left parties are more divided
than are U.S. liberals and conservatives. In two party systems, the

working class may polarize toward one party or waver between parties; in a multi-party system, more wavering is possible. In both systems, workers can disagree over the proper connection between unions and parties. Here the French workers are more divided than U.S. workers. French skilled workers, the unions' strongest supporters, take a more conservative stand on this issue than the less skilled, and foremen and artisans take an even dimmer view of the belt-line connection between unions and parties.

Considerable evidence points to political fragmentation of the French working class. Many workers refuse to divulge their political attitudes, even to their children. Among men in the non-service sector, the unskilled lean toward the Communist party while the skilled are split into Communist and non-communist camps in complicated ways. French working-class women counterbalance male support of the Communist party by endorsing the non-communist left and Gaullism. Supervisors, artisans, and workers in the service sector lean strongly toward center parties and Gaullism. Finally, the strongest union supporters opposed union-party alliances. In a working class where 25 percent are politically withdrawn, 40 percent split into communist and non-communist left, and 35 percent prefer center and rightist parties, the hope of a politically unified working class seems almost as ephemeral as in the U.S.

Conclusions

The hypothesis linking class socioeconomic homogeneity to political consensus has received preliminary support. Although more historical research is needed before arriving at a firm conclusion, the data suggest that the U.S. working class is more homogeneous than the French. Relatively more U.S. workers are employed in the less prosperous peripheral sector of the economy and in the traditional proletarian semiskilled, unskilled, and service occupations. Although more U.S. than French women work in low-skilled jobs, more French women are crowded into lower-paying industries. Finally, U.S. ethnic groups are less industrially and occupationally segregated from the rest of the working class than are the French foreign born.

The larger French cleavages are reflected in greater earnings inequality. The earnings differential between artisans and skilled workers (whether male or female, native or foreign-born) on the one hand, and between skilled and unskilled on the other, are impressively greater in France than in the U.S. Regional earnings inequalities are also much larger in France. Although sex equality in earnings appears to be higher in France, female unemployment and earnings inequality among women is also higher. Finally, although the evidence is mixed, earnings inequality between the FFB and French workers appears to be at least as great as between B–H and other U.S. workers. In short, the U.S. working class resembles the traditional proletariat more than does the French because U.S. workers exhibit greater homogeneity in the earnings of sex, ethnicity, skill, sector, and regional groups and greater political consensus.

While data in this study reveal an association between socioeconomic homogeneity of a class and political consensus, they cannot explain or predict specific class action. That task requires a historical analysis of class conflict at work and an analysis of the interactions among unions, parties, intellectuals, and others who seek to mobilize (or inhibit the mobilization of) working class groups on specific issues. Slowly, data on the structure, beliefs, and experiences of the French working class begin to explain why it can act collectively despite internal disagreements to an extent unparalleled for American workers (Tilly, 1978; Gallie, 1983). During the events of May 1968, for example, the French working class mobilized itself even against the opposition of the dominant union (CGT) leadership.

Obviously, on such occasions even apathetic and mildly conservative workers join activists in movements that threaten the government. Perhaps French workers, whatever their political inclinations, share the belief that class inequalities are greater and more important than are inequalities within the working class. Survey data on this topic are slim (Gallie, 1983), but evidence is available on interclass and intraclass economic inequality. In France, the earnings ratio between the highest paid occupations (managers and administrators) and the lowest paid (unskilled labor) is 4.58; in the U.S., the ratio is 2.39 (Documentation Française, 1976b:49). When these ratios are divided by the skilled/unskilled earnings ratio (1.52 for France and 1.34 for the U.S.) the inequality ratio for France is 3.01 and 1.78 for the U.S. The difference is substantial enough to entertain the hypothesis that class inequality in France is so high that workers see it as more important than intraclass inequality. Gallie's (1983) important study of class radicalism among British and French workers found that workers do not know much about the earnings of different classes, but in every question that dealt with the justice of class income differences, French workers were much more critical of income inequality than were the British. Gallie did not systematically explore differences within the French working class, but his study does place great significance on the grievances that French workers have toward managerial authority in the workplace. The failure of management to legitimize worker participation in factory decisions has been used by activists, unions, and parties to sharpen whatever class feelings workers have.

On the other hand, normally apathetic, nonpolitical, and conservative French workers can also be swayed to withhold their support of the Left during most political crises. Hannaman (1979) pointed out that France has a larger social budget than do Great Britain and West Germany, and that the government rapidly improves the well-being of some workers during political crises. The French state can, independently of the unions and the Left, temporarily alter income inequalities. This Bismarckian policy of concessions during crises makes some parts of the working class loyal to non-left governments.

Compared to France the evidence points to increasing social, economic, and political homogeneity in the American working class. Without basic institutional changes, this drift may produce more class consensus but not necessarily more class politics and more political mobilization. The U.S. lacks several structural features of French society that serve to keep class politics constantly in everyone's mind. One of the most important of these is a cadre of intellectuals in schools and universities, in mass communications, in unions, and in parties who keep class issues salient and teach and lead the working class to work for a different social order. Such a "new" class may be in the making in the United States (*Society*, 1979), but even if it solidifies and gains influence, its success in leading the working class will not be easily achieved—as the French have learned.

Notes

1. In a national survey, INSÉÉ (1975) found that 57 percent of the workers in manufacturing, construction, and public works were employed in establishments with more than 200 employees; 38 percent, in firms with over 500.

2. Problems of illegal immigrants are similar in both countries. Granier and Marciano (1975) estimate that in France they made up 17 percent of the registered foreigners in 1973. The corresponding figure in the United States is probably higher.

3. This situation is not altered by considering agricultural workers. In the United States, less than 4 percent of blacks and six percent of Hispanics work in agriculture (U.S. Bureau of the Census, 1972b:231) compared to 7 percent of the FFB in 1968 (*Hommes et migration*, 1971:56; Butaud, 1972).

4. All but two industries were matched; earnings for France were based on mean hourly wages and mean annual earnings for the United States.

5. The same worker may appear on the report of several employers. Annual income surveys do not overcome all the deficiencies of the INSÉÉ reports.

6. It is not unusual for employers to pay individual workers a 15 percent bonus when they are loyal, produce well, and work regularly.

7. Social benefits are not reported in any tables in this chapter.

8. U.S. data from the Public Use Sample, County File (1/1,000), U.S. Bureau of the Census, 1970. When the artisan/unskilled labor earnings differential is calculated with only self-employed earnings, the ratio drops to 1.01.

9. Measured as French salaries minus immigrant salaries over French salaries.

10. Granier and Marciano (1975) divide the mean monthly earnings of all workers by mean of immigrant workers.

11. All U.S. manual workers earn 26 percent more than B–H; the advantage is 13 percent at the nonmanual level.

12

Conclusions and Prospects

Overview

Sociological research has recognized the internal diversity of the American working class, but it has not systematically traced the impact of this condition on class behavior. Although the working class has become more homogeneous in some respects, it has become more divided in others. Today, as formerly, the class continues to change internally and to drift politically. Class inequalities remain large. The top segments of the class now earn three to four times as much as the most disprivileged full-time workers. Earnings inequality is strongly associated with such variables as self-employment, skill, sector of employment, sex, and race. While the growth of industrial unions since the 1930s improved the lot of some nonskilled workers, it also increased economic inequality in the class.

Foremen, artisans, and skilled workers are part of an aristocracy of labor that remains quite distinct from the mass of manual workers in earnings, social status, and politics. Even nonskilled workers have become more economically stratified than in the past. Males in the nonunionized core sector now earn considerably more than do the heterogeneous group of workers in the competitive sector of the economy, and the marginally employed now form an under-class even in good times. These economic and social status divisions have become large enough to influence class politics.

Scholars predicted that a unified labor movement after World War II would lead to a politically mobilized working class. This appeared to be happening for two decades, but after 1965 the commitment of union members to the Democratic party and liberal causes became unglued. My analysis of the political beliefs and behavior of the rank and file revealed that it was still oriented toward traditional bread and butter issues; its commitment to other political goals was uncertain. Moreover, political commitments varied in the rest of the class. The aristocracy of labor exhibited relatively high voter participation, an independent political position, and ticket-splitting. The nonskilled industrial proletariat vacillated in voting participation and party allegiance. Although nonskilled and nonunionized workers in the economic periphery were the most committed to the economic and political programs of labor, they could not be relied upon consistently to vote their convictions.

Examining structural divisions within the class-conscious French working class showed that it was more internally divided than was the American. In both countries, the historical environment of class relations influenced political tides within the working class. Changes in economic inequality between the classes, rising prosperity, and cyclical unemployment continue to affect working-class politics as in the past.

The Future Working Class

Will the American working class become more economically and socially stratified, and will this affect its politics? In the absence of an adequate theory of structural political change, predictions are risky. However, I shall describe some changes in the working class and evaluate their possible political effect, using working class strata as reference points.

Changes in the economy will change the relative size of working-class divisions. The decline in heavy manufacturing preceded the economic depression of the late 1970s and early 1980s. That decline will continue to reduce the relative size of the nonskilled core stratum. All other strata will probably increase somewhat. Greatest expansion should be in the service industries, enlarging the pool of nonskilled periphery workers there, but a small expansion of foremen, self-employed, and skilled should also be expected. The skilled will expand because a service economy requires more and more workers to maintain and repair the ever-growing number of machines. Self-employed workers also repair appliances, so their numbers should stabilize or increase. Finally, more supervisors are needed as manufacturing and service become more technologically complex. Unless the economy rebounds robustly, the proportion of marginally employed workers should rise because residual underemployment appears to increase after each economic depression.

All these changes point to a more divided working class whose shape will approximate an hour glass, the aristocrats of labor expanding at the top, the proletariat of nonskilled core workers shrinking in the middle, and nonskilled periphery and marginally employed workers expanding at the bottom. The characteristics of the upper working class will increasingly resemble those of white-collar workers while ethnic groups and impoverished women will make up the lower part. As the number of lower white-collar and upper blue-collar workers increase, they will form a middle-status group located at the lower edge of the growing cadres of professional and administrative employees.

How these changes will affect economic inequality within the working class is uncertain. Recently, large numbers of union members in core industries have experienced unemployment and others have suffered wage reductions. Although these trends have received much publicity, workers in core industries comprise a favored group over the long haul. Buchele (1983), who examined four measures of employment stability over an extended period of the business cycle, showed that unemployment in core industries fluctuated more than it did in periphery industries, but it was always lower. Moreover, separation rates and number of job moves were always lower in the core. Again, although downward pressure on union wages has received much publicity, nonunion workers have probably suffered even more unemployment and wage reduction. Consequently, earnings differentials between the unionized and nonunionized sectors should continue to increase somewhat.

In the short run, given their relative scarcity, foremen, the skilled, and possibly the self-employed, should maintain their earning advantages over workers in other strata. Eventually, skilled labor will confront downward wage pressure. Women, blacks, and Hispanic-origin workers are seeking greater access into these privileged jobs, and they will slowly increase their representation. This penetration will weaken traditional bonds among workers in the privileged strata and reduce their ability to resist the market's downward wage pressure. Nonskilled workers in the periphery will also be subjected to downward wage pressure because the supply of unskilled immigrants (mostly Spanish-speaking) is increasing. They are willing to take even the lowest paying jobs. Even if legislation restricts the entry of these workers, illegal immigration will continue at a reduced level. The overall effect will drive wages down in the periphery. Finally, the inability of mature capitalism to absorb all of its workers points to a permanently enlarged stratum of marginally employed. In this pessimistic scenario, I envision most downward wage pressure on the two lowest strata. The above trends point to more economic inequality in the working class as a whole and more inequality in the entire class structure because the salaries of professional and administrative workers probably will not decline appreciably.

The sex and ethnic composition of the working class strata will also change, augmenting intraclass tensions. Clearly, the major new sources of labor recruitment will continue to be women and workers of Hispanic origin. The major stratal destination of white women will be clerical work, while Hispanic origin workers will increase in the periphery and marginally-employed strata. Thus, the bottom of the working class will become more visibly distinct from the middle class. Tensions between black and Hispanic-origin workers will rise as Hispanics increase in number. Given the American record of race prejudice, I expect Hispanic-origin workers to be more upwardly mobile than blacks, increasing competition for the better jobs. Women, of course, are represented in all ethnic groups. They will raise work-group tensions as they increasingly insist on equal treatment.

If present trends continue, the upward mobility of blacks and Hispanic-origin workers will occur more rapidly in the public than in the private sector. This should increase their political power. The second generation of these upwardly mobile groups, especially the well educated, will become increasingly restive, demanding better jobs. They already are the most class-conscious and radical members of the working class, and they will become even more militant in the future. In short, the future working class will be dominated more by ethnic groups that will become more politically effective as they seek upward mobility in the system (see Kornblum, 1974).

Future Working-Class Politics

Any analysis of future working-class politics must assign labor unions a place of central importance. Class grievances have little effect unless they are focused and activated by elites who control organizational resources. Labor unions have both leadership and resources. Some observers have predicted that labor's influence will decline because its membership is declining. This conclusion is simplistic because small groups can wield enormous political influence, and union membership may grow.

The important questions then are, Where will labor unions increase their membership? How will membership growth influence union politics? Union membership will probably grow most in the governmental, educational, and service sectors. Public sector employment will probably grow slowly, as will employment in the government-dependent sector which includes the education and defense industries. Employment stability in these areas makes them attractive targets for unionization. Since the defense industries are already well organized, education remains an attractive target for organization. Segments of the service sector will also attract unionization attempts, especially hospitals, financial services, and even the wholesale and retail trade. In short, union strength may increase in the lower white-collar and nonskilled manual service areas and decrease in the nonskilled core manufacturing area. Women and ethnic minorities will increase their union representation faster than will native-born white males. Therefore, changes in union politics seem inevitable.

Organized labor is currently reexamining its political strategy and its relations with groups in the Democratic party coalition. Under Lane Kirkland, the AFL-CIO decided to become more active in primary elections in order to influence the choice of the Democratic party's presidential nominee. The second tactic seeks to extract more support for labor from groups in the party coalition. Heretofore, labor has willingly supported other liberal groups to pass legislation dealing with environmental pollution, civil rights, gun control, consumer protection, and other causes. Labor has, however, received little reciprocal support for its legislative goals, such as the common-situs picketing bill, implementation of health and safety laws, and tariff protection for industries threatened by foreign competition. In short, labor is asking for more solidarity on the part of the liberal coalition on a number of issues that include those important to labor. Some success on these two fronts can be anticipated, so labor can look forward to increasing political influence.

In assessing labor's future political influence, we must consider the changing industrial, occupational, and ethnic composition of its members and, importantly, the Democratic party's influence on labor. Such influence is particularly important because the party, in response to other pressures, has conservatively affected labor's political stand (Davis, 1980; Harwood, 1982). The question now is, can labor's changing membership and increasing political involvement change the class politics of the Democratic party? The most important change that labor can help bring about is a change in the federal income tax laws that would significantly decrease the taxes or exempt from taxes the poorest third of American families. Labor and the Democratic party have been conspicuously reluctant to attack this fundamental change. Other goals in the working-class political agenda include more welfare aid to the poor, raising the poverty index to take account of growth in productivity as well as inflation, more governmental subsidy to retrain workers for new jobs, a higher minimum wage, more stringent regulation of utility prices with reduced rates for the poor, higher retirement benefits, a truly socialized medical care system, growth of the economy to provide more jobs, and so forth. In short, a working-class agenda requires more shifting of the tax burden from the lowest third of the population to the middle class, the corporations, and the rich.

The experience of the British labor unions and their relation to the Labour party offer instructive analogies on the political future of American labor. In Britain, the decline of union membership in heavy industry and the increase in public sector union membership has been more dramatic than in the United States. Forty percent of the members of Britain's ten largest unions work in the public sector. This statistic probably reflects the large employment in the public sector brought about by earlier Labour governments.

The changing industrial composition of British labor unions and other factors increased factionalism in the Labour party. When in office, the Labour party tried to moderate a serious inflation problem. To keep the support of the middle class, it asked the unions to restrain their wage demands in the national interest. The details of the Social Contract with Labour are not important for the present analysis; more important is the political split that it precipitated. Some union officials thought that the Labour party was not acting in the best interest of its members; others disagreed. In the main, public sector and craft-dominated unions became the conservative wing of the party, and unions in the core manufacturing sector became the radical branch. This split became so deep that a new labor-type party (Social Democratic) arose that now competes with the Labour party for working-class support. While the British scenario is not likely to be repeated in United States, certain parallel tensions may develop (Burton, no date).

Under George Meany, AFL–CIO disputes on public policy were muffled. Unions that disagreed with his moderately liberal but cautious stand either restrained from publicly criticizing him or they left the organization. At one time, as many as one-third of all union members were outside the AFL–CIO, including those in auto, mining, railroad and electrical industries, longshoremen, teamsters, and others. These unions were able to take political stands that departed from those of the AFL–CIO leadership. The return of the UAW to the AFL–CIO and the possible return of other unions may give labor a more united voice than it has had in the recent past, but disagreements will not disappear.

In order to simplify the analysis of political cleavages among American labor unions, they will be classified into five types that reflect their major industrial location: craft, government, education, heavy industry, and light industry and service. The ex-AFL craft unions will continue to exert moderate political influence on AFL--CIO councils because their membership is not declining as fast as that of ex-CIO unions. The conservative pull of craft unions is likely to slacken over time as women, blacks, and Hispanic-origin workers slowly increase their representation in the crafts. But affirmative action programs have been more effective in the governmental than private sector, with the consequence that ethnic groups and women now have a higher representation in government employment. I have shown that these groups are more self-conscious, more politically alert, and more radical than other groups. Moreover, the ready access of government unions to legislators and the executive branch of government enables them to affect the political process directly.

Although minorities are not as highly represented in teachers' unions as in government unions, their representation in both has been increasing. Teachers' unions have grown rapidly, and they are aggressively liberal in their national politics. A danger that both government and teachers' unions face is their dependence on tax revenues. There is always the possibility of a conservative backlash to restrict funding of public services and education. Taxpayer revolts against the high cost of government periodically arise, and when they do, the political liberalism of these unions tends to slacken.

In line with the expectation that women and members of minorities will liberalize union politics, unions in the expanding service sector should also become the most liberal since they contain the largest representation of these groups. If I assess the trends correctly, ex-CIO unions in the heavy manufacturing sector may come to represent a middle ground in the liberal-conservative continuum. Some of the industries that these unions dominate (e.g., auto, steel, chemicals) are economically vulnerable. These unions will be inclined to spend more effort to get tariff protection, government subsidies, and employment protection than legislation to help the poorest segments of the working class. Such a defensive posture would make their politics similar to that of the old craft unions.

In summary, I see an increasing liberal drift in American unions emanating primarily from changes in the sex, ethnic, and industrial composition of their members. The old craft unions will remain the most conservative, and the industrial unions will follow close behind. Unions in government, education, and services will represent a new and stronger left. These are the unions where blacks, Hispanics, and women are increasing their membership the most. This suggests that ethnic politics may become the country's next major spring of political liberalism. The vigor and thrust of ethnic politics emanates from outside the labor movement. Perhaps ethnic organizations will embrace labor unions in their programs rather than labor embracing ethnic groups in the movement as in the past. If this happens, what will it mean for American class formation?

Conclusions

Theories of class formation are abundant, ambiguous, and contradictory. Most scholars are so preoccupied with theorizing about class formation that they neglect doing empirical research on the process. The French Marxists, for example, prolifically produce theories of class formation, but their empirical research remains primitive.

Selecting the best theory of class formation to apply to the United States is difficult. Scholars seem to agree that Thompson's (1963) history of the British working class is an exemplary study, but it is so densely ideographic that it does not provide a clear model to follow. Stinchcombe (1978) skips the study of class formation and argues for examining critical revolutionary events in order to locate "deep causal analogies" that explain challenges to governmental legitimacy. How one uncovers these causal analogies remains a mystery. The dilemma of studying class formation is best illustrated in Przeworski's (1977) review of Marxist theories from Kautsky (1891) to the present. In his attempt to rescue Marxist theory, he concludes that the study of class formation should deal with the interaction of economic, political, social, and ideological forces in specific historical situations. He advises scholars to abandon the idea of class as an entity and to study instead the *process* of class formation. His conclusions should satisfy even the most conservative bourgeois sociologist, but his admonitions are so general that they provide no cues on how to proceed. The most useful approach is that of Tilly (1978, 1981), who emphasizes that class formation must be studied historically in terms of collective actions taken by workers in response to specific factory and community crises. This highly empirical analysis of specific interactions of workers with other local groups over time presents a model that can be followed. Neither the theory nor the method assumes an inexorable working-class movement that will ultimately produce solidarity and political mobilization to control government.

My approach, though not historical, moved in a path similar to that suggested by Tilly. I examined major parts of the working class for the amount and type of interaction they had with each other and found evidence of considerable segmentation. The question now becomes, what is the probability that segmentation will decline, that more consensus will emerge, and that coordinated political class action will occur? These questions and this approach do not require the assumption that a cohesive working class will ever emerge. There is an almost endless litany in the sociological literature: the working class is made up of workers who have become alienated and have had to sell their labor to employers who profit by exploiting them. This litany is historically obvious but not very informative about how workers respond to this situation. Managers exploit or manipulate labor in all industrial societies, whether capitalistic or socialistic. This is what industrial and bureaucratic organization is all about. The research task should search for socially organized segments of the labor force, ask whether they link up with other organized groups for any common purpose, and then attempt to determine whether these links have prospects of becoming permanent and political. Applying this approach, I conclude that the American labor force (the part of the working class that is subject to social organization) will remain divided even though parts of it will gain political influence. I arrived at this conclusion by assessing the probability that each of the five working-class strata and the unions will establish more durable and lasting associations with each other.

Foremen have no horizontal organizational ties that transcend the workplace. They are so immersed in managerial hierarchies that they are incapable of collective action either by themselves or with the workers they supervise. Unless the Taft-Hartley Act is changed, foremen cannot organize into effective unions where, with the help of the skilled and other segments of the working class, they could together exert influence on workplace and national politics.

The self-employed are isolated workers who do not come together politically as French artisans do. If the self-employed cannot act in their self-interest, they cannot link up with other employees to increase working-class political power. The self-employed resemble the skilled: the two groups have some family and informal ties, but they lack formal organization to link their work and political activities.

Skilled workers do have organizational ties and do exert influence in the workplace, union, and the broader community. Although split by craft specialization, the skilled can and do work together when cooperation is mutually beneficial. The successful revolt of the skilled against the UAW leadership in winning the right to veto portions of collective bargaining agreements illustrates their power in the workplace and union. Because the skilled often comprise a true collectivity, they exert workplace influence with or without a union. Where the union exists, it supplements and broadens their influence, but as a stratum, the skilled do not have a political program for labor or American society. By tradition, the skilled have been essentially a defensive and conservative group, seeking to *protect and maintain* their advantages against management's unending drive to reduce their skills through mechanization, automation, and job redesign. Calhoun (1982), in his analysis of the evolution of the British working class, called the skilled "radical conservatives." His attack on Thompson's (1963) analysis of the part that artisans and the skilled played in the formation of the working class strikes me as being essentially correct. These groups were not concerned about advancing the interest, organization, and politics of the working class. They were and still are backward looking, seeking to preserve the privileges of a past era when the rest of the working class was not organized. The skilled were sometimes radical in the sense that they were militant and well organized to protect their interests. In situations where they could not protect their advantages without the active cooperation of other segments of the labor force, the skilled did promote class solidarity both inside and outside of the workplace, but the solidarity was not sustained.

In American organized labor, although the nonskilled outnumbered the skilled, the skilled exerted more influence. The ex-AFL unions in the AFL–CIO were in the majority and exercized a moderating political influence because they were satisfied with the mildly liberal drift of labor under Meany. Now that Meany is gone, it is unlikely that the craft unions will be able to maintain this dominant influence because their relative numbers are declining.

Finally, the three most favored groups in the working class (foremen, self-employed, and skilled) are not going to join forces because they lack common organization. Their self-interests may be parallel and they may vote the same way, but their political behavior does not add up to purposive class action.

The question now is whether unions that represent nonskilled workers in the core will be able to seize the initiative and lead a militant class-oriented political movement. There are signs that these unions have been successful in convincing others to adopt more aggressive tactics in the Democratic party to increase labor's influence. Although some success here is very likely, the signs are not clear that labor will press for narrow gains for labor or whether it will press for legislation that helps the unorganized poor. The latter is more likely to occur if unions that represent nonskilled workers in the periphery and public sector gain in numbers, strength, and political influence in AFL–CIO councils. Given the ethnic makeup of these unions, their growth would nudge ex-CIO unions toward a more class-oriented path. Such an outcome appears likely in the long run, but in the meantime labor still appears to be more militant but still divided.

During the late 1960s and early 1970s, some liberal observers thought that the poor or the marginally employed could be organized into a political force that might lead to the abolition of poverty in America (Alinsky, 1971; Piven and Cloward, 1974). The organizations spawned by the War on Poverty are now part of state and federal establishments, and many once vocal leaders of the poor are now comfortably ensconced in administrative agencies. While these officials might be activated to assert a more militant stance, the fact that they did not do so during the most recent period of high unemployment and increased poverty suggests that they will not act in the future.

The nation's ability to tolerate 10 to 15 percent levels of blue-collar unemployment without serious social reverberations suggests that a serene mood will accompany even modest improvements in the economy. Perhaps workers have endured past spells of unemployment because they felt that a new wave of prosperity would lead to an even higher level of consumption as was the case after World War II. Some observers think that this will not happen again because the American productivity lag will not be easily overcome. They point to the British experience, continuing high levels of unemployment and low productivity, as the future scenario for the United States. It does appear that each new trough in the business cycle in the United States leaves a larger residue of tolerable unemployment.

The Social Security Act of 1935 handled the problems of short economic recessions in the post–World War II period moderately well. I am not certain that these measures will be adequate if unemployment rates rise and maintain themselves over longer periods. At some point, enough groups will define the situation as intolerable and call for legislation to reduce unemployment, stimulate levels of consumption, and give the poor a dignified place in society. Materialist politics will remain the politics of the working class. The problem always has been to coalesce enough organizations to push for it. The post-materialist politics of the middle-class Left (see Lipset, 1981) that call for a cleaner environment, higher quality of education, and human rights at home and abroad represent trivial issues to the working class.

At present, no constellation of organizations has sufficient power to achieve the legislative goals of low unemployment, the removal of poverty, and a higher standard of living for the bottom third of American families. Organizations in or for the working class remain too divided to do that. How much of this class fragmentation results from a strategy of economic and political elites to keep the class divided and how much of it results from genuine divided interests within the class is hard to determine. As Ollman (1970) observed, the American working class does not act in its own interest because it is not anti-capitalistic. To be sure, it is anti-big business, but it is also anti-big labor. Labor, as we have seen, has not been able and probably will not be able to coordinate a coalition to realize the working-class agenda described above. If progress is made in this direction, it will probably come about through the efforts and initiative of other groups that will embrace labor and use its considerable skills and resources to reach some common goals. This strategy may have been more successful in the past than we realize. The most important advances for the working class and for labor were made under the New Deal by the enactment of social security legislation and the Wagner Labor Relations Act which facilitated labor union growth. In no small part, these achievements were coordinated by middle-class liberals and intellectuals in the federal government who were as much interested in preserving social peace as in improving the lot of the working class and the unions.

The next major mobilization of working-class groups will probably be stimulated and coordinated by ethnic organizations. These groups, mostly made up of blacks and Hispanics, have already developed a sense of class awareness. Alert and active, these organizations are experiencing growth in political consciousness and power. In the United States, ethnic identification and loyalty are stronger sources of political commitment than are labor unions. Ethnic organizations are tied into a broader set of community, religious, educational, recreational, and political institutions than are labor unions. When ethnic and class organizations come together, political returns to the working class can be better realized. In some ways, CIO unions built their membership by concentrating on the common grievances of European ethnic groups that dominated the working class of Eastern and Midwestern cities in the 1930s. Although blacks and Hispanics are on the periphery of the labor movement today, they are slowly penetrating it. Perhaps this time around, new ethnic organizations will galvanize the labor movement to work for the working-class agenda described above. Labor may find new working-class friends in the Democratic party coalition to replace their less reliable middle-class friends. Although labor, ethnic groups, and perhaps women's organizations will probably remain divided, they may move in parallel directions sufficiently to improve the lot of the entire working class. I hope so.

References

Abbott, Edith. 1907. *Women in Industry: A Study in American Economic History.* New York: D. Appleton and Company.

Abowd, John M., and Henry S. Farber. 1982. "Queues and union status of workers." *Industrial and Labor Relations Review* 35:354–67.

Adam, Gérard, Frédéric Bon, Jacques Capdevielle, René Moriaux. 1970. *L'ourvriers français en 1970.* Paris: Armand Colin.

Adams, J. Stacey and Sara Freedman. 1976. "Equity theory revisited: comments and annotated bibliography." In *Equity Theory,* ed. L. Berkowitz and E. Walster, 43–90. New York: Academic Press.

Alinsky, Saul David. 1971. *Rules for Radicals.* New York: Vintage.

Almquist, Elizabeth M. and Juanita L. Wehrle-Einhorn. 1978. "The doubly disadvantaged: minority women in the labor force." In *Women Working,* ed. Ann H. Stromberg and Shirley Harkness, 63–88. Palo Alto, Calif.: Mayfield.

Aminzade, Ronald. 1977. "Breaking the chains of dependency: from patronage to class politics, Toulouse, France, 1840–1972." *Journal of Urban History* 3:483–506.

Andrisani, Paul J., and Andrew T. Kohen. 1977. "The effect of collective bargaining as measured for men in blue-collar jobs." *Monthly Labor Review* 100:56–59.

Antos, Joseph R., Mark Chandler, and Wesley Mellow. 1980. "Sex differences in union membership." *Industrial and Labor Relations Review* 33:162–69.

Archer, Margaret Scotford and Salvador Giner, eds. 1971. *Contemporary Europe: Class, Status, and Power.* New York: St. Martin's.

Aron, Raymond. 1955. *Opium of the Intellectuals.* Trans. Terence Kilmartin. London: Seckar and Warburg.

Aronowitz, Stanley. 1971. "Does the United States have a new working class?" In *The Revival of American Socialism,* ed. George Fisher, 199–216. New York: Oxford University Press.

———. 1973. *False Promises: The Shaping of American Working-Class Consciousness.* New York: McGraw-Hill.

Ashenfelter, Orley. 1973. "Discrimination in trade unions." In *Discrimination in Labor Markets,* ed. Orley Ashenfelter and Albert Rees, 88–112. Princeton, N.J.: Princeton University Press.

Averitt, Robert T. 1968. *The Dual Economy.* New York: Norton.

Baker, Elizabeth Faulkner. 1925. *Protective Legislation.* New York: Privately published.

Bakunin, M. 1971. *Bakunin on Anarchy.* New York: Vintage.

Barkan, Alexander E. 1967. "Political activities of labor." *Issues in Industrial Society* 2:23–27.

Barnett, George E. 1926; rpt. 1969. *Chapters on Machinery and Labor.* Carbondale, Ill.: Southern Illinois University Press.

Baron, James N. 1980. "Indianapolis and beyond: a structural model of occupational mobility across generations." *American Journal of Sociology* 85:815–39.

Baron, James N. and William T. Bielby. 1982. "Workers and machines: dimensions and determinants of technical relations in the work place." *American Sociological Review* 47:175–88.

Barrett, Nancy S. 1979. "Women in the job market: unemployment and work schedules." *The Subtle Revolution,* ed. Ralph E. Smith, 63–98. Washington: Urban Institute.

Bartlett, Alton C. 1966. "How rank and file leaders view union political action." *Labor Law Journal* 17:483–93.

Bauman, Zygmunt. 1972. *Between Class and Elite.* Manchester, England: Manchester University Press.

Baxandall, Rosalyn, Linda Gordon, and Susan Reverly, eds. 1976. *America's Working Women.* New York: Vintage.

Bechhofer, F. and B. Elliott. 1976. "Persistence and change: the petite bourgeoisie in industrial society." *Archives européenes de sociologie* 17:74–99.

Becker, Gary S. 1967. *Human Capital and the Personal Distribution of Income.* Ann Arbor, Mich.: University of Michigan Institute of Public Administration.

Beier, A. L. 1978. "Social problems in Elizabethan London." *Journal of Interdisciplinary History* 9:203–21.

Bell, Daniel. 1949. "America's un-Marxist revolution." *Commentary* 12: 207–15.

––––––. 1960. *The End of Ideology.* Glencoe, Ill.: Free Press.

––––––. 1973. *The Coming of Post-Industrial Society.* New York: Basic Books.

Bendix, Reinhard. 1956. *Work and Authority in Industry.* New York: Wiley.

Bennett, Sari J. and Carrille V. Earle. 1980. "The failure of socialism in the U.S.: a geographical interpretation." Working paper no. 4. Geography of American Labor and Industrialization. University of Maryland, Baltimore County.

Berelson, Bernard, Paul F. Lazarsfeld, and William N. McPhee. 1954. *Voting.* Chicago: University of Chicago Press.

Berg, Ivar. 1970. *Education and Jobs.* New York: Praeger.

––––––, ed. 1981. *Sociological Perspectives on Labor Markets.* New York: Academic Press.

Berg, Ivar and David Rogers. 1964. "Former blue-collarites in small business." In *Blue-Collar World*, ed. Arthur B. Shostak and William Gomber, 550–56. Englewood Cliffs, N.J.: Prentice-Hall.

Berger, Susanne and Michael J. Piore. 1980. *Dualism and Discontinuity in Industrial Societies*. Cambridge: Cambridge University Press.

Berquist, Virginia A. 1974. "Women's participation in labor organization." *Monthly Labor Review* 97:3–9.

Bibb, Robert C. 1981. "Industrial organization, market structure, and economic performance: empirical foundations of the dual economy." Unpublished manuscript. Nashville, Tenn.: Sociology Department, Vanderbilt University.

Bibb, Robert C. and William H. Form. 1977. "The effects of industrial, occupational, and sex stratification on wages in blue collar markets." *Social Forces* 55:974–96.

Bielby, William T. and James N. Baron. 1982. "Organization, technology and worker attachment to the firm." In *Research in Social Stratification and Mobility*, ed. Donald J. Treiman and Robert V. Robinson, vol. 3, 77–113. Greenwich, Conn.: JAI Press, 1983.

Bielby, William T. and Robert M. Hauser. 1977. "Response error in earnings functions for nonblack males." *Sociological Methods and Research* 6:241–80.

Bingham, Alfred M. 1935. *Insurgent America: The Revolt of the Middle Classes*. New York: Harper.

Blackburn, R. M. and Michael Mann. 1979. *The Working Class in the Labor Market*. London: Macmillan.

Blaine, Harry and Frederick Zeller. 1965. "Who uses the UAW public review board?" *Industrial Relations* 4:95–104.

Blau, Francine. 1978. "Data on women workers, past, present and future." In *Women Working*, ed. Ann Stromberg and Shirley Harkness, 29–62. Palo Alto, Calif: Mayfield.

Blau, Peter. 1968. "The hierarchy of authority in organizations." *American Journal of Sociology* 73:453–67.

Blau, Peter and Otis Dudley Duncan. 1967. *The American Occupational Structure*. New York: Wiley.

Blauner, Robert. 1964. *Alienation and Freedom: The Factory Worker and His Industry*. Chicago: University of Chicago Press.

———. 1972. *Racial Oppression in America*. New York: Harper and Row.

Bloch, Farrell E. and Mark S. Kuskin. 1978. "Wage determination in the union and nonunion sectors." *Industrial and Labor Relations Review* 31:183–92.

BLS [Bureau of Labor Statistics] 1966. *Labor Developments Abroad*. Washington: U.S. Government Printing Office.

———. 1972. *Work Experience of the Population in March 1972*. Washington: U.S. Government Printing Office.

Bluestone, Barry. 1970. "The tripartite economy: labor markets and the working poor." *Poverty and Human Relations Abstracts* 5:221–38.

Blumberg, Paul. 1980. *Inequality in an Age of Decline.* New York: Oxford University Press.

Blume, Norman. 1970. "The impact of a local union on its membership in a local election." *Western Political Quarterly* 23:138–50.

_____. 1973a. "Union worker attitudes toward open housing: the case of the UAW in the Toledo metropolitan area." *Phylon* 34:63–72.

_____. 1973b. "Control and satisfaction and their relation to rank and file support for union political action." *Western Political Quarterly* 26:51–63.

Bok, Derek C. and John T. Dunlop. 1971. *Labor and the American Community.* New York: Simon and Schuster.

Bonacich, Edna. 1972. "A theory of ethnic antagonism: the split labor market." *American Sociological Review* 37:547–59.

_____. 1976. "Advanced capitalism and black/white race relations in the United States: a split labor market interpretation." *American Sociological Review* 41:34–51.

Borjas, George J. 1979. "Job satisfaction, wages, and unions." *Journal of Human Resources* 14:21–40.

Bowles, Samuel. 1972. "Unequal education and the reproduction of the hierarchical division of labor." In *The Capitalist System,* ed. Richard C. Edwards et al., 219–99. Englewood Cliffs, N.J.: Prentice-Hall.

Braverman, Harry. 1974. *Labor and Monopoly Capital: The Degradation of Work in the Twentieth Century.* New York: Monthly Review Press.

_____. 1975. "Work and unemployment." *Monthly Review* 27:18–31.

Braverman Symposium. 1978. *Insurgent Sociologist* 8:33–50.

Breckenridge, S. P. 1933. "The activities of women outside the home." In *Recent Social Trends in the United States.* Vol. 1, 709–50. New York: McGraw-Hill.

Breiger, Ronald. L. 1981. "The social class structure of occupational mobility. *American Journal of Sociology* 86:578–607.

Bridenbaugh, Carl. 1950. *Cities in the Wilderness: The First Century of Urban Life in America.* Boston: Houghton, Mifflin.

Briefs, Goetz. 1937. *The Proletariat.* New York: McGraw-Hill.

Brissenden, Paul F. 1929. *Earnings of Factory Workers 1899 to 1927.* Census Monograph X. Washington: U.S. Government Printing Office.

Brooks, Robert R. R. 1937. *When Labor Organizes.* New Haven, Conn.: Yale University Press.

Brooks, Thomas. 1970. "Black upsurge in the unions." *Dissent* 17:124–34.

Brown, Henry Phelps. 1977. *The Inequality of Pay.* Berkeley: University of California Press.

Brown, Stanley H. 1967. "Walter Reuther: 'He's got to walk that last mile.' " *Fortune* 76:86–89, 141–49.

Buchele, Robert. 1983. "Economic dualism and employment stability." *Industrial Relations* 2:410–18.

Bulmer, Martin, ed. 1975. *Working-Class Images of Society.* London: Routledge and Kegan Paul.

Bunel, Jean. 1973. *La mensualisation: Une réforme tranquille.* Paris: Edition Economie et Humanisme.

Bunzel, John J. 1962. *The American Small Businessman.* New York: Knopf.

Burawoy, Michael. 1978. "Toward a Marxist theory of the labor process: Braverman and beyond." *Politics and Society* 8:247–312.

———. 1979. *Manufacturing Consent: Change in the Labor Process under Monopoly Capitalism.* Chicago: University of Chicago Press.

Burke, Donald R. and Lester Rubin. 1973. "Is contract rejection a major collective bargaining problem?" *Industrial and Labor Relations Review* 26:820–33.

Burton, John. No date (1982?). *The Political Future of American Unions.* Washington: Heritage Foundation.

Butaud, Jean Phillippe. 1972. "Les resources des travailleurs étrangers." *Hommes et migrations* 827:5–21.

Butler, D. E. and Richard Rose. 1960. *The British General Election of 1959.* London: Macmillan.

Cain, Glen G. 1976. "The challenge of segmented labor market theories to orthodox theory: a survey." *Journal of Economic Literature* 14:1213–57.

Cain, Pamela S. and Donald J. Treiman. 1981. "The dictionary of occupational titles as a source of occupational data." *American Sociological Review* 46:253–78.

Calhoun, Craig. 1982. *The Question of Class Struggle.* Chicago: University of Chicago Press.

Calkins, Fay. 1952. *The CIO and the Democratic Party.* Chicago: University of Chicago Press.

Campbell, Angus et al. 1964. *The American Voter.* New York: Wiley.

Campbell, Angus, Philip E. Converse, and Willard R. Rodgers. 1976. *The Quality of American Life.* New York: Russell Sage Foundation.

Carol, Arthur and Samuel Parry. 1968. "The economic rationale of occupational choice." *Industrial and Labor Relations Review* 21:183–96.

Carr-Saunders, A. M. and D. C. Jones. 1937. *A Survey of the Social Structure of England and Wales.* Oxford: Oxford University Press.

Case, John. 1973. "Workers' control: toward a North-American movement." In *Workers' Control*, ed. Gerry Hunnius, G. David Garson, and John Case, 438–68. New York: Vintage.

Castles, Stephan and Godula Hosack. 1973. *Immigrant Workers and Class Structure in Western Europe.* New York: Oxford University Press.

Catchpole, Terry. 1968. *How to Cope with COPE.* New York: Arlington House.

Centers, Richard. (1949) *The Psychology of Social Classes.* Princeton, N.J.: Princeton University Press.

Central Intelligence Agency. 1963. *Average Annual Money Earnings of Wage Workers in Soviet Industry, 1928–61.* Washington, D.C.

CERC [Centre d'Étude des revenus et des coûts] 1971. *La hiérachie des salaires.* Document 12. Paris: La Documentation Française.

———. 1973. "Les connaissances et opinions des français dans le domaine des revenus." No. 19, 20. Paris: La Documentation Française.

CFDT. 1977. *La hiérarchie.* Paris: Montholon Services.

Charraud, Alain. 1974. "Travail feminin et revendications feministes." *Sociologie du travail* 3:291–321.

Charters, W. W. 1952. "A study of role conflict among foremen in a heavy industry." Ph.D. Dissertation, University of Michigan, Ann Arbor, Mich.

Chinoy, Ely. 1955. *Automobile Workers and the American Dream.* Garden City, N.J.: Doubleday.

Chronicle of Higher Education. 1982. "Survey of 1982 entrants in France to colleges and universities." 17 Feb.

Clawson, Dan. 1980. *Bureaucracy and the Labor Process.* New York: Monthly Review Press.

Cloward, Richard A. and Frances Fox Piven. 1974. *The Politics of Turmoil.* New York: Vintage.

Cohen, Jacob. 1968. "Multiple regression as a general data analytic system." *Psychological Bulletin* 70:426–43.

Commons, John R. et al. 1918. *A History of Labor in the United States.* 2 vols. New York: Macmillan.

Conell, Carol and Kim Voss. 1982. "Craft organization and class formation: impact of craft locals on working-class organization in the Knights of Labor." Unpublished manuscript. Stanford: Sociology Department, Stanford University.

Conk, Margo Anderson. 1978. "Occupational classification in the U.S.: 1870–1910." *Journal of Interdisciplinary History* 9:111–30.

Converse, Philip E. 1976. *The Dynamics of Party Support.* Beverly Hills, Calif.: Sage.

Converse, Philip E. and Georges Dupeaux. 1962. "Politicization of the electorate in France and the United States." *Public Opinion Quarterly* 26:1–23.

Cook, Alice. 1963. *Union Democracy: Practice and Ideal: An Analysis of Four Union Locals.* Cornell Studies in Industrial and Labor Relations 11. Ithaca, N.Y.: Cornell University Press.

————. 1968. "Women and American trade unions." *Annals of the American Academy of Political and Social Sciences* 375:124–32.

Cook, Steven L. 1975. *What is the Impact of the AFL–CIO and Local Control Body Political Endorsement on the Rank and File?* Institute for Labor Studies, West Virginia University (Morgantown) Information Series No. 9.

Cook, W. N. 1979. "Turnover and earnings: some empirical evidence." *Industrial Relations* 18:220–26.

Corey, Lewis. 1934. *The Decline of American Capitalism.* New York: Covici, Friede.

Cullen, Donald E. 1956. "The interindustry wage structure: 1899–1950." *American Economic Review* 46:353–69.

Currie, Robert. 1979. *Industrial Politics.* Oxford: Clarendon.

Curtin, Richard. 1977. *Income Equity among U.S. Workers.* New York: Praeger.

Dahrendorf, Ralf. 1959. *Class and Class Conflict in Industrial Society.* Stanford: Stanford University Press.

Daubigny, J. B. 1969. "Actualité du système 'Parodi' dans les comportements salariaux des entreprises." *Revue économique* 20:697–714.

Davidson, Percey and J. Dewey Anderson. 1937. *Occupational Mobility in an American Community.* Stanford: Stanford University Press.

Davies, Margery. 1974. "Women's place is at the typewriter." *Radical America* 8:1–28.

Davis, E. and J. C. Taylor. 1976. "Technology, organization, and job structure." In *Handbook of Work, Organization, and Society,* ed. R. Dubin, 379–420. Chicago: Rand McNally.

Davis, Mike. 1980. "The barren marriage of American labour and the Democratic Party." *New Left Review* 124:45–84.

DeFronzo, James. 1973. "Embourgeoisement in Indianapolis?" *Social Problems* 21:269–83.

Della Fave, L. Richard. 1974. "On the structure of egalitarianism." *Social Problems* 22:199–203.

Deming, Donald D. 1977. "Reevaluating the assembly line." *Supervisory Management* 22:2–7.

Denitch, Bogdan. 1973. "Is there a new working class?" In *Workers' Control,* ed. Gerry Hunnius, G. David Garson, and John Case, 429–38. New York: Vintage.

Derber, Milton. 1963. "Worker participation in Israeli management." *Industrial Relations* 3:51–72.

Dissent. Winter 1972. "The World of the Blue-Collar Worker," 9–304.

Dix, Kenneth and Abram Flory. 1970. "Political attitudes of West Virginia AFL–CIO members." *West Virginia University Bulletin,* Series 71.

Dobson, C. R. 1980. *Masters and Journeymen: A Pre-History of Industrial Relations: 1717–1800.* Totowa, N.J.: Rowen and Littlefield.

Documentation Française. 1976a. *Rémunérations des travailleurs manuels.* Paris: Group d'Étude.

————. 1976b. *Rémunérations des travailleurs manuels: Annexes.* Paris: Group d'Étude.

Doeringer, Peter B. and Michael Piore. 1971. *Internal Labor Markets and Manpower Analysis.* Lexington, Mass.: Heath.

Dollard, John. 1937. *Caste and Class in a Southern Town.* New Haven, Conn.: Yale University Press.

Douty, H. M. 1953. "Union impact on wage structures." *Proceedings of the Industrial Relations Research Association* 12:61–76.

————. 1961. "Sources of occupational wage and salary dispersion within labor markets." *Industrial and Labor Relations Review* 15:67–74.

Drake, St. Clair and Horace R. Cayton. 1945. *Black Metropolis.* New York: Harcourt, Brace.

Dubin, Robert. 1956. "Industrial workers' worlds: a study of 'central life interests' of industrial workers." *Social Problems* 3:131–42.

Duncan, Gregory M. and Duane E. Leigh. 1980. "Wage determination in the union and nonunion sectors: a sample selectivity approach." *Industrial and Labor Relations Review* 34:24–34.

Dunkerly, David. 1975. *The Foreman: Aspects of Task and Structure.* London: Routledge and Kegan Paul.

Dunlop, John T. 1944. *Wage Determination under Trade Unions.* New York: Macmillan.

Durand, Claude. 1971. *Conscience ouvrière et action syndicale.* Paris: Morton.

Durkheim, Emile. 1902; rpt. 1964. *The Division of Labor in Society.* Trans. George Simpson. Glencoe, Ill.: Free Press.

Eby, Kermit. 1950. "Research in labor unions." *American Journal of Sociology* 56:222–28.

Edelman, Murray. 1969. "The conservative political consequences of labor conflict." In *Essays in Industrial Relations Theory,* ed. Gerald G. Somers, 163–76. Ames, Iowa: Iowa State University Press.

Edelstein, J. David and Malcolm Warner. 1979. *Comparative Union Democracy.* New Brunswick, N. J.: Transaction Books.

Edwards, Alba. 1943. *Comparative Occupation Statistics for the United States: 1870–1940.* U.S. Bureau of the Census. Washington: U.S. Government Printing Office.

Edwards, Richard. 1979. *Contested Terrain: The Transformation of the Workplace in the Twentieth Century.* New York: Basic Books.

Ellul, Jacques. 1967. *The Technological Society.* Trans. John Wilkinson. New York: Vintage.

Engels, Friedrick. 1893. "Why there is no large socialist party in America." In *Basic Writings on Politics and Philosophy: Karl Marx and Friedrick Engels,* ed. Lewis A. Feuer, 457–58. Garden City, N.Y.: Anchor.

Fain, T. S. 1980. "Self-employed Americans: their number has increased." *Monthly Labor Review* 103:3–8.

Faunce, William A. 1958. "Automation in the automobile industry." *American Sociological Review* 23:401–7.

Featherman, David L. and Robert M. Hauser. 1978. *Opportunity and Change.* New York: Academic Press.

Feuille, Peter, Wallace E. Hendricks, and Lawrence M. Kahn. 1981. "Wage and nonwage outcomes in collective bargaining: determinants and tradeoffs." *Journal of Labor Research* 2:39–53.

Figaro. 25 Oct. 1977. "Barre et les artisans."

Foner, Philip S. 1976. *Labor and the American Revolution.* Westport, Conn.: Greenwood.

Foote, Nelson N. 1953. "The professionalization of labor in Detroit." *American Journal of Sociology* 58:371–80.

Form, William H. 1972. "Technology and social behavior of workers in four countries; a sociotechnical perspective." *American Sociological Review* 37:727–38.

——. 1973. "The internal stratification of the working class." *American Sociological Review* 38:697–711.

———. 1974. "Review of 'Work in America.'" *Report of a Special Task Force to the Secretary of Health, Education, and Welfare*. Cambridge, Mass.: MIT. In *American Journal of Sociology* 79:1550–2.

———. 1976a. *Blue-Collar Stratification: Auto Workers in Four Countries*. Princeton, N.J.: Princeton University Press.

———. 1976b. "Conflict within the working class: the skilled as a special interest group." In *The Uses of Controversy in Sociology*, ed. Lewis A. Coser and Otto N. Larson, 51–73. New York: Free Press.

———. 1979. "Comparative industrial sociology and the convergence hypothesis." *Annual Review of Sociology* 5:1–25.

———. 1980. "Resolving ideological issues on the division of labor." In *Sociological Theory and Research*, ed. Hubert M. Blalock, Jr., 140–55. New York: Free Press.

———. 1982. "Self-employed manual workers: petty bourgoisie or working class?" *Social Forces* 60:1050–69.

Form, William H. and Joan Althous Huber. 1976. "Occupational power." In *Handbook of Work, Organization, and Society*, ed. Robert Dubin, 751–830. Chicago: Rand McNally.

Form, William H. and David Byron McMillen. 1983. "Women, men, and machines." *Work and Occupations* 10:147–78.

Fortune. 1940. "The people of the United States—a self portrait." Vol. 21, passim.

Foster, James Caldwell. 1975. *The Union Politic—The CIO Political Action Committee*. Columbia, Mo.: University of Missouri.

Freedman, Francesca. 1975. "Internal structure of the American proletariat." *Socialist Revolution* 5:41–85.

Freedman, Marcia. 1976. *Labor Markets: Segments and Shelters*. Montclair, N.J.: Allanheld, Osmun.

Freeman, Richard B. 1978. "Job satisfaction as an economic variable." *American Economic Review* 68:135–41.

———. 1980. "Unionism and the dispersion of wages." *Industrial and Labor Relations Review* 34:3–24.

———. 1981. "The effects of unionism on fringe benefits." *Industrial and Labor Relations Review* 34:489–509.

Friedmann, Georges. 1955. *Industrial Society*. Harold L. Sheppard, ed. Glencoe, Ill.: Free Press.

Galbraith, John Kenneth. 1958. *The Affluent Society*. Boston: Houghton-Mifflin.

Gallie, Duncan. 1983. *Social Inequality and Class Radicalism in France and Great Britain*. Cambridge: Cambridge University Press.

Gamm, Sara. 1979. "The election base of national union executive boards." *Industrial and Labor Relations Review* 23:295–311.

Gani, Léon. 1972. *Syndicats et travailleurs immigrés*. Paris: Éditions Sociales.

Gans, Herbert J. 1962. *Urban Villagers*. New York: Free Press.

Garden, Maurice. 1975. *Lyon et les Lyonnais au XVIIIe siècle*. Paris: Flammariou.

Garson, Barbara. 1975. *All the Live-Long Day: The Meaning and Demeaning of Work*. New York: Doubleday.

Geiger, Kent. 1969. "Social class differences in family life in the U.S.S.R." In *Socially Structured Inequality*, ed. Celia S. Heller, 284–96. New York: Macmillan.

Geruson, Richard T. and Dennis McGrath. 1977. *Cities and Urbanization*. New York: Praeger.

Geschwender, James A. and Rhonda F. Levine. 1983. "Rationalization of sugar production in Hawaii, 1946–60: a dimension of class struggle." *Social Problems* 30:352–68.

Giles, William E. 1975. "Managers: China's Achilles' Heel?" *Wall Street Journal*, 21 July.

Glass, D. V. and J. R. Hall. 1954. "Social mobility in Britain: a study of inter-generational changes in status." In *Social Mobility in Britain*, ed. D. V. Glass, 177–260. Glencoe, Ill.: Free Press.

Glenn, Evelyn Nakamo and Roslyn L. Feldberg. 1977. "Degraded and deskilled: the proletarianization of clerical work." *Social Problems* 25:52–64.

Glenn, Norval D. and Jon P. Alston. 1968. "Cultural distances among occupational categories." *American Sociological Review* 33:365–82.

Goldman, Robert B. 1976. *A Work Experiment: Six Americans in a Swedish Plant*. New York: Ford Foundation.

Goldthorpe, John H. 1966. "Attitudes and behavior of car assembly workers: a deviant case." *British Journal of Sociology* 17:227–44.

Goldthorpe, John H., David Lockwood, Frank Bechhofer, and Jennifer Platt. 1969. *The Affluent Worker and the Class Structure*. Cambridge: Cambridge University Press.

Goode, Bill. 1976. "The skilled auto worker: a social portrait." *Dissent* 23:392–97.

Goode, William H. and Irving Fowler. 1949. "Incentive factors in a low morale plant." *American Sociological Review* 14:618–23.

Gordon, David M. 1972. *Theories of Poverty and Unemployment*. Lexington, Mass.: Heath.

Gorz, André. 1973. "Workers' control is more than just that." In *Workers' Control*, ed. Gerry Hunnius, G. David Garson, and John Case, 325–43. New York: Vintage.

Gottdiener, M. 1983. "Understanding metropolitan decentralization: a clash of paradigms." *Social Science Quarterly* 64:227–46.

Gouldner, Alvin W. 1954. *Patterns of Industrial Bureaucracy*. New York: Free Press.

Granier, R. and J. P. Marciano. 1975. "The earnings of immigrant workers in France." *International Labour Review* 111:143–66.

Granovetter, Mark. 1981. "Toward a sociological theory of income differences." In *Sociological Perspectives on Labor Markets*, ed. Ivan Berg, 11–47. New York: Academic Press.

Greeley, Andrew M. 1972. "The new ethnicity and blue collars." *Dissent* 19:270–77.

Greenstone, J. David. 1977. *Labor in American Politics.* Chicago: University of Chicago Press.

Gregory, Charles O. 1949. *Labor and Law.* New York: Norton.

Griffen, Clyde. 1969. "Workers divided: the effect of craft and ethnic differences in Poughkeepsie, New York 1850–80." In *Nineteenth Century Cities,* ed. Stephen Thernstrom and Richard Sennett, 49–97. New Haven: Yale University Press.

Gruenberg, Barry. 1980. "The happy workers: an analysis of educational and occupational differences in determinants of job satisfaction." *American Journal of Sociology* 86:247–71.

Gunter, H. 1964. "Changes in occupational wage differentials." *International Labour Review* 64:136–55.

Gustman, Alan L. and Martin Segal. 1974. "The skilled-unskilled wage differential in construction." *Industrial and Labor Relations Review* 27:261–75.

Hall, Kenneth and Isabel Miller. 1975. *Retraining and Tradition: The Skilled Worker in an Era of Change.* London: George Allen and Unwin.

Hall, R. E. 1972. "Turnover in the labor force." *Brookings Papers on Economic Activity* 3:709–56. Washington: Brookings Institution.

Hall, Richard A. 1969. *Occupations and the Social Structure.* Englewood Cliffs, N.J.: Prentice-Hall.

Hamilton, Richard F. 1963. "The income difference between skilled and white collar workers." *British Journal of Sociology* 14:363–73.

———. 1964. "The behavior and values of skilled workers." In *Blue-Collar World,* ed. Arthur B. Shostack and William Gomberg, 43–57. Englewood Cliffs, N.J.: Prentice-Hall.

———. 1965a. "Affluence and the worker: the West German case." *American Journal of Sociology* 71:144–52.

———. 1965b. "Skill level and politics." *Public Opinion Quarterly* 31:390–99.

———. 1966. "The marginal middle class: a reconsideration." *American Sociological Review* 31:192–99.

———. 1967. *Affluence and the French Worker in the Fourth Republic.* Princeton, N.J.: Princeton University Press.

———. 1972. *Class and Politics in the United States.* New York: Wiley.

———. 1975. *Restraining Myths.* New York: Wiley.

Hamilton, Richard F. and James Wright. 1982. "The state of the masses." Unpublished manuscript. Montreal: Sociology Department, McGill University.

Hammer, Tove Helland. 1978. "Relationships between local union characteristics and worker behavior and attitudes." *Academy of Management Journal* 21:560–77.

Hanagan, Michael P. 1977. "The logic of solidarity: social structure in Le Chambon-Feugerolles." *Journal of Urban History* 3:409–26.

———. 1980. *The Logic of Solidarity.* Urbana, Ill.: University of Illinois Press.

Hannaman, Robert. 1979. "Inequality and Development in Britain, France, and Germany." Ph.D. diss., University of Wisconsin, Madison.

Hardman, J. B. S. 1959. "An emerging synthesis." In *Unions and Union Leadership*, ed. Jack Barbash, 36–39. New York: Harper.

Hardman, J. B. S. and Maurice Neufeld, eds. 1951. *The House of Labor*. New York: Prentice Hall.

Harrington, Michael. 1962. *The Other America*. New York: Macmillan.

Harris, Roy J. 1983. "Boeing accord attacks narrowing pay gap between skilled and less skilled workers." *Wall Street Journal*, 11 Oct.

Harrison, Bennett. 1974. "The theory of the dual economy." In *The Worker in "Post-industrial" Capitalism*, ed. Bertram Sherman and Murray Yanowitch, 269–87. New York: Free Press.

Hartmann, G. W. and T. Newcomb, eds. 1939. *Industrial Conflict*. New York: Cordon.

Harvard University Program on Technology and Society. 1970. *Technology and Work*, Research Review No. 2. Cambridge, Mass.: Harvard University Press.

Harvey, Edward B. 1975. *Industrial Society*. Homewood, Ill.: Dorsey.

Harwood, Edwin. 1982. "Union political action and member political attitudes: a parting of the ways?" Unpublished manuscript. Macon, Ga.: Department of Sociology, Mercer University.

Hauser, Robert M. 1980. "On 'stratification in a dual economy.' " Comment, *American Sociological Review* 45:702–12.

Hauser, Robert M. and David L. Featherman. 1977. *The Process of Stratification*. New York: Academic Press.

Haworth, Charles T. and Carol Jean Reuther. 1967. "Industrial concentration and interindustry wage determination." *Review of Economics and Statistics* 60:85–95.

Hedges, J. N. and S. E. Bemis. 1974. "Sex stereotyping: its decline in skilled trades." *Monthly Labor Review* 97:14–22.

Heldman, Dan C. and Deborah L. Knight. 1980. *Unions and Lobbying*. Arlington, Va.: Foundation for the Public Trust.

Herriot, R. A. and F. Spiers. 1975. "Measuring the impact on income statistics of reporting differences between the current population survey and administrative sources." *Proceedings of the Social Statistical Section of the American Statistical Association* 18:147–58.

Heydebrand, Wolf V. 1973. *Comparative Organizations*. Englewood Cliffs, N.J.: Prentice-Hall.

Hill, Stephen. 1976. *The Dockers*. London: Heinemann.

Hirsch, Susan E. 1978. *Roots of the American Working Class: The Industrialization of Crafts in Newark, 1800–1860*. Philadelphia: University of Pennsylvania Press.

Hochschild, Jennifer L. 1981. *What's Fair?* Cambridge, Mass.: Harvard University Press.

Hodge, Robert W. and Donald J. Treiman. 1968. "Class identification in the United States." *American Journal of Sociology* 73:538–48.

Hodson, Randy. 1983. *Workers' Earnings and Corporate Economic Structure.* New York: Academic Press.

Hodson, Randy and Robert L. Kaufman. 1981. "Circularity in the dual economy." Comment. *American Journal of Sociology* 86:881–87.

Hoffman, Stanley, ed. 1963. *In Search of France.* Cambridge, Mass.: Harvard University Press.

——. 1974. *Decline or Renewal: France Since the 1930s.* New York: Viking.

Homans, George Caspar. 1961. *Social Behavior.* New York: Harcourt, Brace.

Hommes et migration. 1971. Les mal logés, no. 117.

——. 1972. Document, No. 825.

Huber, Joan and William H. Form. 1973. *Income and Ideology.* New York: Free Press.

Huber, Joan and Glenna Spitze. 1983. *Sex Stratification.* New York: Academic Press.

Hull, Frank M., Natalie S. Friedman, and Teresa Rogers. 1982. "The effect of technology on alienation from work." *Work and Occupations* 9:131–57.

Hunnius, Gerry G., David Garson, and John Case, eds. 1973. *Workers' Control.* New York: Vintage.

Hunter, L. D. and D. J. Robertson. 1969. *Economics of Wages and Labour.* New York: Augustus M. Kelley.

Hyman, Herbert H. 1966. "The value systems of different classes." In *Class, Status, and Power,* ed. Reinhard Bendix and Seymour Martin Lipset, 488–92. New York: Free Press.

ILO [International Labour Office]. 1956. *Problems of Wage Policy in Asian Countries.* Studies and Reports. New Series, No. 43. Geneva, Switzerland.

——. 1958. *Statistical Supplement. International Labour Review.* July. Geneva, Switzerland.

——. 1974. *Yearbook of Labour Statistics, 1974.* Geneva, Switzerland.

——. 1976. *Yearbook of Labour Statistics, 1976.* Geneva, Switzerland.

INSÉÉ [Institut national de la statistique et des études économiques]. 1972. *Les collections,* M-60.

——. 1974. *Les collections,* D-32. R. Tohl, C. Théot, M. F. Jouset. "Enquête formation qualification professionnelle 1970."

——. 1975. *Les collections,* M 43–44. Elisabeth Vlassenko. "La structure des salaires dans l'industrie en 1972."

Israel, Joachim. 1971. *Alienation: From Marx to Modern Sociology.* Boston: Allyn and Bacon.

Jackman, Mary R. and Robert W. Jackman. 1983. *Class Awareness in the United States.* Berkeley: University of California Press.

Jasso, Guillermina and Peter H. Rossi. 1977. "Distributive justice and earned income." *American Sociological Review* 42:639–52.

Jehlin, Elizabeth. 1974. "The concept of working-class embourgeoisement." *Studies in Comparative International Development* 9:1–19.

Jencks, Christopher. 1972. *Inequality*. New York: Basic Books.

Johnson, G. E. and K. C. Youmans. 1971. "Union relative wage effects by age and education." *Industrial and Labor Relation Review* 24:171-9.

Jones, Alfred Winslow. 1941. *Life, Liberty, and Property*. Philadelphia: Lippincott.

Kahn, Lawrence M. 1977. "Union impact: a reduced form approach." *Review of Economics and Statistics* 59:503-7.

―――. 1978. "The effects of unions on the earnings of nonunion workers." *Industrial and Labor Relations Review* 31:205-16.

―――. 1980. "Union spillover effects on unorganized labor markets." *Journal of Human Resources* 15:87-98.

Kalleberg, Arne L. and Larry Griffin. 1978. "Positional sources of inequality in job satisfaction." *Sociology of Work and Occupations* 5:371-401.

Kanter, Rosabeth Moss. 1977. *Men and Women of the Corporation*. New York: Basic Books.

Karsh, Bernard. 1968. "Human relations versus management." In *Institutions and Persons*, ed. Howard S. Becker, Blanche Geer, David Riesman, and Robert S. Weiss, 35-48. Chicago: Aldine.

Katona, George F., Charles A. Lininger, and Eva Mueller. 1964. *Survey of Consumer Finances*. Monograph 34. Institute for Social Research. Ann Arbor, Mich.: University of Michigan.

Kautsky, Karl. (1891) 1971. *The Class Struggle*. New York: Norton.

Kemper, Theodore. 1972. "The division of labor: a post-Durkheimian analytical view." *American Sociological Review* 37:739-53.

Kerr, Clark, John T. Dunlop, Frederick H. Harbison, and Charles A. Myers. 1960. *Industrialism and Industrial Man*. Cambridge, Mass.: Harvard University Press.

Kluegel, James R. and Eliot R. Smith. 1981. "Beliefs about stratification." *Annual Review of Sociology* 7:29-56.

Knapp, Vincent J. 1976. *Europe in the Era of Social Transformation: 1700-Present*. Englewood Cliffs, N.J.: Prentice-Hall.

Knowles, William H. 1955. *Personnel Management*. New York: American Book.

Kohn, Melvin. 1969. *Class and Conformity*. Homewood, Ill.: Dorsey.

Kohn, Melvin and Carmi Schooler. 1978. "The reciprocal effects of substantive complexity of work and intellectual flexibility: a longitudinal assessment." *American Journal of Sociology* 84:24-82.

Kolaja, Jiri. 1965. *Workers' Councils: The Yugoslav Experience*. London: Tavistock.

Kornblum, William. 1974. *Blue Collar Community*. Chicago: University of Chicago Press.

―――. 1977. "Why the insurgents lost in steel." *Dissent* 24:135-37.

Kornhauser, Arthur. 1965. *Mental Health of the Industrial Worker*. New York: Wiley.

Kornhauser, Arthur, Harold L. Sheppard, and Albert J. Mayer. 1956. *When Labor Votes*. New York: University Books.

Kraus, Henry. 1947. *The Many and the Few*. Los Angeles: Plantin.

Kreps, Juanita. 1971. *Sex and the Marketplace*. Baltimore: Johns Hopkins University Press.

Kuczynski, Jürgen. 1971. *The Rise of the Working Class*. Trans. C. T. A. Ray. New York: McGraw-Hill.

Kusterer, Ken C. 1978. *Know-How on the Job: the Important Working Knowledge of "Unskilled" Workers*. Boulder, Colo.: Westview.

Lambert, Richard. 1963. *Workers, Factories, and Social Change in India*. Princeton, N.J.: Princeton University Press.

Landes, D. S. 1966. "Technological change and industrialization." pp. 585–601 In *Cambridge Economic History of Europe*, ed. H. J. Habakuk and M. Posten, 545–601. Cambridge: Cambridge University Press.

Landsberg, Henry A. 1950. *Hawthorne Revisited*. Ithaca, N.Y.: Cornell University Press.

Lane, David and Felicity O'Dell. 1978. *The Soviet Worker*. New York: St. Martin's.

Lane, Robert E. 1959. "The fear of equality." *American Political Science Review* 53:35–51.

———. 1962. *Political Ideology*. New York: Free Press.

Laslett, John H. M. and Seymour M. Lipset, eds. 1974. *Failure of a Dream?* Garden City, N.Y.: Doubleday-Anchor.

Lawler, Edward E. 1971. *Pay and Organizational Effectiveness: A Psychological View*. New York: McGraw-Hill.

Lee, Alfred McClung. 1972. "An obituary for alienation." *Social Problems* 20:121–27.

Leggett, John C. 1968. *Class, Race, and Labor*. New York: Oxford University Press.

Lenin. 1943. *Selected Works*. Vol. 10. New York: International Publishers.

Lenski, Gerhard E. 1955. "American social classes: statistical strata or social groups?" *American Journal of Sociology* 58:139–44.

Levasseur, E. 1900; rpt. 1977. *The American Workman*. Baltimore: Johns Hopkins University Press.

Levine, Gene. 1963. *Workers' Vote: The Political Behavior of Men in the Printing Trade*. Totowa, N.J.: Bedminster.

Levison, Andrew. 1974. *Working-Class Majority*. New York: Coward, McCann and Geohagan.

Levitan, Sar A., ed. 1971. *Blue-Collar Workers*. New York: McGraw-Hill.

Lewis, H. Gregg. 1968. "Labor unions: influence on wages." *International Encyclopedia of the Social Sciences*. Vol. 8. New York: Macmillan and Free Press.

Liaisons Sociales. 1975a. Documents 74/76 R. "Immigration en France."

———. 1975b. Documents 65/75 R. "La formation professionelles des adults."

———. 1975c. Documents 86/75 R. "Le travail et l'emploi des femmes."

———. 1976. Documents 104/76 R. "Sondage de l'Agence national pour l'emploi."

———. 1978. Documents 29/78 T. "Population active selon le status en 1975."

Lindert, Peter H. and Jeffrey G. Williamson. 1977. "Three centuries of American inequality." In *Research in Economic History*, ed. Paul Uselding, vol. 1, 69–233. Greenwich, Conn.: JAI Press.

Linhart, Robert. 1978. *L'établi*. Paris: Les Éditions de Minuit.

Lipset, Seymour Martin. 1960. *Political Man*. New York: Doubleday.

————. 1970. *Revolution and Counterrevolution*. Garden City, N.Y.: Doubleday.

————. 1977. "Why no socialism in the United States?" In *Sources of Contemporary Radicalism*, ed. Seweryn Bialer and Sophis Sluzar, 31–149. Boulder, Colo.: Westview Press.

————. 1981. "Whatever happened to the proletariat?" *Encounter* 56:18–34.

Lipset, Seymour Martin and Reinhard Bendix. 1959. *Social Mobility in Industrial Society*. Berkeley: University of California Press.

Lipset, Seymour Martin and William Schneider. 1983. *The Confidence Gap*. New York: Free Press.

Lipset, Seymour Martin, Martin A. Trow, and James A. Coleman. 1956. *Union Democracy*. Glencoe, Ill.: Free Press.

Lipsitz, Lewis. 1965. "Working-class authoritarianism: a re-evaluation." *American Sociological Review* 30:103–9.

Lockwood, David 1981. "The weakest link in the chain: some comments on the Marxist theory of action." In *Research in the Sociology of Work*, ed. Richard L. Simpson and Ida Harper Simpson, 435–81. Greenwich, Conn.: JAI.

Lord, George F. and William W. Falk. 1982. "Hidden income and segmentation: structural determinants of fringe benefits." *Social Science Quarterly* 63:208–24.

Lorwin, Val. R. 1954. *The French Labor Movement*. Cambridge, Mass.: Harvard University Press.

Low-Beer, John R. 1978. *Protest and Participation: The New Working Class in Italy*. Cambridge: Cambridge University Press.

Lupton, T. 1963. *On the Shop Floor*. New York: Macmillan.

Lynd, Robert S. and Helen M. Lynd. 1929. *Middletown*. New York: Harcourt, Brace.

————. 1937. *Middletown in Transition*. New York: Harcourt, Brace.

McClosky, Herbert. 1960. "Consensus and ideology in American politics." *American Political Science Review* 30:548–68.

Machlup, F. 1967. "Theories of the firm: marginalist, behavioral, managerial." *American Economic Review* 57:3–33.

McKenny, Ruth. 1939. *Industrial Valley*. New York: Harcourt, Brace.

Mackenzie, Gavin. 1973. *The Aristocracy of Labor*. Cambridge: Cambridge University Press.

McLaughlin, Steven D. 1978. "Occupational sex identification and the assessment of male and female earnings." *American Sociological Review* 43:909–21.

McNamee, Stephen J. 1975. "Skill level and politics: a replication. PASS Working Paper, 1222. Sociology Department, University of Illinois at Urbana-Champaign.

Magaud, Jacques. 1974. "Vrais et faux salaires." *Sociologie du travail* 16:1–18.

Mahler, John E. 1961. "The wage pattern in the United States." *Industrial and Labor Relations Review* 15:3–20.

Main, Jackson T. 1966. "The class structure of revolutionary America." In *Class Status and Power*, ed. Reinhard Bendix and Seymour Martin Lipset, 111–21. New York: Free Press.

Mallet, Serge. 1969. *La nouvelle classe ouvrière*. Paris: Seuil.

———. 1975. *The New Working Class*. Nottingham: Spokesman Books.

Mann, Michael. 1973. *Consciousness and Action Among the Western Working Class*. London: Macmillan.

Marglin, Steven. 1974. "What do bosses do?" *Review of Radical Economics* 6:33–60.

Marshall, Ray. 1963. "Union structure and public policy: the control of union racial practices." *Political Science Quarterly* 78:444–58.

———. 1967. "Union racial problems in the South." *Industrial Relations* 1:117–28.

———. 1968. "Racial practices of unions." In *Negroes and Jobs*, ed. Louis Ferman, Joyce A. Kornbluh, and J. A. Miller, 277–98. Ann Arbor, Mich.: University of Michigan Press.

———. 1972. "Black workers and the union." *Dissent* 19:295–302.

Marx, Karl. 1951. *The Eighteenth Brumaire of Louis Bonaparte*. Trans. Daniel DeLeon. New York: New York Labor News.

———. 1956. "Social Class and Class Conflict." In *Karl Marx: Selected Writings in Sociology and Social Philosophy*, ed. T. B. Bottomore, 178–202. New York: McGraw-Hill.

———. 1844, rept. 1963. *Early Writings*, ed and trans. T. B. Bottomore. New York: McGraw-Hill.

———. 1967. *Capital*. Vol. 1. New York: International Publishers.

Marx, Karl and Friedrich Engels. 1936. *Selected Works*. Moscow: Publications of Foreign Workers in the USSR.

Mathewson, Stanley B. 1931; rpt. 1969. *Restriction of Output Among Unorganized Workers*. Carbondale, Ill.: Southern Illinois University Press.

Matza, David. 1971. "Poverty and dispute." In *Contemporary Social Problems*, ed. Robert K. Merton and Robert Nisbet, 601–56. New York: Harcourt Brace Jovanovich.

Matza, David and Henry Miller. 1967. "Poverty and the proletariat." In *Contemporary Social Problems*, ed. Robert K. Merton and Robert Nisbet, 639–74. New York: Harcourt Brace Jovanovich.

Maupeau-Abbud, Nicole de. 1974. "Grèves et rapports sociaux de travail: modeles classiques ou schémas nouveaux." *Sociologie du travail* 16:265–90.

Mayer, Kurt B. 1956. "Recent changes in the class structure of the United States." *Transactions of the Third World Congress of Sociology* 3:66–86.

Mayer, Kurt B. and Walter Buckley. 1955. *Class and Society*. New York: Random House.

Mayer, Kurt B. and S. Goldstein. 1964. "Manual workers as small business-men." In *Blue-Collar World*, ed. Arthur B. Shostak and William Gomberg, 537–50. Englewood Cliffs, N.J.: Prentice-Hall.

Mayo, Elton. 1945. *The Social Problem of an Industrial Civilization*. Boston: Harvard University Press.

Meissner, Martin. 1969. *Technology and the Worker*. San Francisco: Chandler.

———. 1976. "The language of work." In *Handbook of Work, Organization and Society*, ed. R. Dubin, 205–80. Chicago: Rand McNally.

Michelat, Guy and Michel Simon. 1975. "Catégories socio-professionnelles en milieu ouvrier et comportement politique d'après enquêtes de l'IFOP. *Revue française de science politique* 25:291–316.

Michels, Robert. 1959. *Political Parties*. Trans. Eden Paul and Cedar Paul. New York: Dover.

Miller, Ann R., Donald J. Treiman, Pamela S. Cain, and Patricia A. Roos, eds. 1980. *Work, Jobs, and Occupations: A Critical Review of the Dictionary of Occupational Titles*. Washington: National Academy Press.

Miller, Delbert C. and William H. Form. 1980. *Industrial Sociology*. New York: Harper and Row.

Miller, Herman P. 1966. *Income Distribution in the United States*. Washington: U.S. Bureau Census. U.S. Government Printing Office.

Miller, Joanne. 1980. "Individual and occupational determinants of job satisfaction." *Sociology of Work and Occupations* 7:337–66.

Miller, S. M. 1964. "The American lower classes: a typological approach." In *Blue-Collar World*, ed. Arthur B. Shostak and William Gomberg, 9–23. Englewood Cliffs, N.J.: Prentice-Hall.

Miller, S. M. and Martin Rein. 1966. "Poverty, inequality, and policy." In *Social Problems*, ed. Howard S. Becker, 426–516. New York: John Wiley.

Mills, C. Wright. 1942. "Review of W. Lloyd Warner and Paul S. Lunt, The Social Life of a Modern Community." *American Sociological Review* 7:262–71.

———. 1948a. "The contribution of sociology to studies of industrial relations." *Proceedings of the Industrial Relations Research Association*: 1:199–222.

———. 1948b. *The New Men of Power*. New York: Harcourt, Brace.

———. 1956. *White Collar*. New York: Oxford University.

Minces, Juliette. 1973. *Les travailleurs étrangers en France*. Paris: Éditions du Seiul.

Moch, Leslie Page. 1979. "Migrants in the city: newcomers to Nîmes, France, at the turn of the century." Ph.D. diss., University of Michigan, Ann Arbor.

Montagna, Paul D. 1977. *Occupations and Society*. New York: Wiley.

Moore, Thomas S. 1982. "The structure of work life 'ordeal': an empirical assessment of class criteria." *Insurgent Sociologist* 11:73–83.

Moore, Wilbert E. 1951. *Industrial Relations and the Social Order*. New York: Macmillan.

_____. 1970. *The Professions: Roles and Rules.* New York: Russell Sage Foundation.

More, Charles. 1980. *Skill and the English Working Class, 1870–1914.* New York: St. Martin's.

Morgan, Glenn. 1981. "Class theory and the structural location of black workers." *Insurgent Sociologist* 10:21–34.

Mothé, Daniel. 1972. *Les O.S.* Paris: Les Éditions du Cerf.

Moussez-Lavau, Janine, and Mariette Sineau. 1976. "Les femmes et la politique." *Revue française de science politique* 26:929–50.

Mowry, George E. 1969. "Social democracy, 1900–1918." In *The Comparative Approach to American History*, ed. C. Vann Woodward, 271–84. New York: Basic Books.

Mueller, Eva et al. 1969. *Technological Advance in an Expanding Economy.* Ann Arbor, Mich.: Braun-Brumfield.

Mumford, Lewis. 1938. *The Culture of Cities.* New York: Harcourt, Brace.

Nash, Al. 1977. "A unionist remembers: militant unionism and political factions." *Dissent* 4:181–89.

National Commission for Manpower Policy. 1978. *Manpower and Immigration Policies in the United States.* Special Report No. 20. Washington, D.C.

Nie, Norman H., Sidney Verba, and John R. Petrocik. 1979. *The Changing American Voter.* Cambridge, Mass.: Harvard University Press.

Noble, David F. 1979. "Social choice in machine design." In *Case Studies in the Labor Process*, ed. Andrew Zimbalist, 18–50. New York: Monthly Review Press.

North, D. and W. Weissert. 1973. *Immigrants and the American Labor Market.* Washington: Trans-Century.

Nyden, Paul. 1979. "An internal colony: labor conflict and capitalism in Appalachian coal." *Insurgent Sociologist* 4:33–43.

Ober, Harry. 1948. "Occupational wage differentials, 1907–47." *Monthly Labor Review* 67:127–34.

O'Connor, James. 1973. *The Fiscal Crisis of the State.* New York: St. Martin's.

O'Donnell, Laurence G. 1974. "UAW internal battle looms as unit says skilled workers can't veto new contracts." *Wall Street Journal,* 15 Apr.

Ollman, Bertell. 1970. "Toward class consciousness next time: Marx and the working class. In *The Politics and Society Reader*, ed. Ira Katz-Nelson, Gordon Adams, Philip Brenner, Alan Wolfe, 305–25. New York: David McKay.

Olson, Mancur, Jr. 1965. *The Logic of Collective Action.* Cambridge, Mass.: Harvard University Press.

Oppenheimer, Martin. 1974. "The sub-proletariat: dark skins and dirty work." *Insurgent Sociologist* 4:6–20.

Oppenheimer, Valerie Kincade. 1970. *The Female Labor Force in the United States.* Berkeley, Calif.: Institute of International Studies, University of California Press.

Osterman, Paul. 1975. "An empirical study of market segmentation." *Industrial and Labor Relations Review* 28:508–21.

Ozanne, Robert A. 1962. "A century of occupational differentiation in manufacturing." *Review of Economics and Statistics* 44:292–99.

Parker, Richard. 1972. *The Myth of the Middle Class*. New York: Harper and Row.

Parkin, Frank. 1979. *Marxism and Class Theory: A Bourgeois Critique*. New York: Columbia University Press.

Parnes, Herbert S. 1976. *The National Longitudinal Surveys Handbook.* Center for Human Resources Research, College of Administrative Science. Columbus, Ohio: Ohio State University Press.

Parodi, Maurice. 1962. *Croissance économique et nivellement hiérarchique des salaires ouvriers*. Paris: Rivière.

Parsons, Talcott. 1968. *Professions*. International Encyclopedia of the Social Sciences. New York: Free Press and Macmillan.

Parsons, Talcott and Neil J. Smelser. 1965. *Economy and Society*. New York: Free Press.

Peck, Sidney M. 1963. *The Rank-and-File Leader*. New Haven, Conn.: College and University Press.

Perlman, Richard. 1958. "Forces widening occupational wage differentials." *Review of Economics and Statistics* 40:107–15.

Perlman, Selig. 1928. *A Theory of the Labor Movement*. New York: Augustus M. Kelley.

Perlman, Selig and Philip Taft. 1935. *History of Labor in the United States, 1896–1932*. New York: Macmillan.

Perrow, Charles. 1970. *Organizational Analysis*. Belmont, Calif.: Wadsworth.
———. 1978. "The Society of Organizations." Unpublished manuscript. Sociology Department, State University of New York at Stony Brook.

Pfeffer, Jeffrey and Jerry Ross. 1981. "Unionization and income inequality." *Industrial Relations* 20:271–85.

Pfeffer, Richard M. 1979. *Working for Capitalism*. New York: Columbia University Press.

Phelps, Orme W. 1957. "A structural model of the U.S. labor market." *Industrial and Labor Relations Review* 10:402–23.

Pirenne, Henri. 1934. "Guilds: European." In *Encyclopedia of the Social Sciences*, 209–14. New York: Macmillan.

Piven, Frances Fox and Richard A. Cloward. 1971. *Regulating the Poor: The Functions of Public Welfare*. New York: Random House.

Point de jour. 1977. "La vérité par la feuille de paye." 22 Nov.

Polaskoff, Murray. 1959. "Internal pressures on the Texas CIO council, 1937–1955." *Industrial and Labor Relations Review* 12:227–42.

Pomper, Gerald M. 1975. *Voters' Choice*. New York: Dodd, Mead.

Portes, Alejandro. 1971. "Political primitivism, differential socialization, and lower-class leftist radicalism." *American Sociological Review* 36:820–35.

Poulantzas, Nicos. 1975. *Class in Contemporary Capitalism*. London: New Left Books.

Przeworski, Adams. 1977. "Proletariat into a class." *Politics and Society* 7:343–403.

Ra, Jong Oh. 1978. *Labor at the Polls*. Amherst, Mass.: University of Massachusetts.

Raphael, Edna E. 1974. "Working women and their membership in labor unions." *Monthly Labor Review* 97:27–33.

Ray, R. N. 1975. "A report on self-employed Americans in 1973." *Monthly Labor Review* 98:49–54.

Reder, Melvin. 1955. "The theory of occupational wage differentials." *American Economic Review* 45:833–52.

Rees, Albert. 1962. *The Economics of Trade Unionism*. Chicago: University of Chicago Press.

Reiss, Albert, J., Jr. 1961. *Occupations and Social Status*. Glencoe, Ill.: Free Press.

Reynaud, Jean-Daniel. 1975. "Trade unions and political parties in France: some recent trends." *Industrial and Labor Relations Review* 28: 208–25.

Roberts, Kenneth. 1978. *The Working Class*. London: Longman.

Roethlisberger, Fritz J. 1945. "The foreman: master and victim of double talk." *Harvard Business Review* 23:283–98.

Rogoff, Natalie. 1953. *Recent Trends in Occupational Mobility*. Glencoe, Ill.: Free Press.

Rones, P. L. 1978. "Older men—the choice between work and retirement." *Monthly Labor Review* 101:3–10.

Roomkin, Myron and Gerald G. Somers. 1974. "The wage benefits of alternative sources of skill development." *Industrial and Labor Relations Review* 27:228–41.

Rosen, Sherwin. 1970. "Unionism and the occupational wage structure in the United States." *International Economic Review* 11:269–86.

Rosenberg, Sam. 1980. "Male occupational standing and the dual labor market." *Industrial Relations* 19:34–49.

Rothbaum, Melvin. 1957. "National wage structure comparisons." In *New Concepts in Wage Determination*, ed. George W. Taylor and Frank C. Pierson, 299–327. New York: McGraw-Hill.

Roy, Donald. 1952. "Quota restriction and goldbricking in a machine shop." *American Journal of Sociology* 57:427–42.

Rubin, Lillian B. 1976. *Worlds of Pain*. New York: Basic Books.

Rumberger, Russell W. 1981. "The changing skill requirements of jobs in the U.S. economy." *Industrial and Labor Relations Review* 34: 578–90.

Russett, Bruce M. et al. 1964. *World Handbook of Political and Social Indicators*. New Haven, Conn.: Yale University Press.

Sable, Charles F. 1982. *Work and Politics*. Cambridge: Cambridge University Press.

Sayles, Leonard R. 1963. *Behavior of Industrial Work Groups*. New York: Wiley.

Schervish, Paul G. 1981. "The structure of employment and unemployment." In *Sociological Perspectives on Labor Markets*, ed. Ivar Berg, 153–86. New York: Academic Press.

Schlozman, Kay Lehman and Sidney Verba. 1979. *Injury to Insult: Unemployment, Class, and Political Response*. Cambridge, Mass.: Harvard University Press.

Schmidt, Peter and Robert Strauss. 1976. "The effects of unions on earnings and earnings on unions: a mixed logit approach." *International Economic Review* 17:204–12.

Schoeplein, Robert N. 1977. "Secular changes in the skill differentials in manufacturing, 1952–1973." *Industrial and Labor Relations Review* 30:314–24.

Scoble, Harry M. 1967. *Ideology and Electoral Action*. San Francisco: Chandler.

Scoville, James G. 1972. *Manpower and Occupational Analysis: Concepts and Measurements*. Lexington, Mass.: Heath.

Seeman, Melvin. 1959. "On the meaning of alienation." *American Sociologist Review* 24:783–91.

―――. 1971. "The urban alienations: some dubious theses from Marx to Marcuse." *Journal of Personality and Social Psychology* 19:135–43.

―――. 1975. "Alienation studies." *Annual Review of Sociology* 1:91–124.

―――. 1977. "Some real and imaginary consequences of social mobility: a French-American comparison." *American Journal of Sociology* 82: 757–82.

Seidman, Joel et al. 1958. *The Worker Views His Union*. Chicago: University of Chicago Press.

Sellier, François. 1973. "The French workers' movement and political unionism." In *The International Labor Movement in Transition*, ed. Adolf Sturmthal and James G. Scoville, 79–100. Urbana, Ill.: University of Illinois Press.

Sewell, William H. and Robert M. Hauser. 1975. *Education, Occupation, and Earnings*. New York: Academic Press.

Sexton, Brendon. 1971. "Unions and the black power brokers." *Dissent* 18:41–49.

Sexton, Brendon and Patricia Cayo Sexton. 1971. *Blue Collars and Hard Hats: The Workingclass and the Future of American Politics*. New York: Random House.

Sexton, Patricia Cayo. 1977. *Women and Work*. R & D Monograph 46. U.S. Department of Labor, Employment and Training Administration. Washington: U.S. Government Printing Office.

Shepard, Jon M. 1971. *Automation and Alienation*. Cambridge, Mass.: MIT Press.

―――. 1977. "Technology, alienation, and job satisfaction." *Annual Review of Sociology* 3:1–22.

Sheppard, Harold L. and Neil Herrick. 1972. *Where Have all the Robots Gone?* New York: Free Press.

Sheppard, Harold L. and Nicholas A. Masters. 1959. "Political attitudes and preferences of union members: the case of the Detroit auto workers." *American Political Science Review* 53:437–46.

Shostak, Arthur B. 1969. *Blue-Collar Life.* New York: Random House.

Shostak, Arthur B. and William Gomberg, eds. 1964. *Blue-Collar World.* Englewood Cliffs, N.J.: Prentice-Hall.

Silver, Alan. 1979. "Work and ideology among engineers: an international comparison of the new working class." Unpublished manuscript. Department of Sociology, Columbia University, N.Y.

Silver, Catherine Bodard. 1977. "France: contrasts in familial and societal roles." In *Women: Roles and Status in Eight Countries,* ed. Janet Zollinger Giele and Audrey Chapman Smock, 257–300. New York: Wiley.

Simkin, William E. 1968. "Refusals to ratify contracts." *Industrial and Labor Relations Review* 21:518–40.

Simmel, George. 1950. *The Sociology of George Simmel.* Ed. and trans. Kurt H. Wolff. Glencoe, Ill.: Free Press.

Small, Sylvia. 1976. "Black Workers in labor unions—a little less separate, a little more equal." *Ethnicity* 3:174–96.

Smith, Adam. 1776; rpt. 1937. *An Inquiry into the Nature and Causes of the Wealth of Nations.* New York: Modern Library.

Smith, David L. and Robert E. Snow. 1976. "The division of labor: conceptual and methodological issues. *Social Forces* 55:520–28.

Society. 1979. "Is there a new class?" 16, May–June.

Sombart, Werner. 1906. *Warum Gibt es in den vereinigten Staaten Keinen Socialismus?* Tübingen: Mohr.

Spaeth, Joe L. 1979. "Vertical differentiation among occupations." *American Sociological Review* 44:746–62.

Spenner, Kenneth I. 1979. "Temporal changes in work content." *American Sociological Review* 44:968–75.

Spilerman, Seymour. 1977. "Careers, labor market structure and socioeconomic achievement." *American Journal of Sociology* 83:551–93.

Spinrad, William. 1960. "Correlates of trade union participation: a summary of the literature." *American Sociological Review* 25:237–44.

Stevenson, M. H. 1978. "Wage differences between men and women: economic theories. In *Women Working,* ed. Ann H. Stromberg and Shirley Harkness, 89–107. Palo Alto, Calif.: Mayfield.

Stinchcombe, Arthur L. 1965. "Social structure and organizations." In *Handbook of Organizations,* ed. James G. March, 142–293. Chicago: Rand-McNally.

———. 1978. *Theoretical Methods in Social History.* New York: Academic Press.

———. 1979. "Social mobility in industrial labor markets." *Acta Sociologica* 22:217–45.

Stoddart, Jennifer. 1978. "Feminism in Paris." *Canadian Newsletter for Research on Women* 7:62–67.

Stolzenberg, Ross M. 1975. "Education, occupation, and wage differences between white and black men." *American Journal of Sociology* 81: 229–323.

Stone, Katherine. 1974. "The origins of job structures in the steel industry." *Review of Radical Political Economics* 6:113–73.

Sturmthal, Adolf. 1964. *Workers' Councils*. Cambridge, Mass.: Harvard University Press.

————. 1983. *Left of Center: European Labor Since World War II*. Urbana: University of Illinois Press.

Survey Research Center. 1970. *Survey of Working Conditions*. Ann Arbor, Michigan: University of Michigan Press.

Sweet, James A. 1973. *Women in the Labor Force*. New York: Seminar Press.

Szymanski, Albert. 1974. "Race, sex, and the U.S. working class." *Social Problems* 21:706–25.

————. 1978. "Braverman as a neo-Luddite." *Insurgent Sociologist* 8:45–50.

Taira, Koji. 1970. *Economic Development and the Labor Market in Japan*. New York: Columbia University Press.

Tannenbaum, Arnold S. and Robert L. Kahn. 1958. *Participation in Union Locals*. Evanston, Ill.: Row, Peterson.

Tapinos, Georges, 1975. *L'immigration étrangère en France: 1946–73*. Institut national d'études démographiques 71. Paris: Universitaires de France.

Tapper, Owen and James Neal. 1977. *Political Attitudes of West Virginia CIO Union Members*. Institute for Labor Studies. Morgantown, W.Va.: West Virginia University.

Taylor, Frederick W. 1911. *Principles of Scientific Management*. New York: Harper.

Temme, Lloyd V. 1975. *Occupation: Meanings and Measures*. Washington: Bureau of Social Science Research.

Thernstrom, Stephan. 1964. *Poverty and Progress*. Cambridge, Mass.: Harvard University Press.

Thompson, E. P. 1963. *The Making of the English Working Class*. New York: Vintage.

Thurman, J. E. 1977. "Job satisfaction: an international overview." *International Labour Review* 116:249–67.

Thurow, Lester C. 1975. *Generating Inequality*. New York: Basic Books.

Tillery, Winston. 1974. "Internal affairs hold the spotlight at the UAW convention." *Monthly Labor Review* 97:52–54.

Tilly, Charles. 1978. *From Mobilization to Revolution*. Reading, Mass.: Addison-Wesley.

————. 1981. *As Sociology Meets History*. New York: Academic Press.

Tilly, Louise A. 1977. "Urban growth, industrialization, and women's employment in Milan, Italy, 1881–1911." *Journal of Urban History* 3:467–84.

Tolbert, Charles. 1983. "Industrial segmentation and men's intergenerational mobility. *Social Forces* 61:1119–138.

Tolbert, Charles, Patrick M. Horan, and E. M. Beck. 1980. "The structure of economic segmentation: a dual economy approach." *American Journal of Sociology* 85:1095–1116.

Tourraine, Alain. 1971. *The Post-Industrial Society.* New York: Random House.

Treiman, Donald J. and Kermit Terrell. 1975. "Sex and the process of status attainment: a comparison of working men and women." *American Sociological Review* 40:174–200.

Trotsky, Leon. 1932. *The History of the Russian Revolution.* Vol. 1. Trans. Max Eastman. New York: Simon and Schuster.

Tyree, Andrea and Billy G. Smith. 1978. "Occupational hierarchy in the United States: 1789–1969." *Social Forces* 56:881–99.

UAW Proceedings. 1974. Twenty-fourth Constitutional Convention. Los Angeles, Calif.: UAW.

United Nations. 1973. *The Determinants and Consequences of Population Trends.* New York: Department of Economic and Social Affairs, Population Studies 50.

U.S. Bureau of the Census. 1970. *United States Summary: Detailed Characteristics.* Washington: U.S. Government Printing Office.

————. 1970a. *U.S. Summary, Detailed Characteristics.* PC (1)-D 1. Washington: U. S. Government Printing Office.

————. 1970b. *Occupational Characteristics.* Public Use Sample, 1/1,000.

————. 1970c. *Subject Report, National Origin and Language.* Washington: U. S. Government Printing Office.

————. 1972. *Subject Reports: Occupation by Industry.* PC(2) 7C. Washington: U. S. Government Printing Office.

————. 1972a. *Work Experience of the Population in March 1972.* Washington: U. S. Government Printing Office.

————. 1972b. *Statistical Abstract of the United States: 1972.* Washington: U. S. Government Printing Office.

————. 1972c. *Population, Subject Reports: Part 7A Occupational Characteristics.* PC (2)-7A. Washington: U. S. Government Printing Office.

————. 1972d. *Current Population Reports: Consumer Income.* Series P-60. No. 85. Characteristics of Low-Income Population 1971. Washington: U. S. Government Printing Office.

————. 1972e. *Subject Reports: Occupation by Industry.* PC (2)-7C. Washington: U. S. Government Printing Office.

————. 1973. *Census of Population: 1970. Subject Reports: Earnings by Occupation and Education.* Washington: U. S. Government Printing Office.

————. 1973a. *Occupations of Persons with High Earnings.* PC (2)-7F. Washington: U. S. Government Printing Office.

————. 1973b. *Subject Reports: Earnings by Occupation and Education.* PC (2)-8B. Washington: U. S. Government Printing Office.

————. 1973c. *Current Population Reports: Consumer Income.* Series P-60, Dec., No. 90. Washington: U. S. Government Printing Office.

————. 1974. *Current Population Reports: Special Studies.* Series P-23, No. 54. Washington: U. S. Government Printing Office.

————. 1975. *Historical Statistics of the United States: Colonial Times to 1970.* Bicentennial Edition, Pt. 1. Washington: U. S. Government Printing Office.

————. 1976. *Current Population Reports: Consumer Income.* Series P-60, No. 101. *Money Income in 1974 of Families and Persons in the United States.* Washington: U. S. Government Printing Office.

————. 1976a. Current Population Reports: Population Profile of the United States: 1975. Washington: U. S. Government Printing Office.

————. 1978a. *Current Population Reports.* Series P-20, No. 322. Mar. Washington: U. S. Government Printing Office.

————. 1978b. *Current Population Reports: Population Characteristics.* P-20. No. 324, Apr. Washington: U. S. Government Printing Office.

————. 1979. *Current Population Reports.* Series P-60, No. 118, "Money income in 1977 of families and persons in the United States." Washington: U. S. Government Printing Office.

————. 1981. *Current Population Reports: Consumer Income.* Series P-60, No. 137. Washington: U. S. Government Printing Office.

U.S. HEW [Department of Health, Education and Welfare]. 1973. *Work in America: Report of a Special Task Group to the Secretary.* Cambridge, Mass.: MIT Press.

U.S. Department of Labor. 1956. *Study of Consumer Expenditures Incomes and Savings 4: Summary of Family Expenditures for Housing and Household Operations.* Philadelphia: University of Pennsylvania.

————. 1974. *Educational Attainment of Workers, March 1974.* Special Labor Force Report, No. 17, Washington: U. S. Government Printing Office.

————. 1975. *1975 Handbook on Women Workers.* Bulletin 297. Washington: Women's Bureau.

U.S. Department of the Treasury. 1979. *Estimates of Income Unreported on Individual Income Tax Returns.* Internal Revenue Service. Washington: U. S. Government Printing Office.

U.S. Small Business Administration. 1980. *Requirements for Eligibility.* Washington: Department of Commerce.

Van Doorn, Jacques A. S. 1956. "The changed position of unskilled workers in the social structure of the Netherlands." *Transactions of the Third World Congress of Sociology* 3:113–24.

Vanneman, Reeve. 1977. "The occupational composition of American classes: results from cluster analysis." *American Journal of Sociology* 83:783–807.

Veblen, Thorstein. 1921; rpt. 1940. *The Engineers and the Price System.* New York: Viking.

Vlassenko, É., and S. Volkoff. 1975. "Les salaries des étrangers en France en 1972." *Economie et statistique* 70:47–53.

Walker, Charles R., and Robert H. Guest. 1952. *The Man on the Assembly Line.* Cambridge, Mass.: Harvard University Press.

Wallace, Michael and Arne L. Kalleberg. 1982. "Industrial transformation and the decline of craft." *American Sociological Review* 47:307–424.

Wall Street Journal. 1974. "UAW internal battle looms as unit says skilled workers can't veto new contracts." 15 Apr.

Warner, W. Lloyd and J. O. Low. 1947. *The Social System of the Modern Factory.* New Haven, Conn.: Yale University Press.

Warner, W. Lloyd and Paul S. Lunt. 1941. *The Social Life of a Modern Community.* New Haven, Conn.: Yale University.

Weaver, Charles N. 1979. "The irony of the job satisfaction of females." *Personnel Administrator* 1179:70–4.

Webb, Sidney. 1981 "Alleged differences in the wages paid to men and women for similar work." *Economic Journal* 1:630–62.

Weber, Arnold. 1963. "The craft-industrial issue revisited: a study of union government." *Industrial and Labor Relations Review* 16:381–404.

Weber, Max. 1922; rpt. 1978. "Status groups and classes." In *Economy and Society,* ed. Guenther Roth and Claus Wittich, 302–7. Berkeley: University of California Press.

———. 1946. "Class, status and party." In *From Max Weber: Essays in Sociology,* ed. and trans. H. H. Gerth and C. Wright Mills, 180–95. New York: Oxford University Press.

Weir, Stanley. 1973. "Rebellion in American labor rank and file." In *Workers' Control,* ed. Gerry Hunnius, G. David Garson, and John Case, 45–61. New York: Vintage.

Weitz, Peter R. 1975. "Labor and politics in a divided movement: the Italian case." *Labor and Industrial Relations Review* 28:226–42.

Wesolowski, Wlodzimierz. 1969. "Strata and strata interest in socialist society." In *Structured Social Inequality,* ed. Celia S. Heller, 465–77. New York: Macmillan.

Westley, William A. and Margaret W. Westley. 1971. *The Emerging Worker.* Montreal: McGill-Queen's University Press.

Widick, B. J. 1972. "Black city, black union?" *Dissent* 19:138–45.

Wilensky, Harold L. 1960. "Work, careers, and social integration." *International Social Science Journal* 12:3–20.

———. 1961. "Orderly careers and social participation: the impact of work history on social integration in the middle mass." *American Sociological Review* 26:251–539.

———. 1966. "Class, class consciousness, and American workers." In *Labor in a Changing America,* ed. William Haber, 12–44. New York: Basic Books.

———. 1975. *The Welfare State and Equality.* Berkeley: University of California Press.

———. 1976. *The 'New Corporatism,' Centralization, and the Welfare State.* London: Sage.

Wilson, Graham K. 1979. *Unions in American Politics.* New York: St. Martin's.

Wolfbein, Seymour. 1969. *Work in American Society.* Glenview, Ill.: Scott, Foresman.

Woofter, T. J., Jr. 1933. "The status of racial and ethnic groups." In *Recent Social Trends in the United States,* Vol. 1, 553–601. New York: McGraw-Hill.

Wright, Erik Olin. 1976. "Class boundaries in advanced capitalist societies." *New Left Review* 98:3–41.

———. 1979. *Class Structure and Income Determination.* New York: Academic Press.

Wright, Erik Olin and Lucca Peronne. 1977. "Marxist class categories and income inequality." *American Sociological Review* 42:32–55.

Wright, James D. 1972. "The working class, authoritarianism and the Vietnam war." *Social Problems* 20:133–50.

Wright, James D. and Richard F. Hamilton. 1979. "Education and job attitudes among blue-collar workers." *Sociology of Work and Occupations* 6:59–83.

Yellowitz, Irwin. 1977. *Industrialization and the American Labor Movement: 1850–1900.* Port Washington, N.Y.: Kennikat Press.

Zaleznik, A. 1951. *Foremen Training in a Growing Enterprise.* Boston: Harvard University Press.

Zarca, B. 1977. "Données statistiques sur l'artisant." *Annales du CREDOC* 3:91–111. Paris.

Zeitlin, Maurice. 1967. *Revolutionary Politics and the Cuban Working Class.* Princeton, N.J.: Princeton University Press.

Subject Index

Author Index

A Note on the Author

William Form is professor emeritus of the Sociology Department and the Institute of Labor and Industrial Relations at the University of Illinois. He is now teaching at Ohio State University. In the past he has studied industrial workers in Argentina, France, India, Italy, Mexico, and the United States. Currently he is doing research on American labor politics, work in the welfare state, and changing skill patterns. Among his previous publications are articles in the *American Sociological Review* and the *American Journal of Sociology*. He is also the author of *Income and Ideology*, with Joan Huber (1973), *Blue-Collar Stratification* (1976), and, with D. C. Miller, *Industrial Sociology* (1980).